Through The Lens of a Photojournalist

2nd Edition

John Jochimsen

First published in 2013
© Copyright 2013, 2014
John Jochimsen

The right of John Jochimsen to be identified as the author of this work has been asserted by him in accordance with Copyright, Designs and Patents Act 1998.

All rights reserved. No reproduction, copy or transmission of this publication may be made without written permission. No paragraph of this publication may be reproduced, copied or transmitted save with the written permission or in accordance with the provisions of the Copyright Act 1956 (as amended).
Any person who does any unauthorised act in relation to this publication may be liable to criminal prosecution and civil claims for damage.

Paperback ISBN13 978-1-78092-713-8

Published in the UK by MX Publishing,
335, Princess Park Manor, Royal Drive, London, N11 3GX
www.mxpublishing.co.uk
Cover by www.staunch.com

Authors note

I was born just before the start of the Thirties, during the days of the General Strike and a world recession. Living through a world war and national service I then became a photojournalist, retiring at the age of sixty-seven.

My father, a journalist on *The Times* during the Thirties and the war had a great influence over my formative years, though I very rarely saw him for months on end for during that time he was relief correspondent in Paris and sometimes Berlin. During the war my mother had to raise me as best she could and during the London Blitz we would sleep under the stairs every night with the backdrop of noise from the guns and bombs getting ever nearer. My father worked in London during the war and would return on the paper van at all hours of the night.

Having no idea what I would do after leaving school at sixteen, I struggled with suggestions before intuition steered me into photography, first cine and then stills.

After fifty years of photography and an extraordinary life of travel and adventure for which I received many accolades, I enjoyed a career in a creative art form that gave me immense pleasure and satisfaction. But now at the age of eighty four I write as a hobby and a short time ago published my first book, a fictional wartime adventure called *King's Flight*.

I published my memoirs, *80 Years Gone in a Flash*, in September 2011. A history of my life and fifty years of photography entwined with my memories of a richly unique and dangerous life, lived both here and abroad.

This picture book is a collection of some of my images taken throughout my career before photography became digitalized. Most of the colour transparencies taken in East Africa and Malaya in the 1950's are as good today as they were when they were taken.

Often my assignments led me into precarious situations in order to get the desired shot. Below is just one instance of this when I was standing on the unguarded ledge of the filter near the top of one of the Windscale chimneys at Sellafield, photographing Calder Hall below. The chimneys were approximately 290ft in height as seen in the picture below.

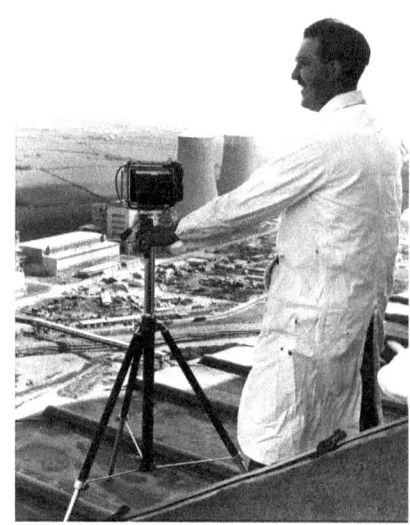

Many of my older shots took me over eighteen months to find as they were in various archives and photo libraries around Britain. But with the help of a lot of people I managed to find quite a few.

Unfortunately though I was not able to find some of my more pertinent pictures of the time, such as those I took of Princess Elizabeth at Tree Tops in Kenya when she became Queen or the ones of Sir Gerald Templer when I was seconded to him in Malaya during the terrorist uprising in 1954.

I hope you enjoy this collection of pictures I have put together and if there is anyone who remembers me from the past or would like to talk about those old days, please get in touch and let's chat about the old ways of taking pictures.

johnjoch@tesco.net

I dedicate this book to the memory of my wife Chris and to my children Paul, Sally, Jane and Rob.

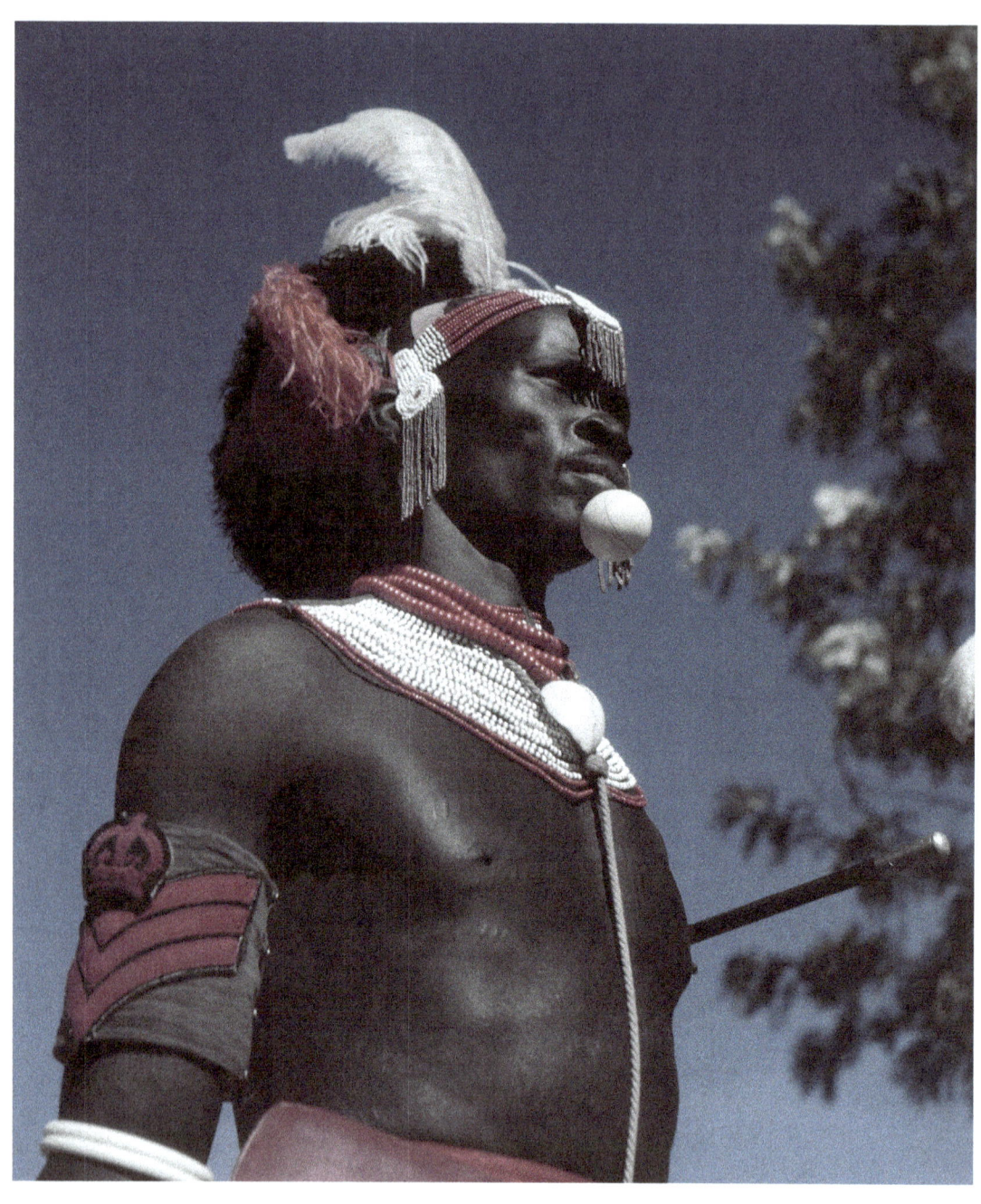

A Sergeant-Major of the Kings African Rifles in Nairobi, Kenya, 1952

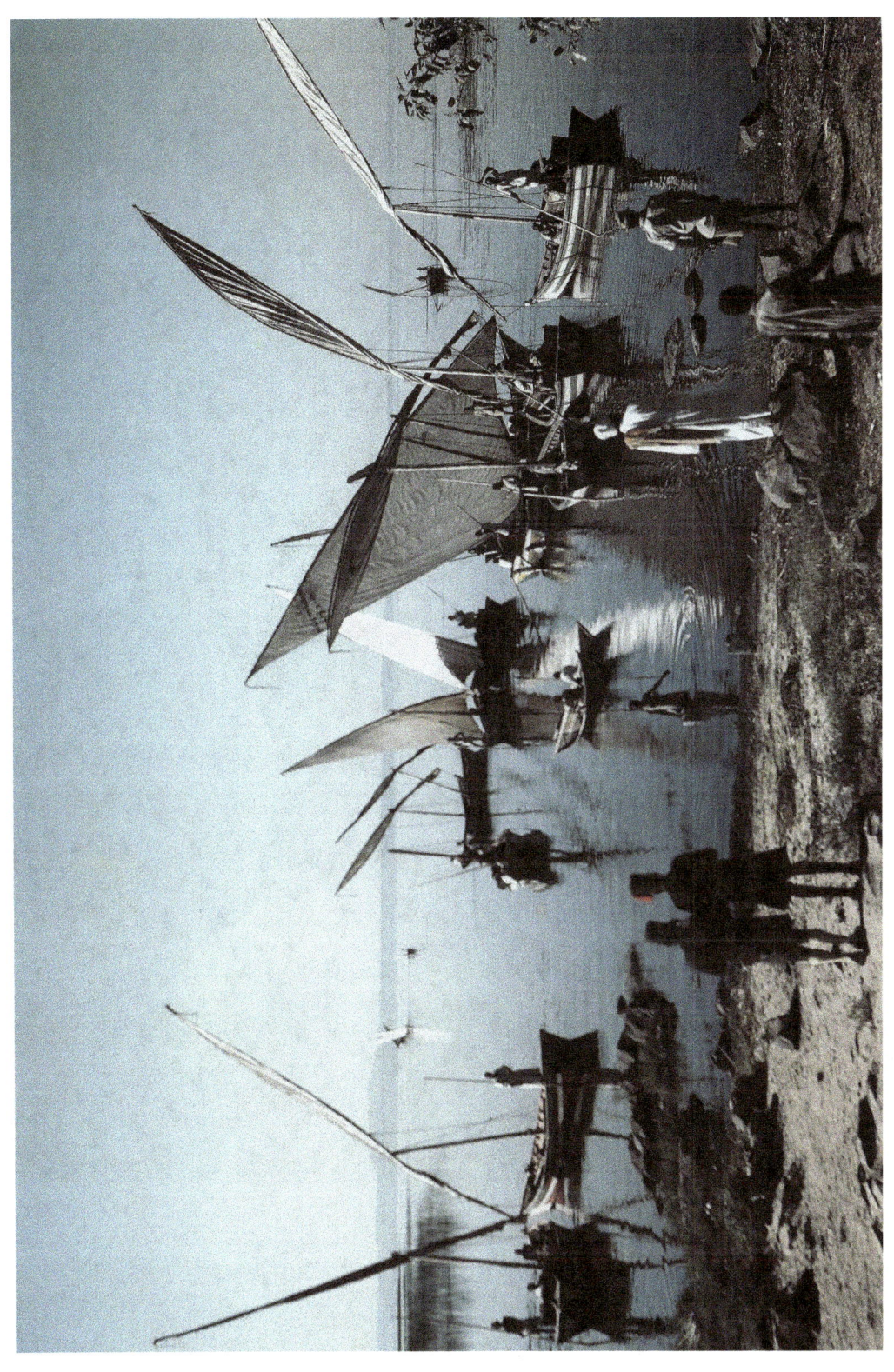

Boats coming in after all night fishing on Lake Victoria, Uganda, 1952

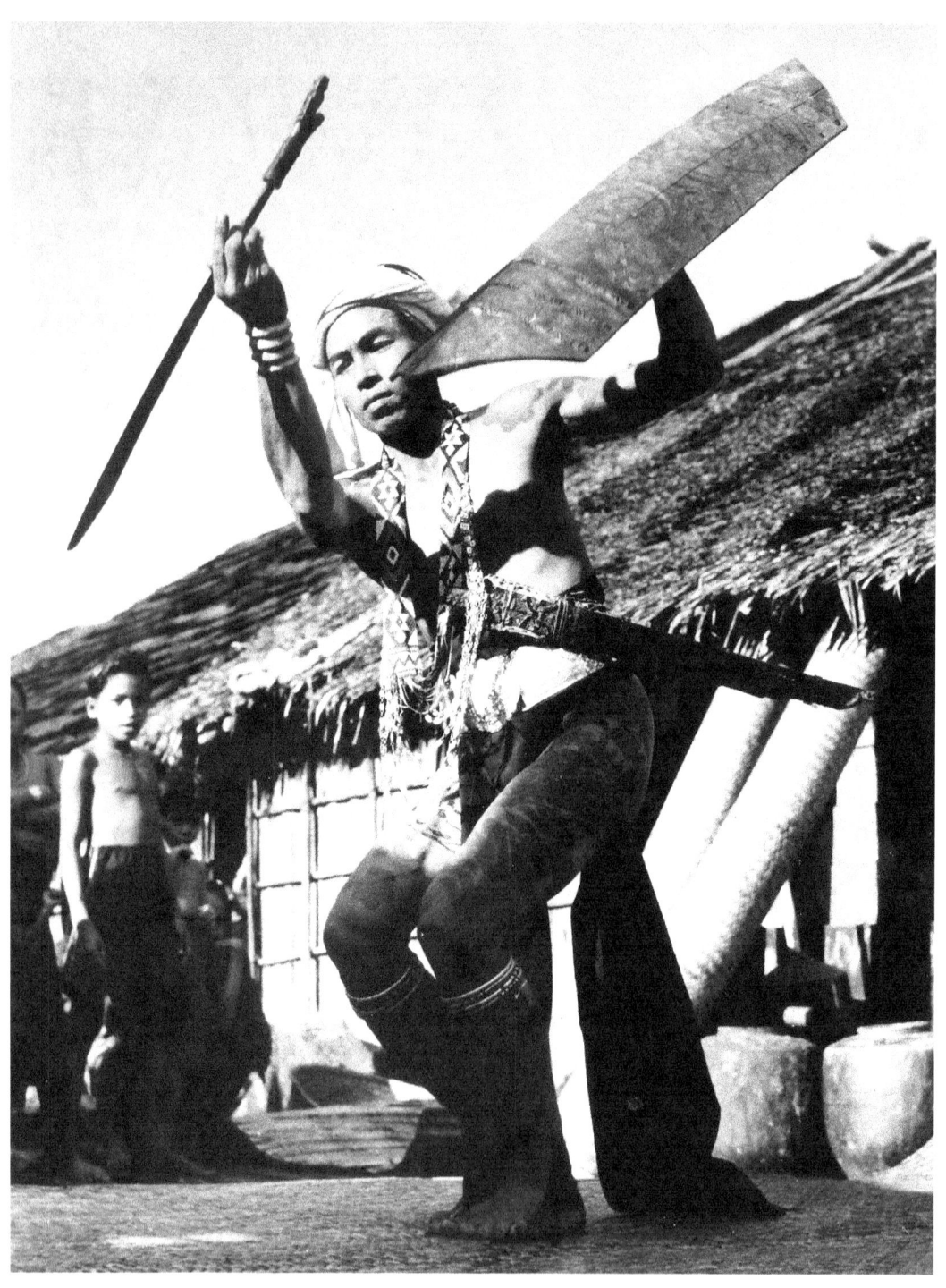

A war dance by a Dyak warrior in Sarawak, 1954

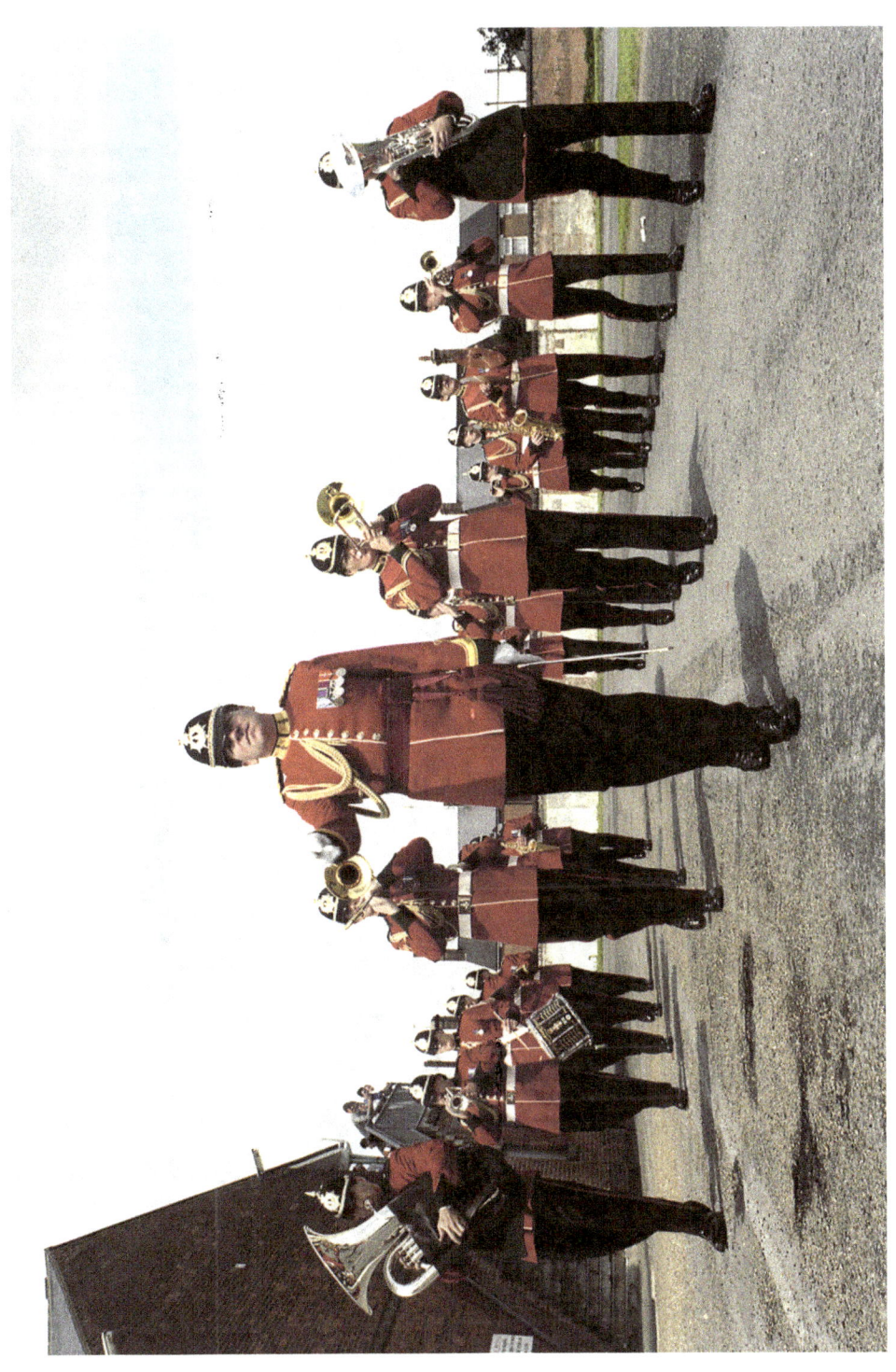

The Green Howard's band at Colchester Garrison on parade, 1983

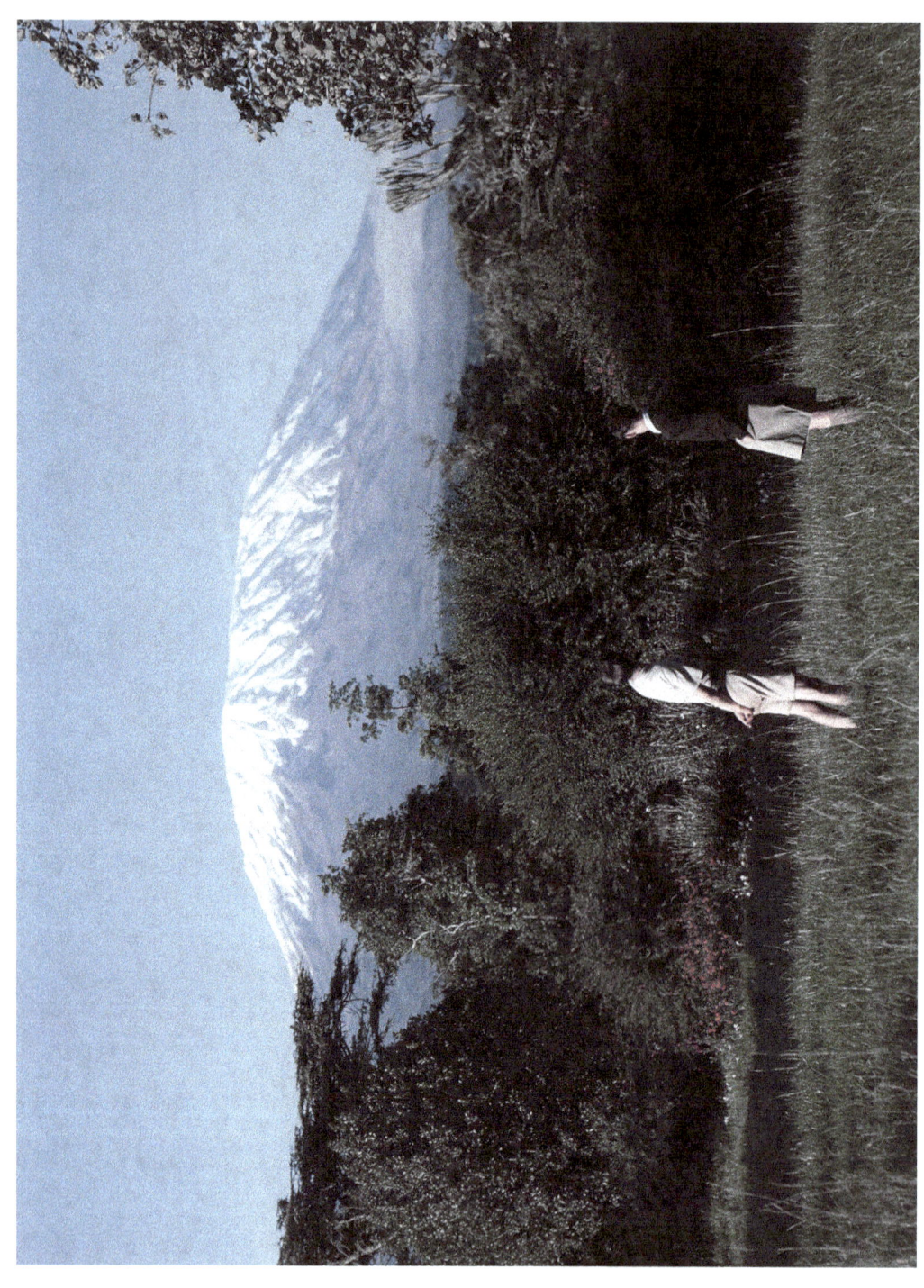

Mount Kilimanjaro, Uganda, 1952

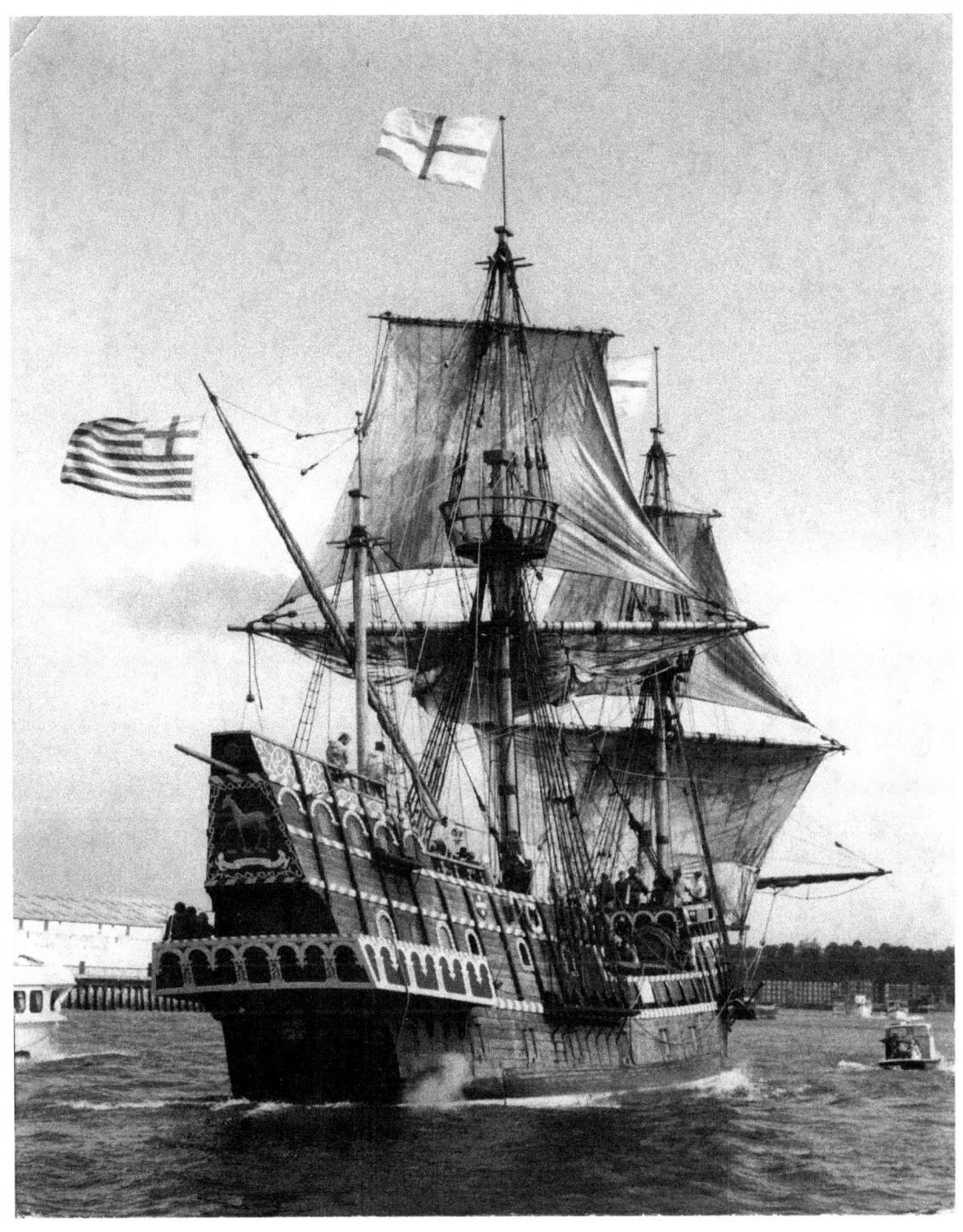

The re-build of the Golden Hinde on it first sail down the Thames on its way to Greenwich

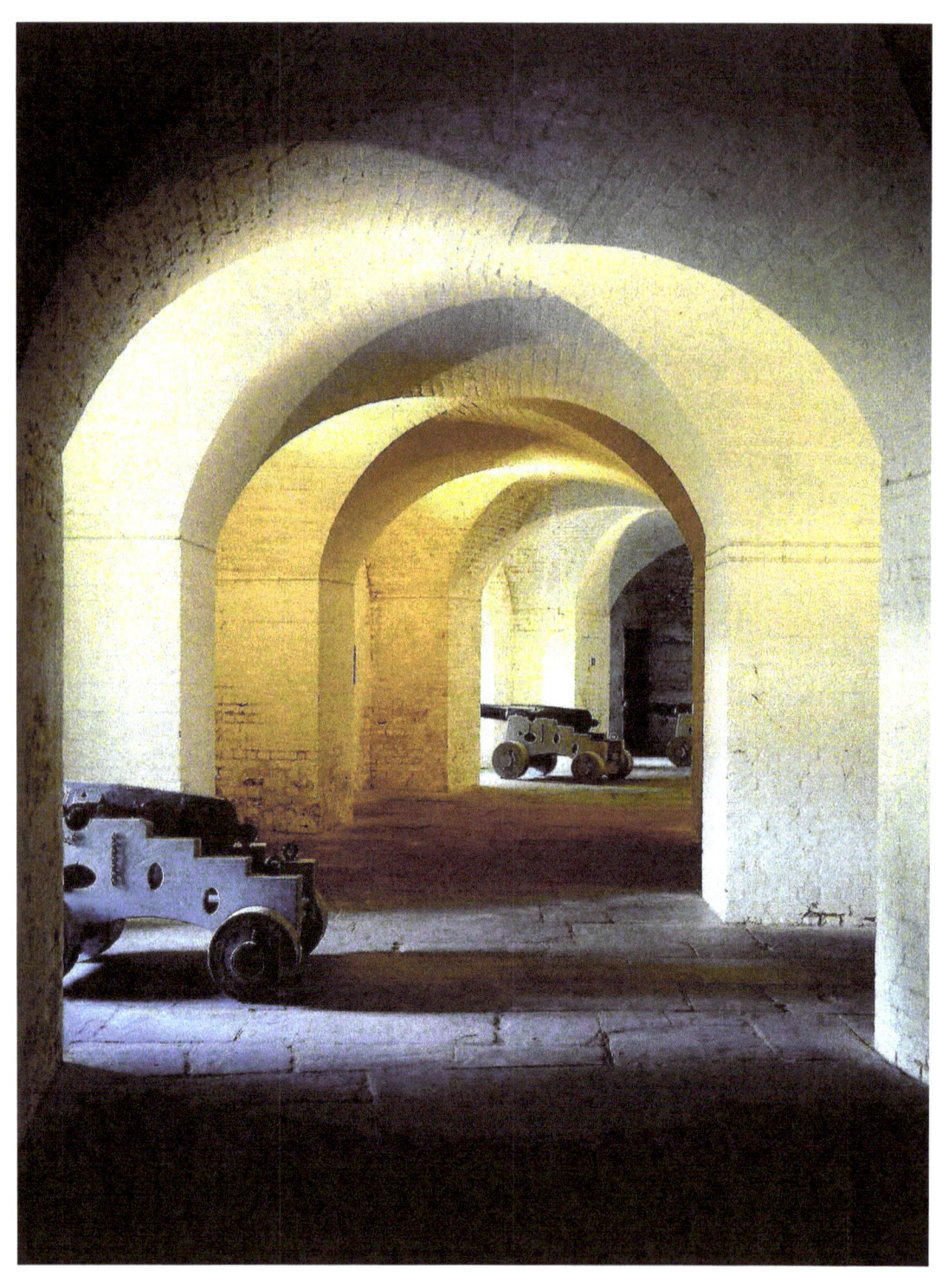

Interior of Fort Brockhurst, Gosport

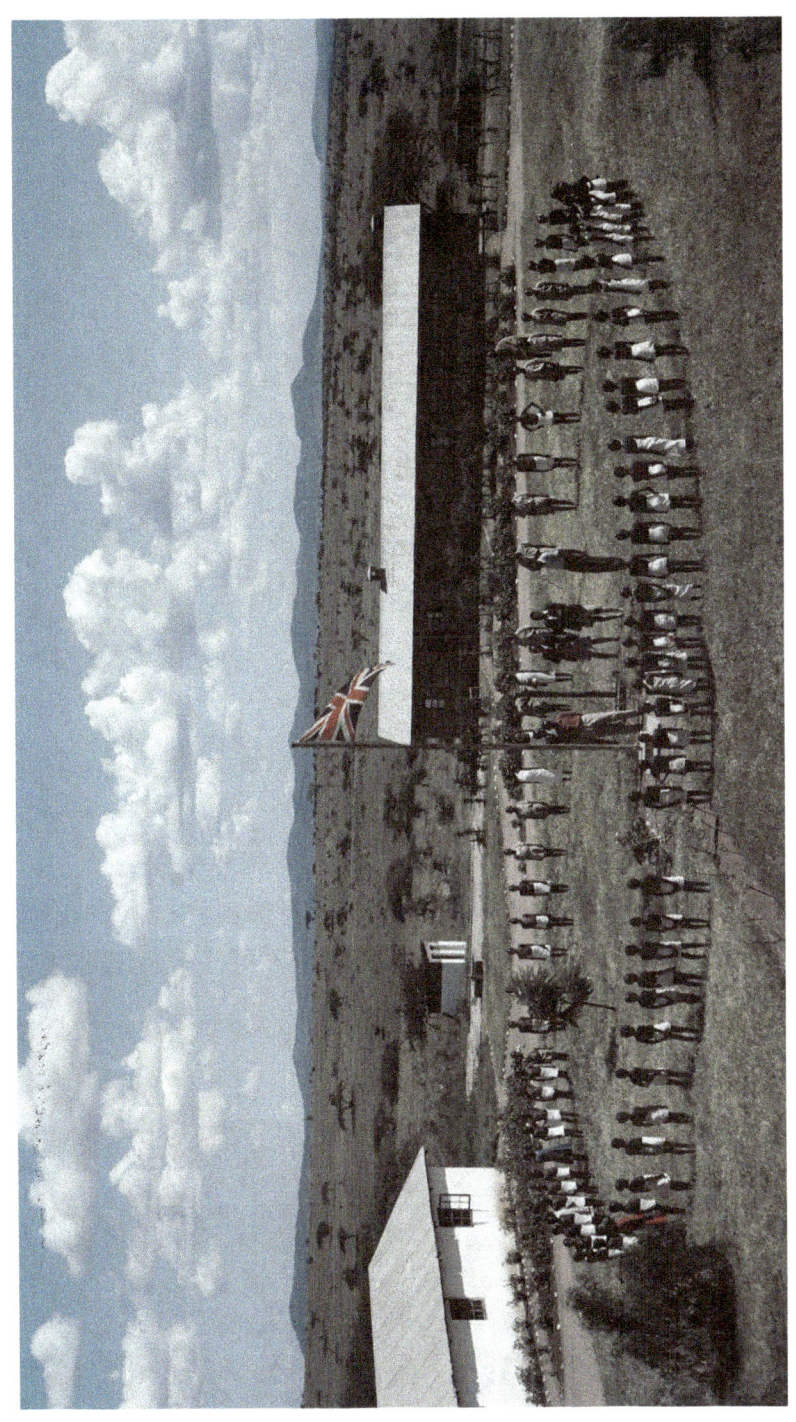

The first boarding school for Maasai children in the Kajiado district of the Rift Valley, Kenya, 1952

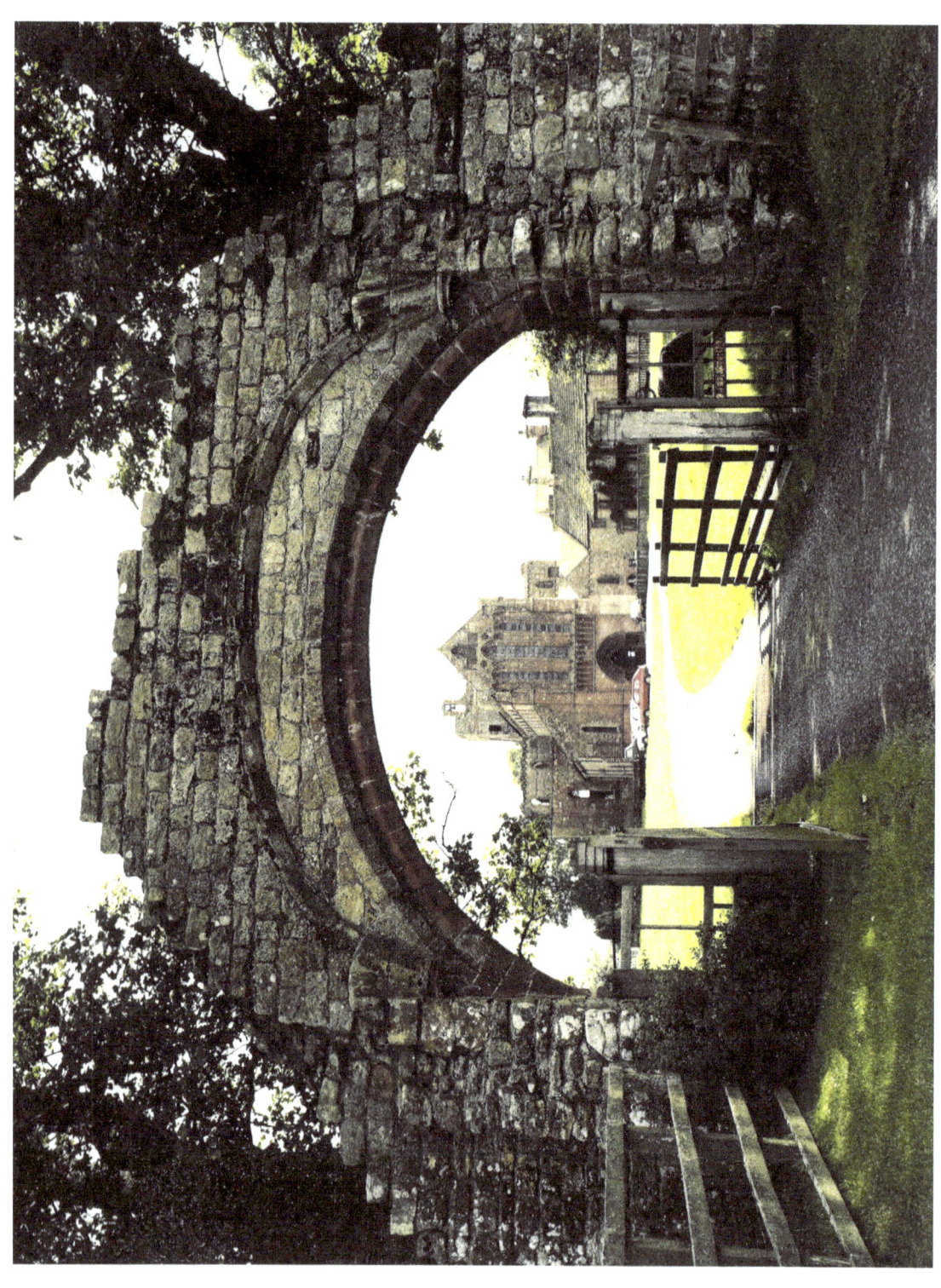

The ruins of Lanercost Priory in Brampton, Cumbria

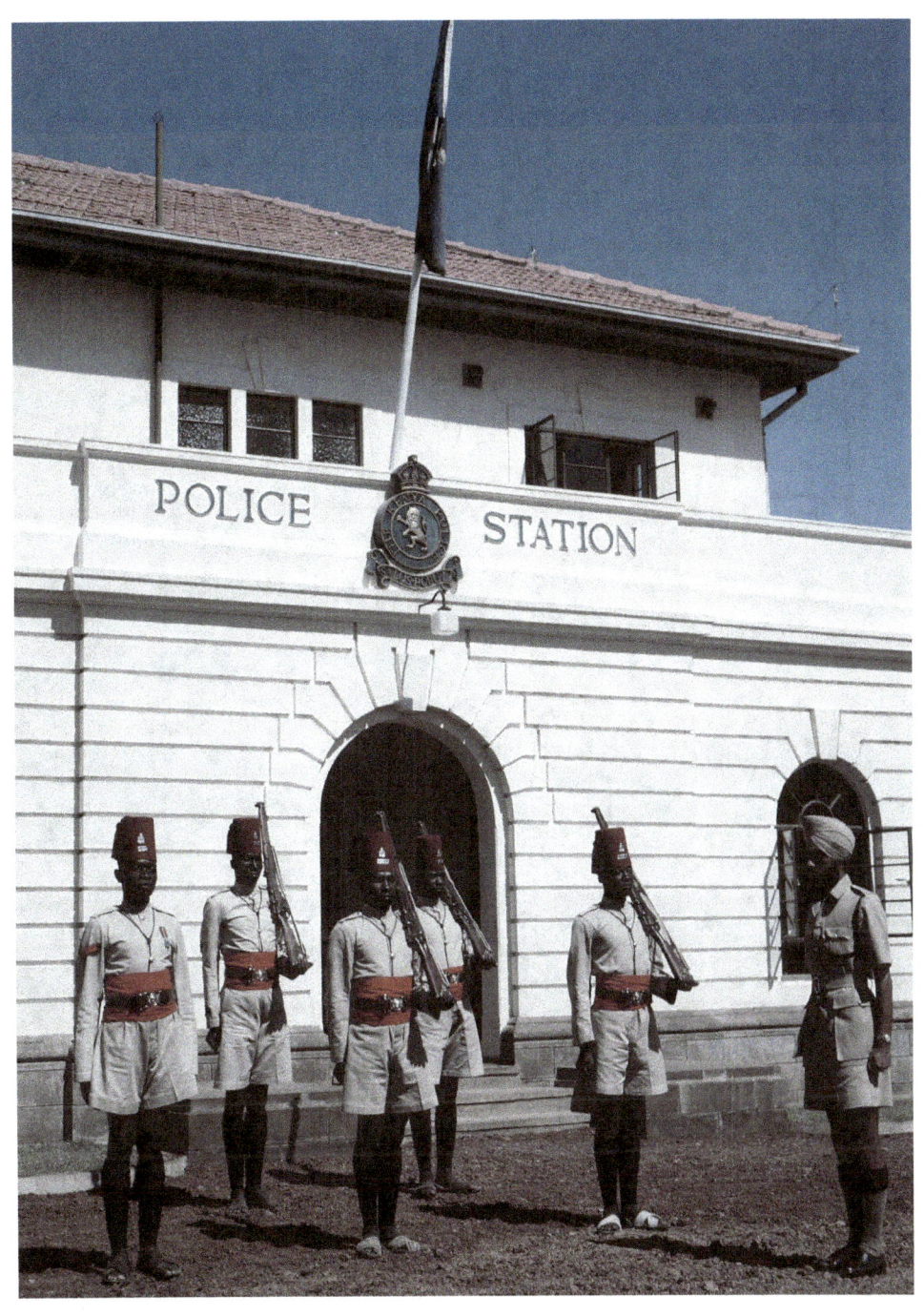

A new Police Station outside Nairobi, Kenya, 1952

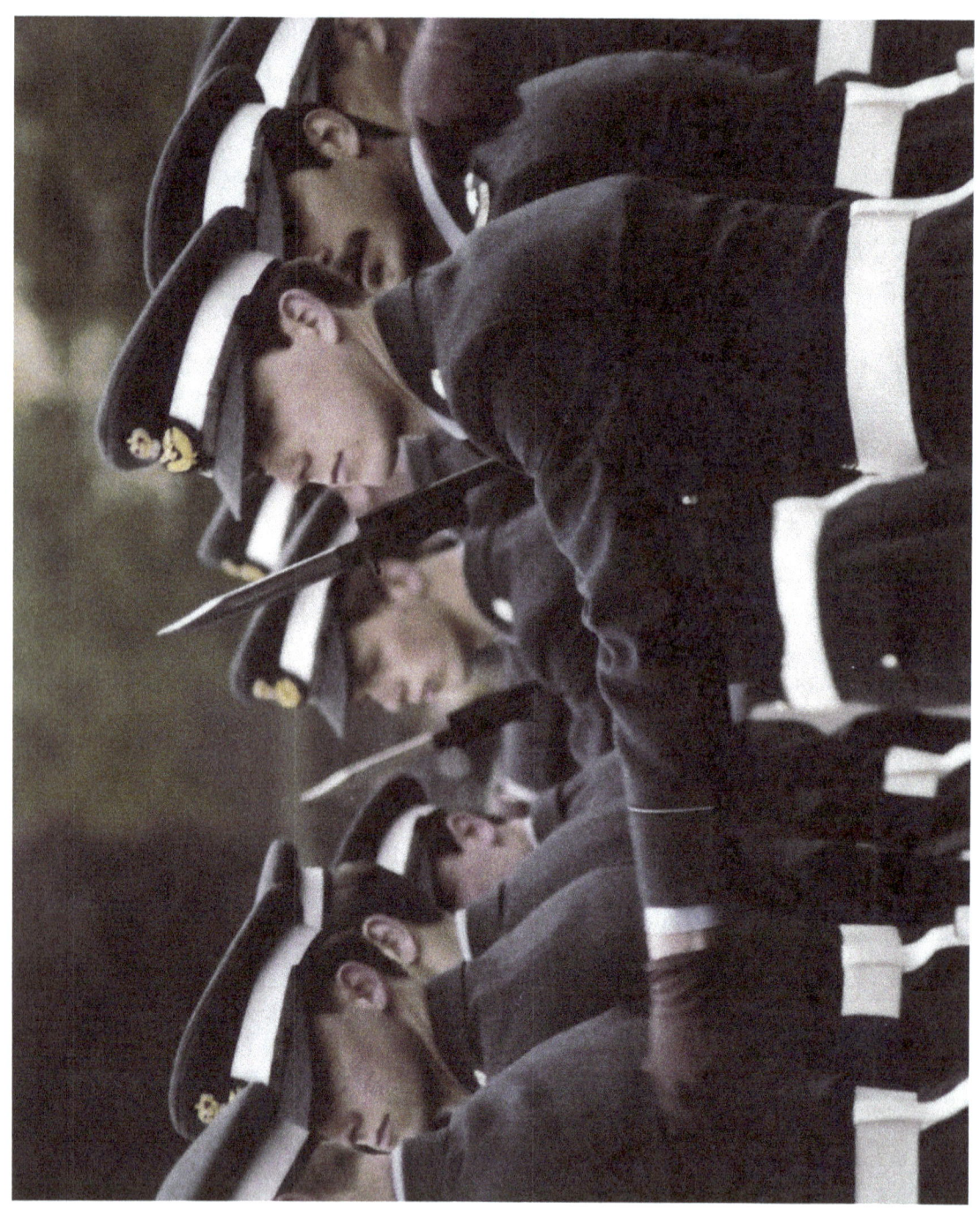

The last passing out parade held at RAF Henlow, 24th April 1980

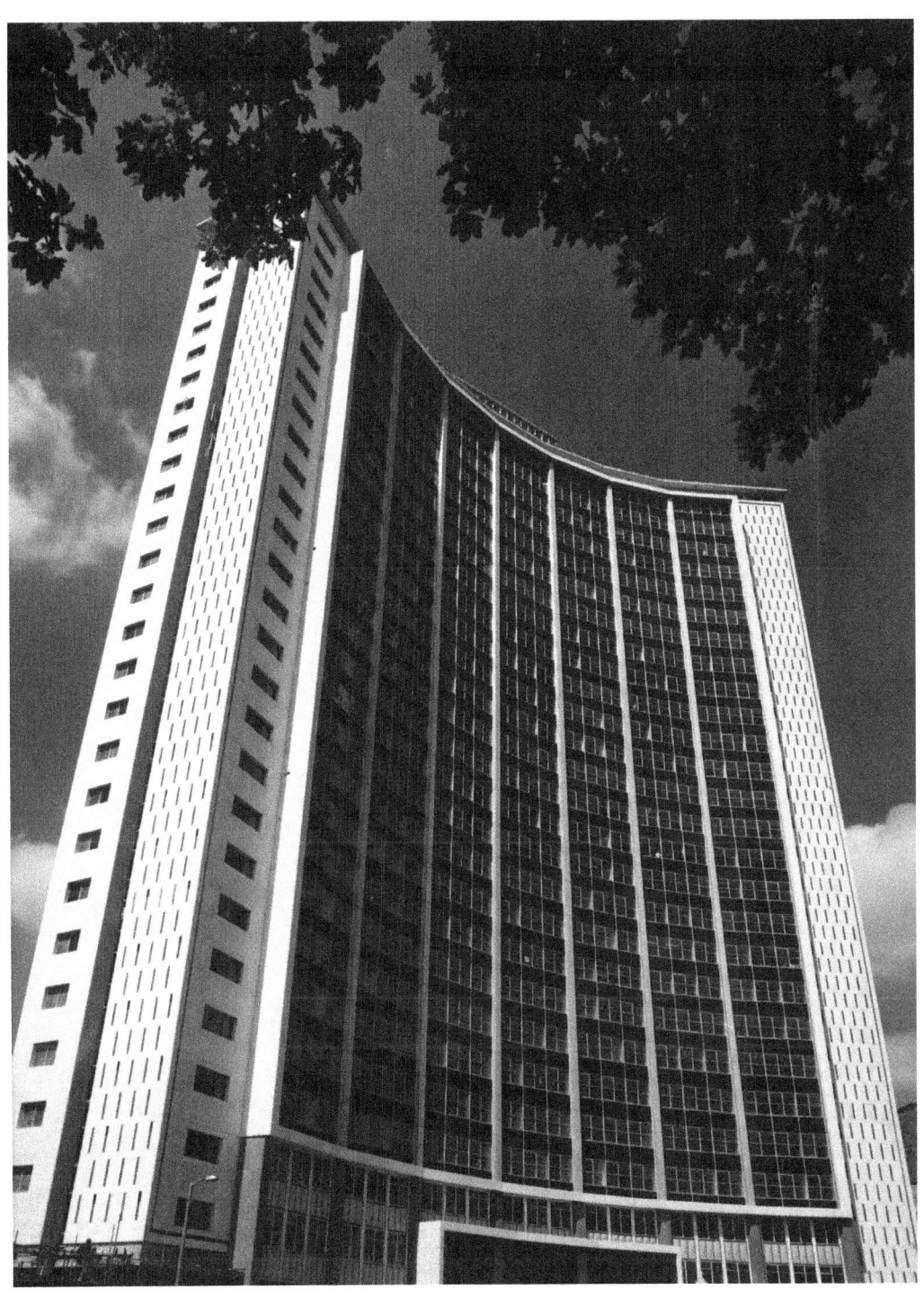

Earls Court Building in South London

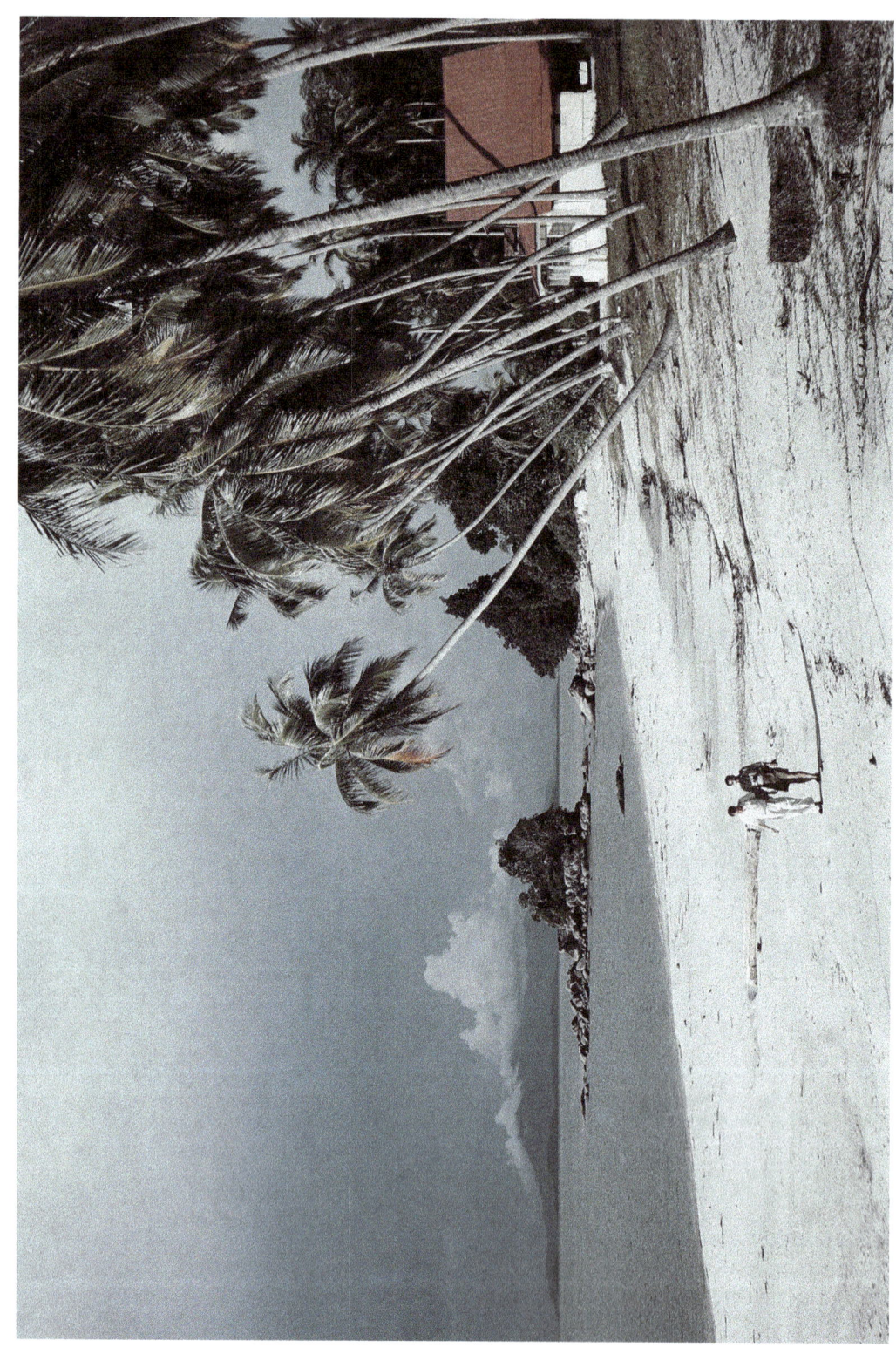

Walkers on the white sand of a beach in Penang, Malaysia

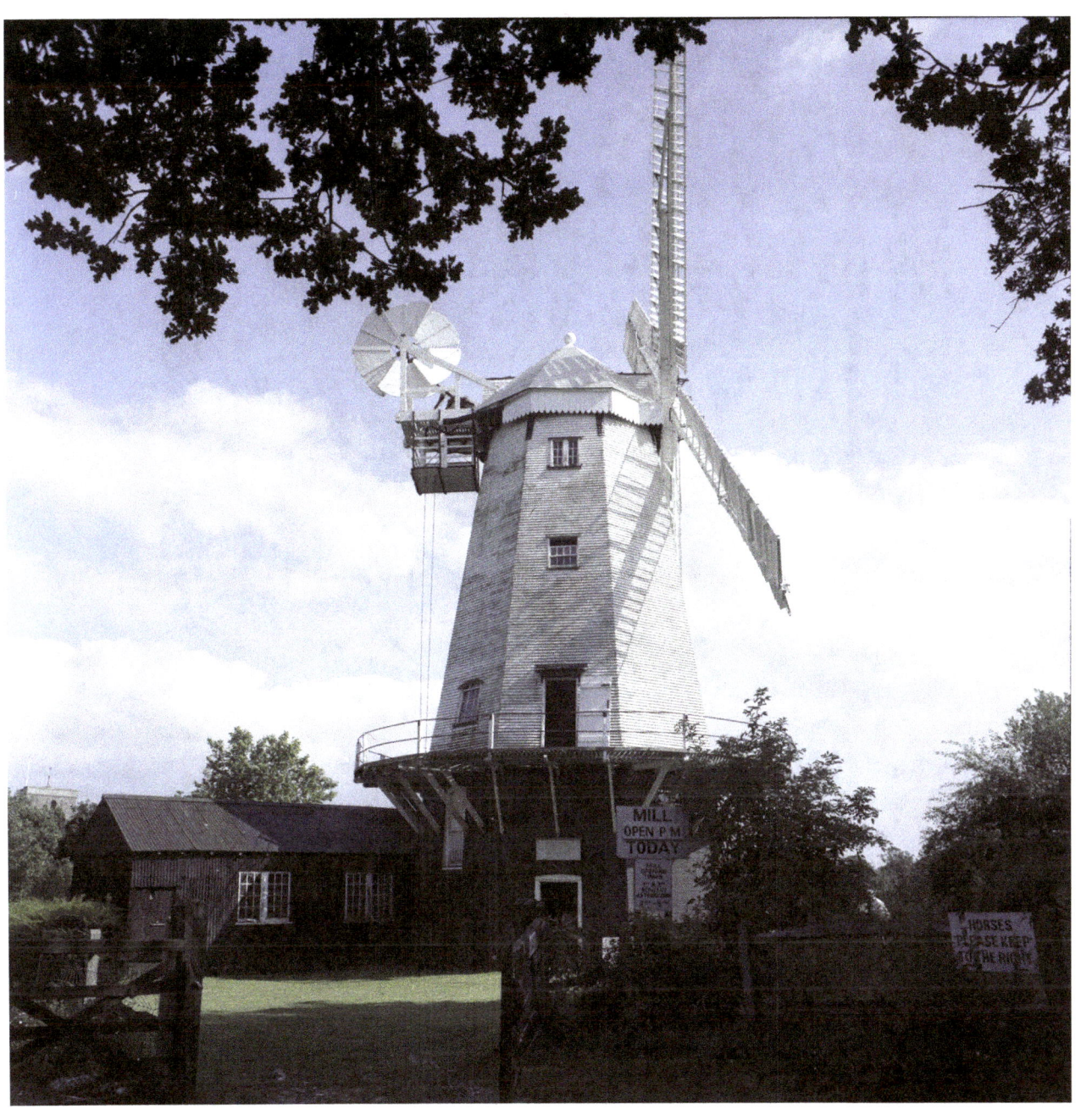

Shipley Windmill near Southwater, West Sussex

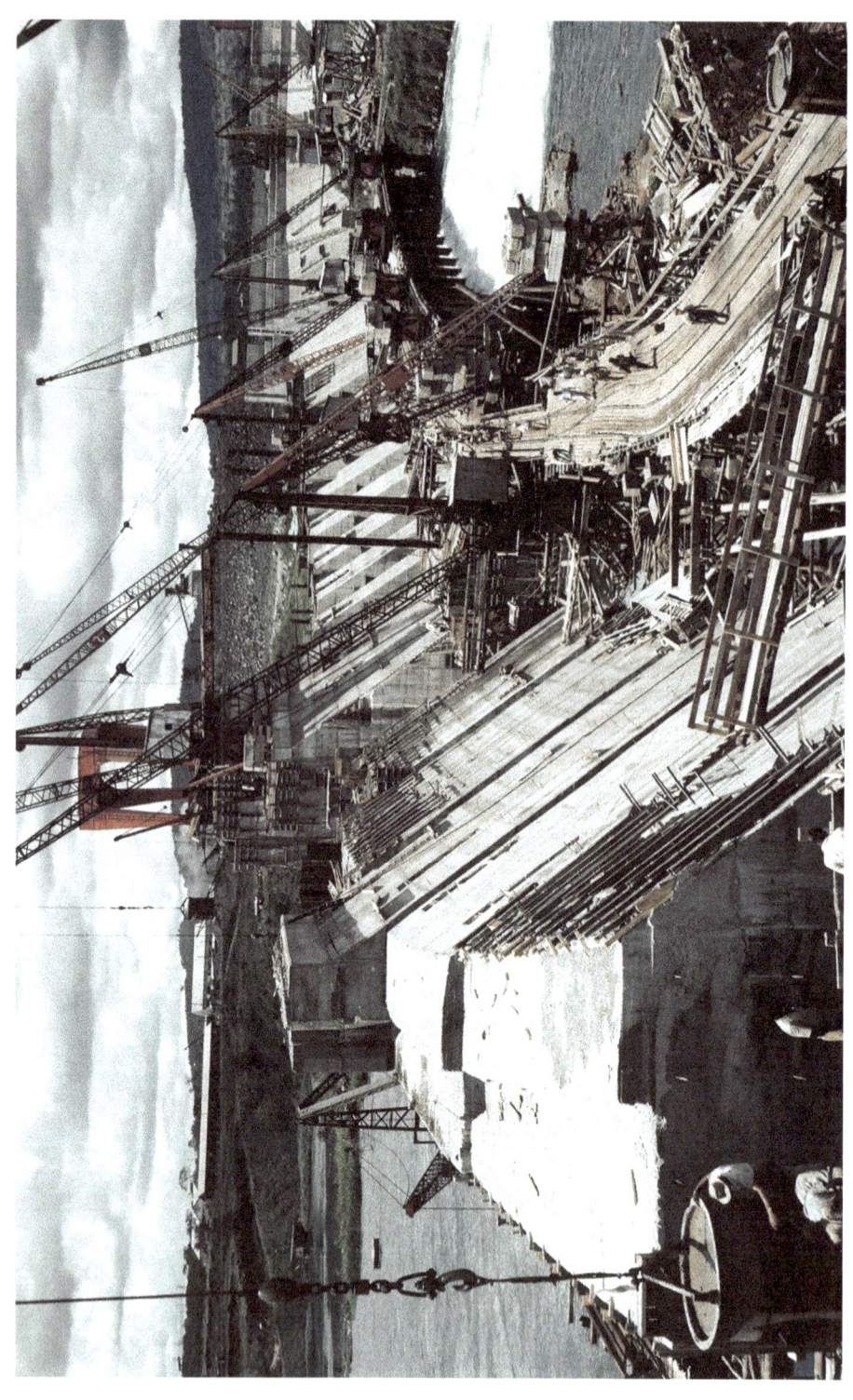

The Owen Falls dam project nearing completion at Jinga, Uganda in 1952

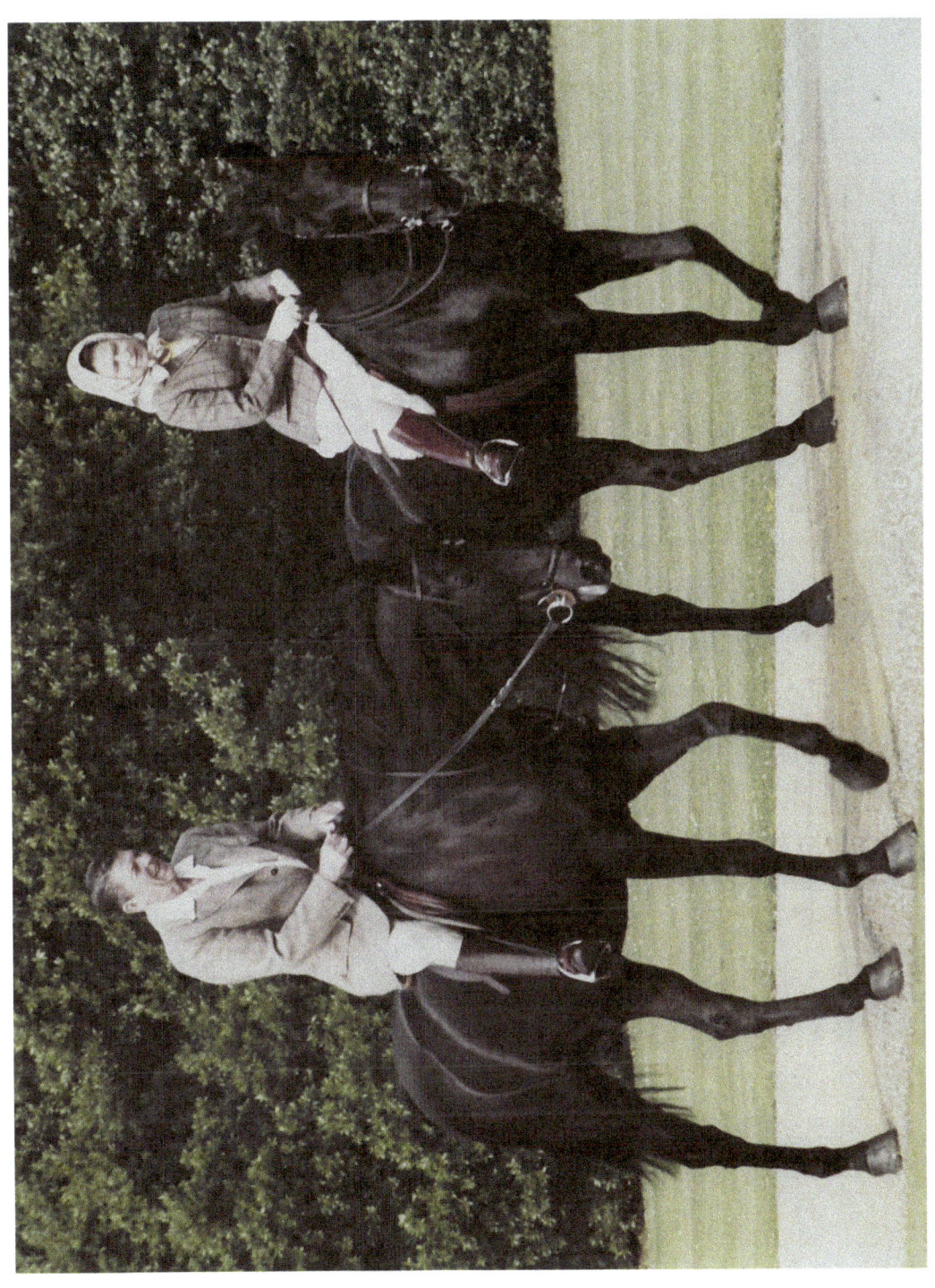

The Queen and Ronald Reagan ride out together in Windsor Great Park

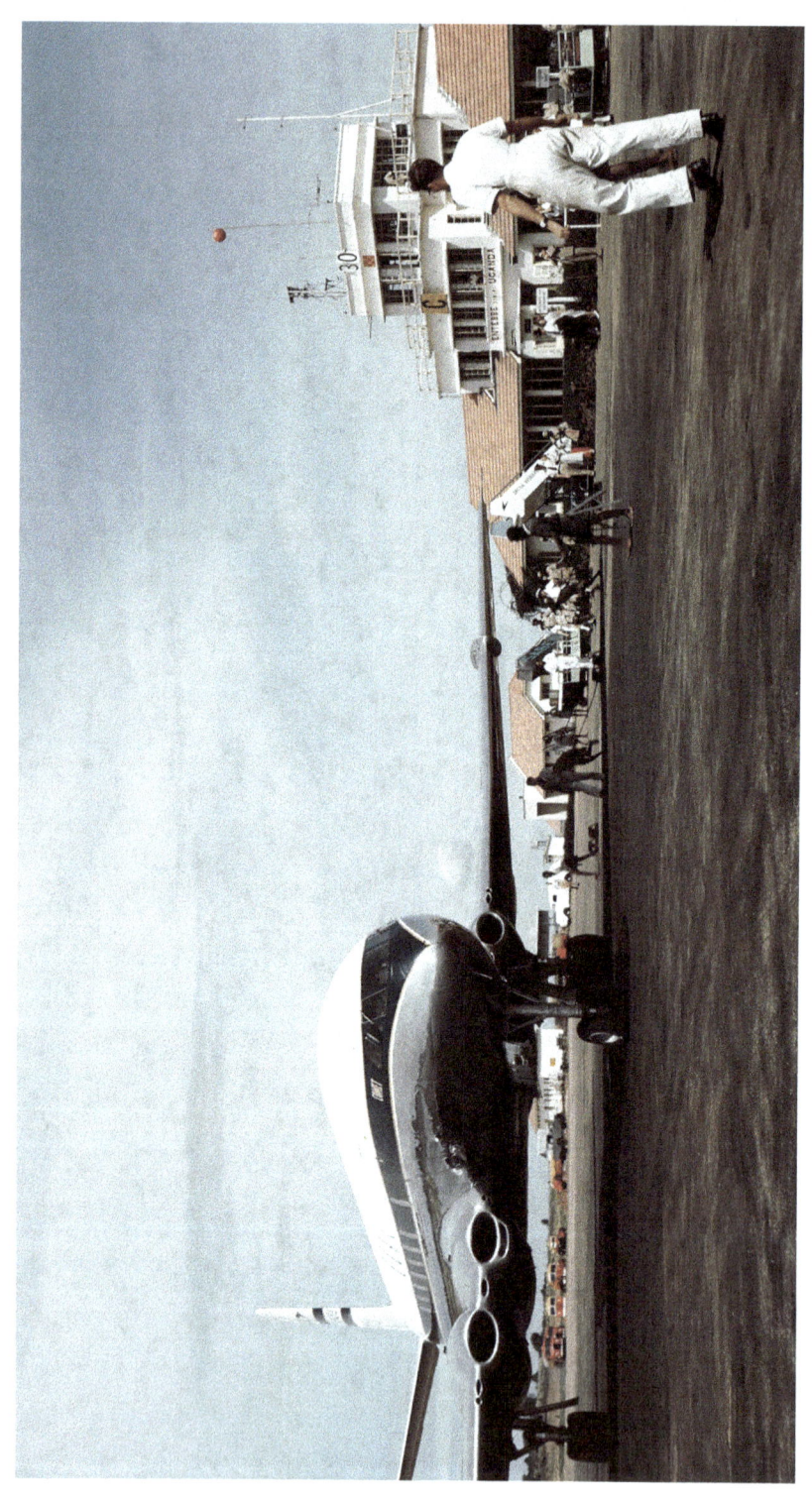

The BOAC Comet airliner G- ALYU lands at the new airport Entebbe, Uganda on it's way to Johannesburg, 1952

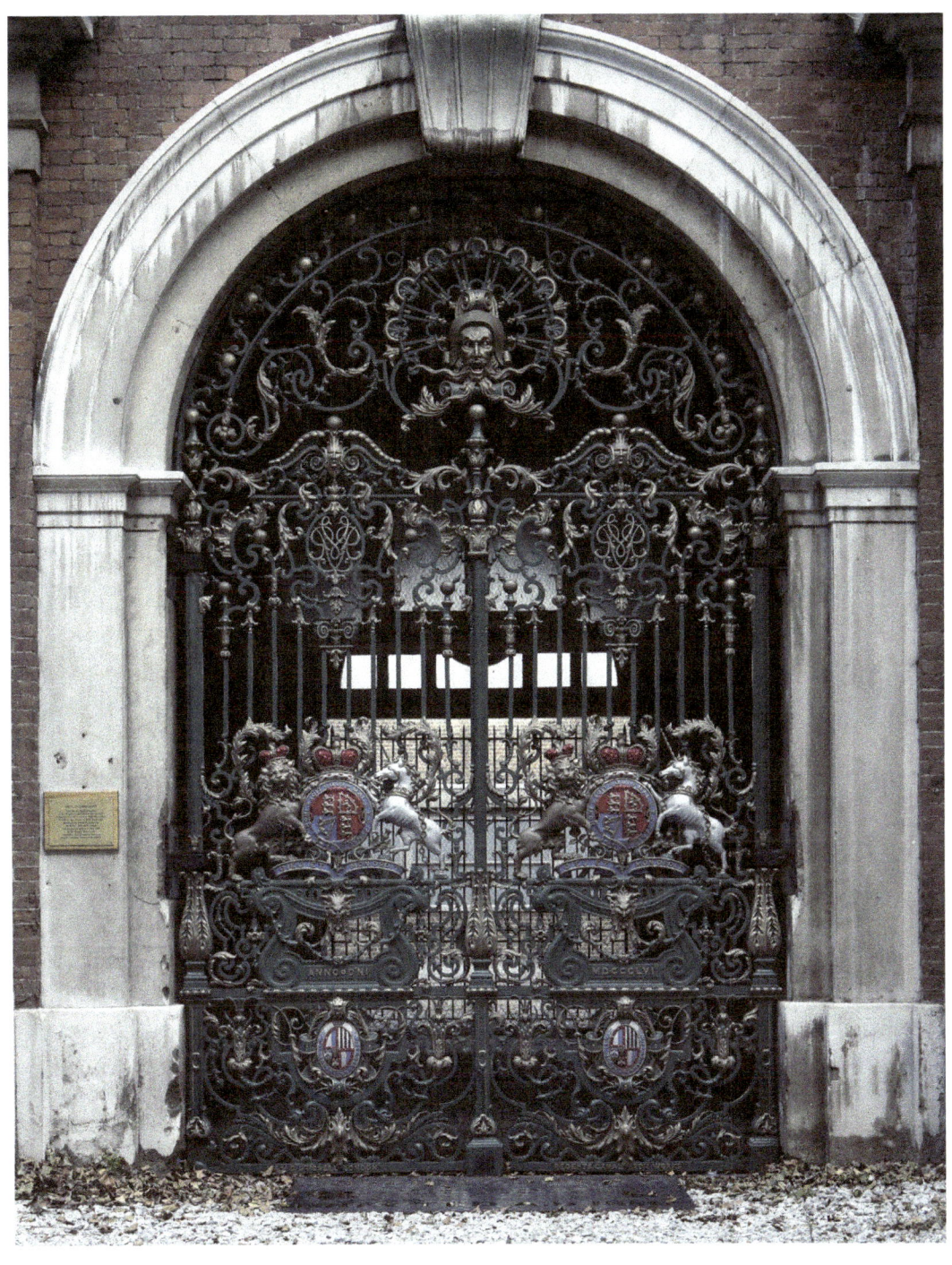

The original front gate of the Royal Arsenal, Woolwich

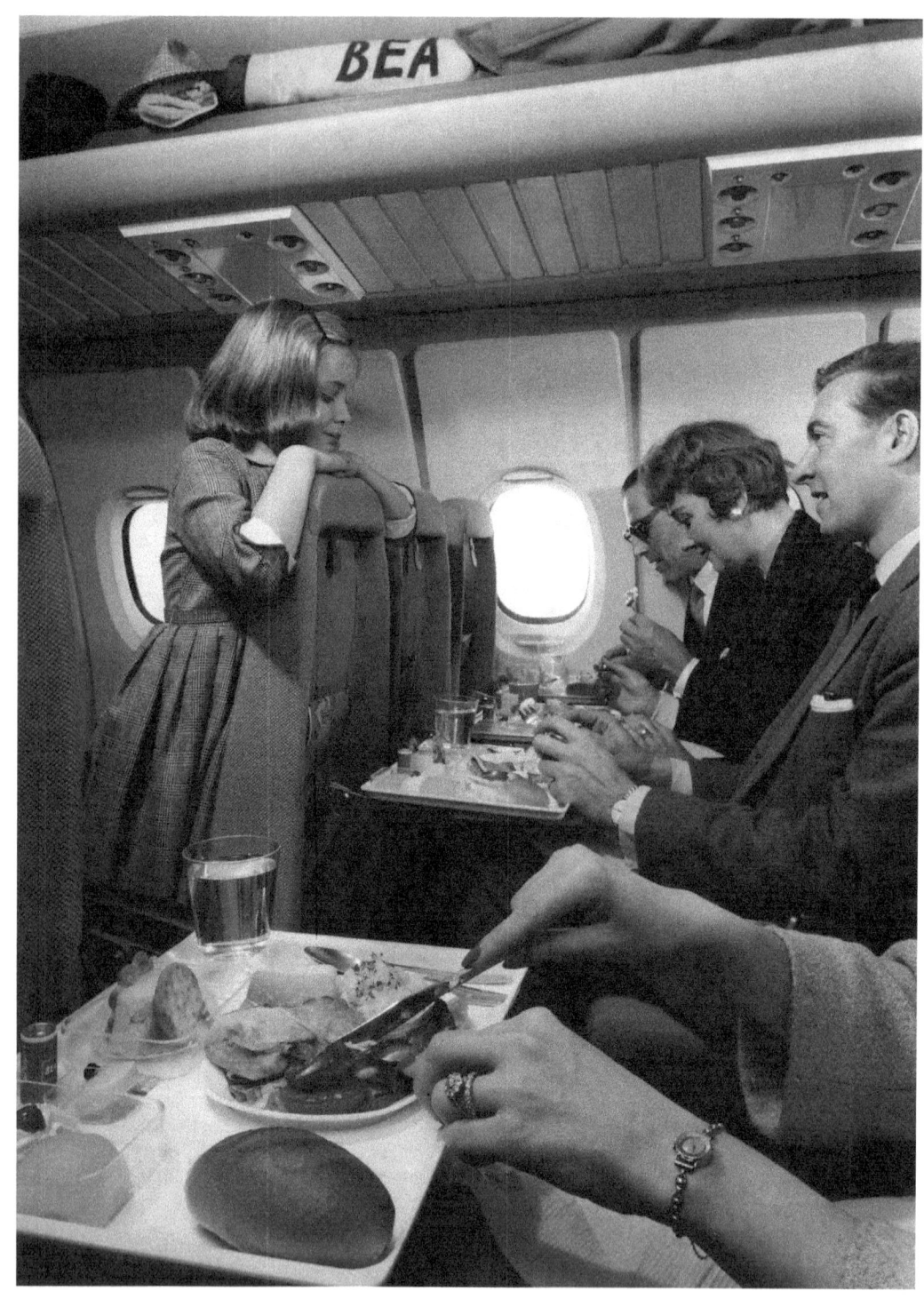

A mock up of the interior of the De Havilland Trident aircraft

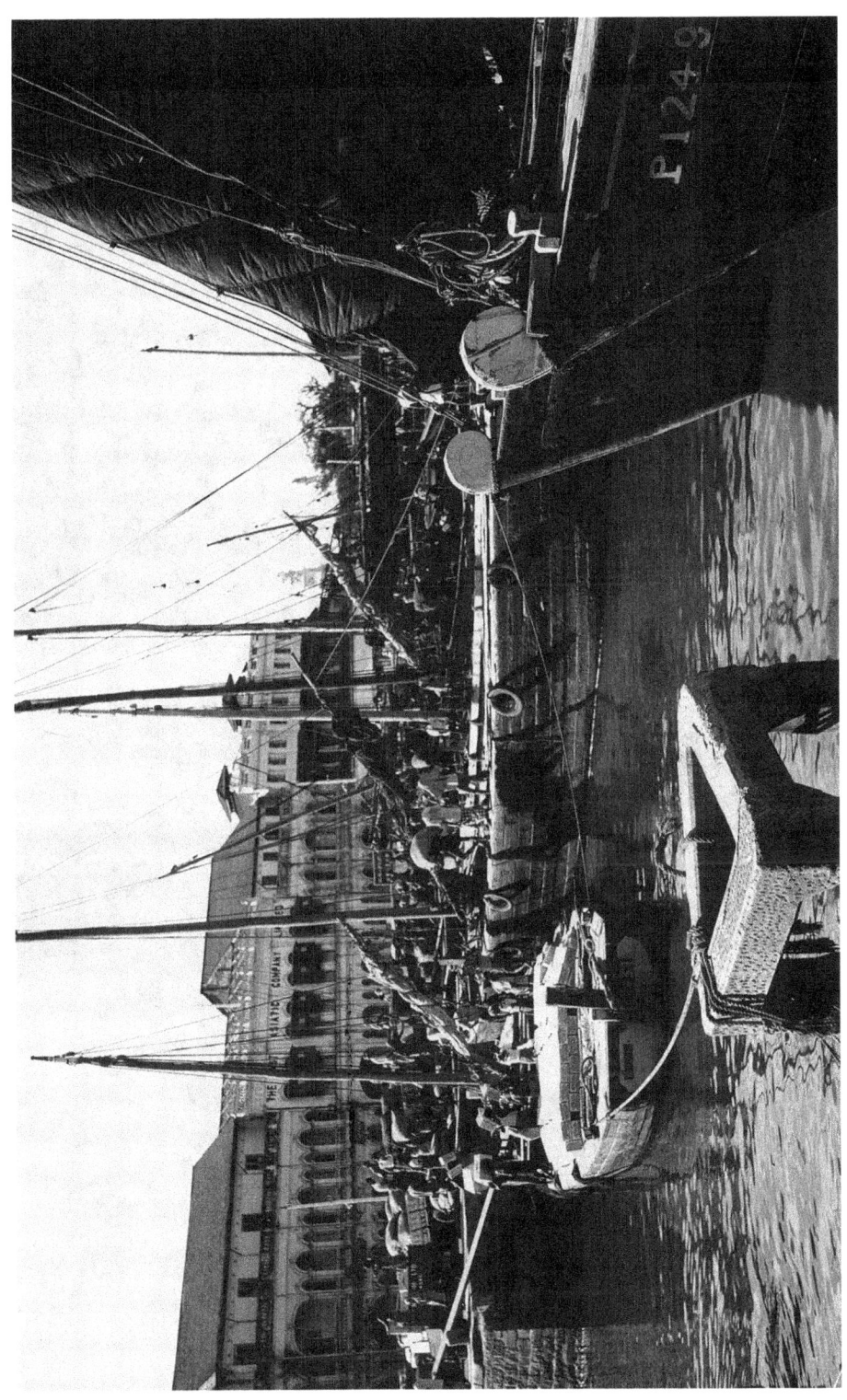

Boats in the harbour at George Town, Penang, Malaya showing dockside buildings, 1954

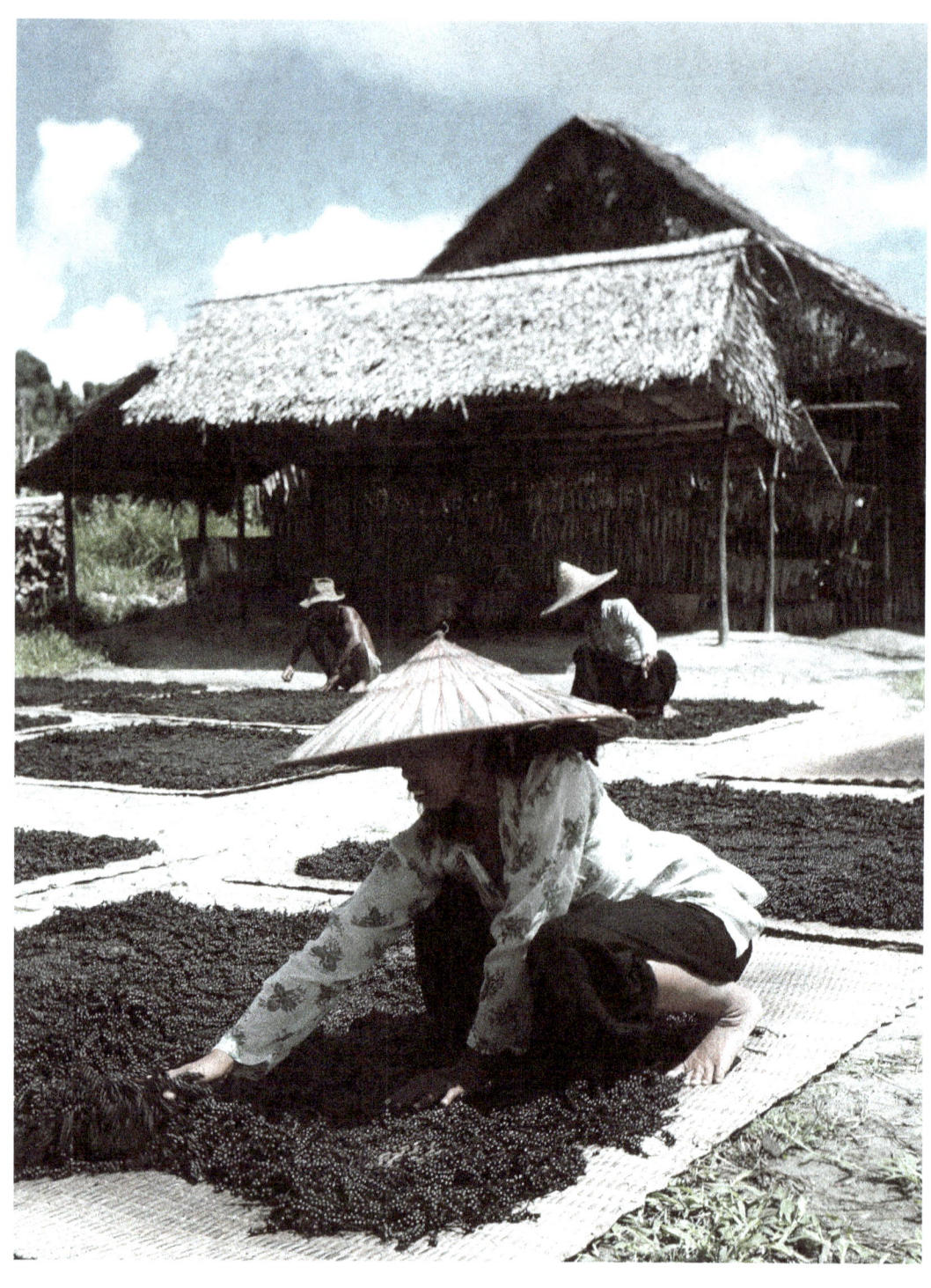

Spreading pepper to dry in the sun at the Semegok resettlement between Serian and Kuching, Sarawak, 1954

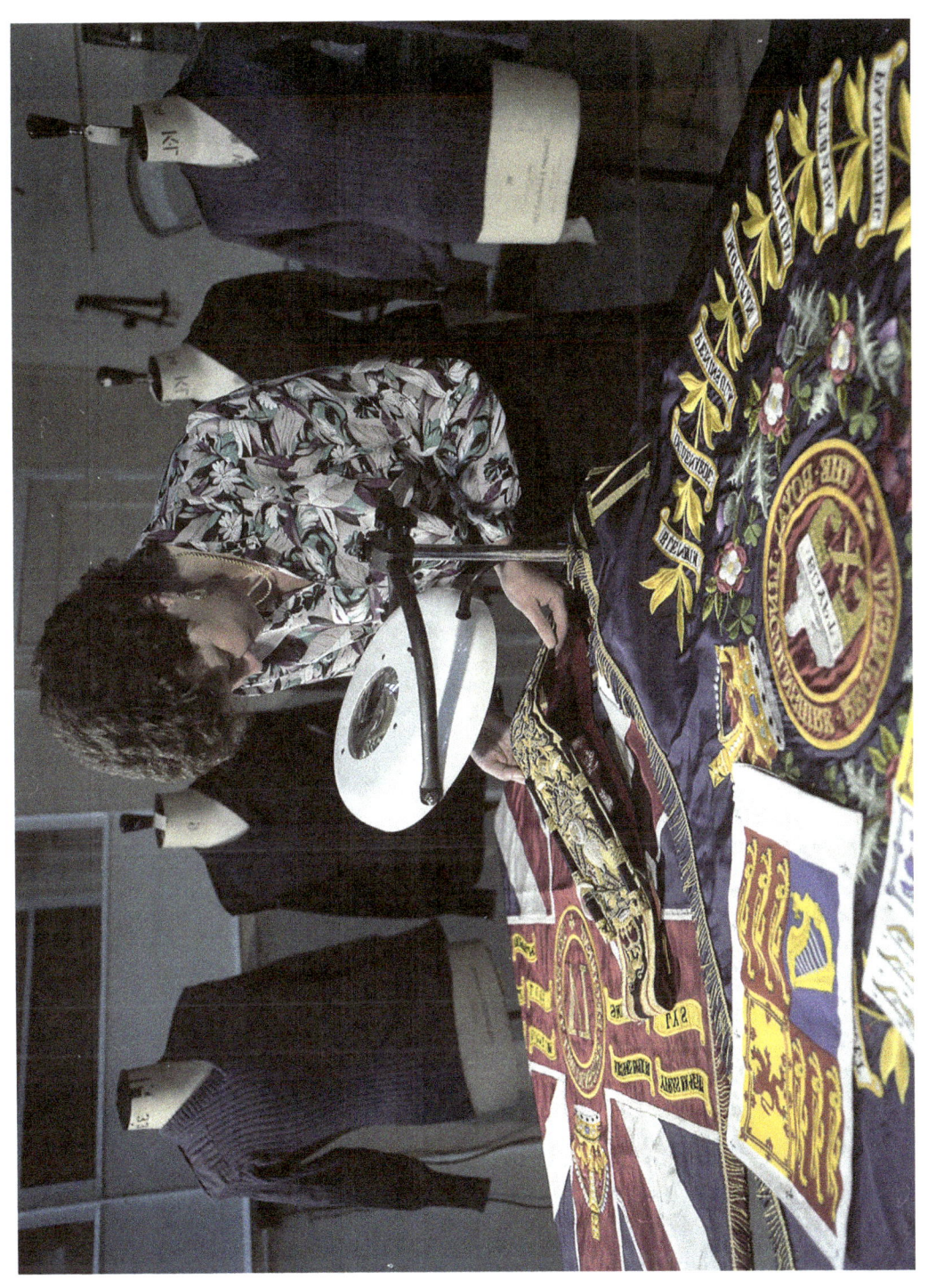

QAD Didcot, checking the needle work on regimental colours

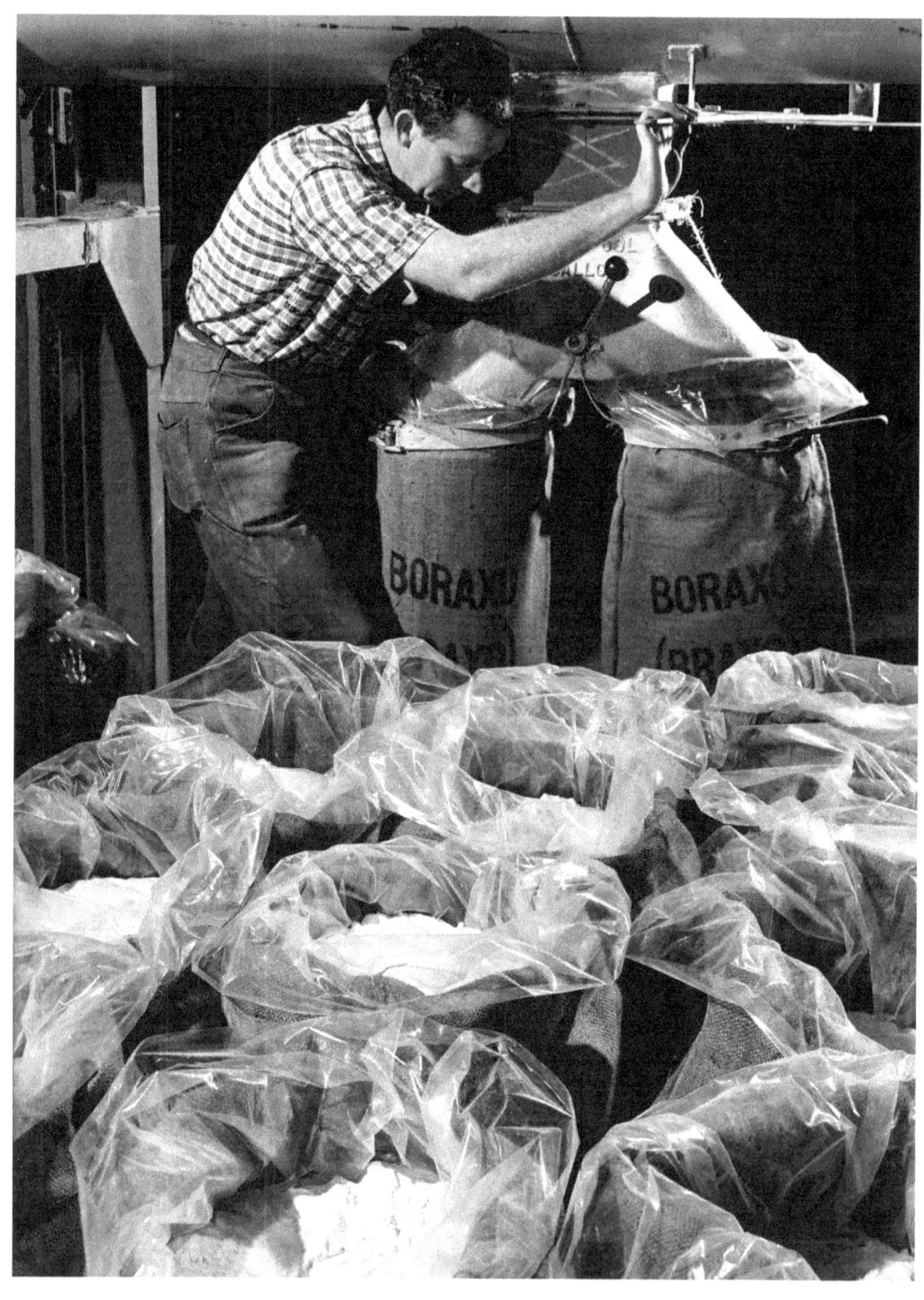

Animal feed being loaded into sacks for delivery to farms

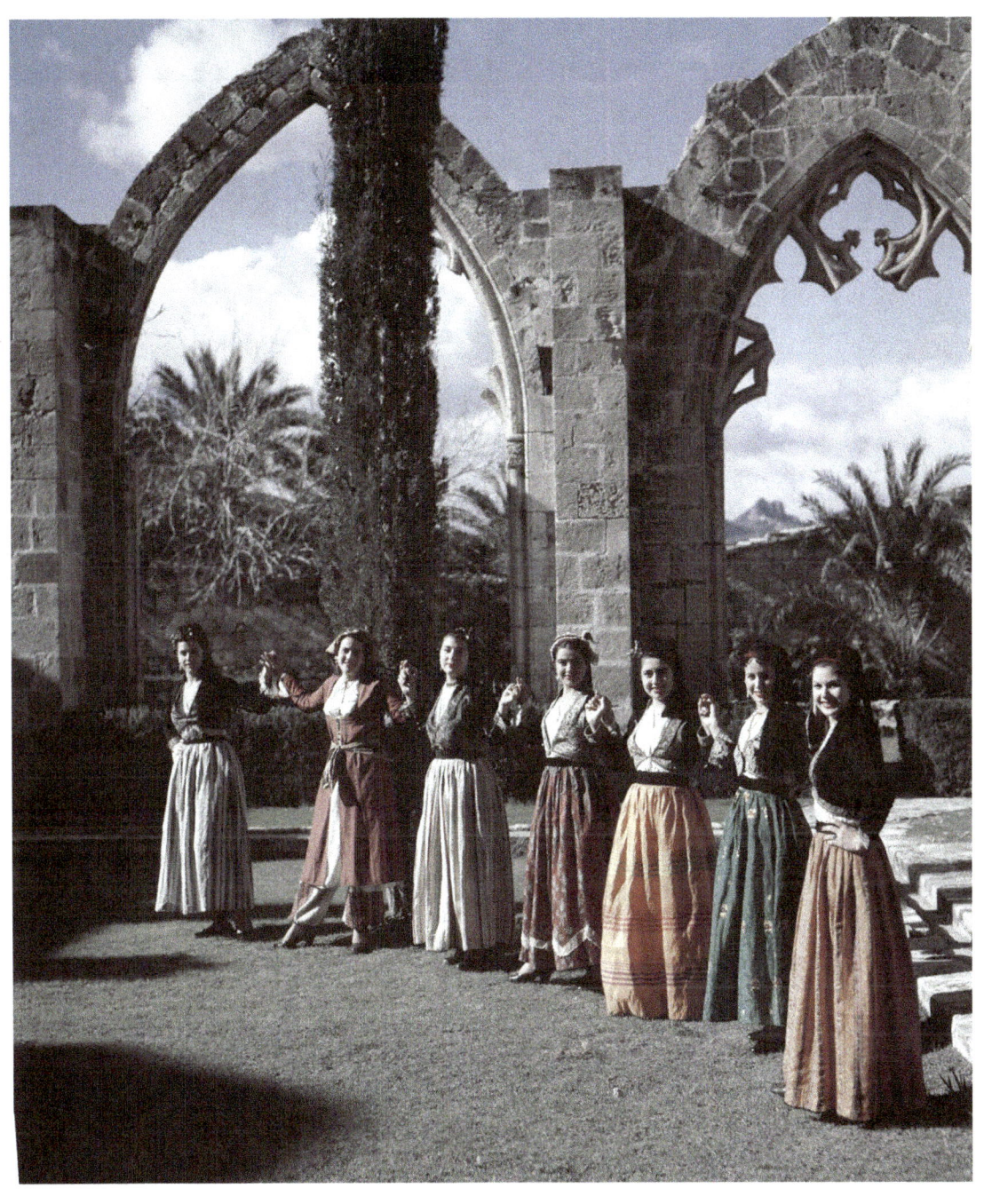

Girls in traditional costume at Bellapais Abbey near Kyrenia, Cyprus, 1953

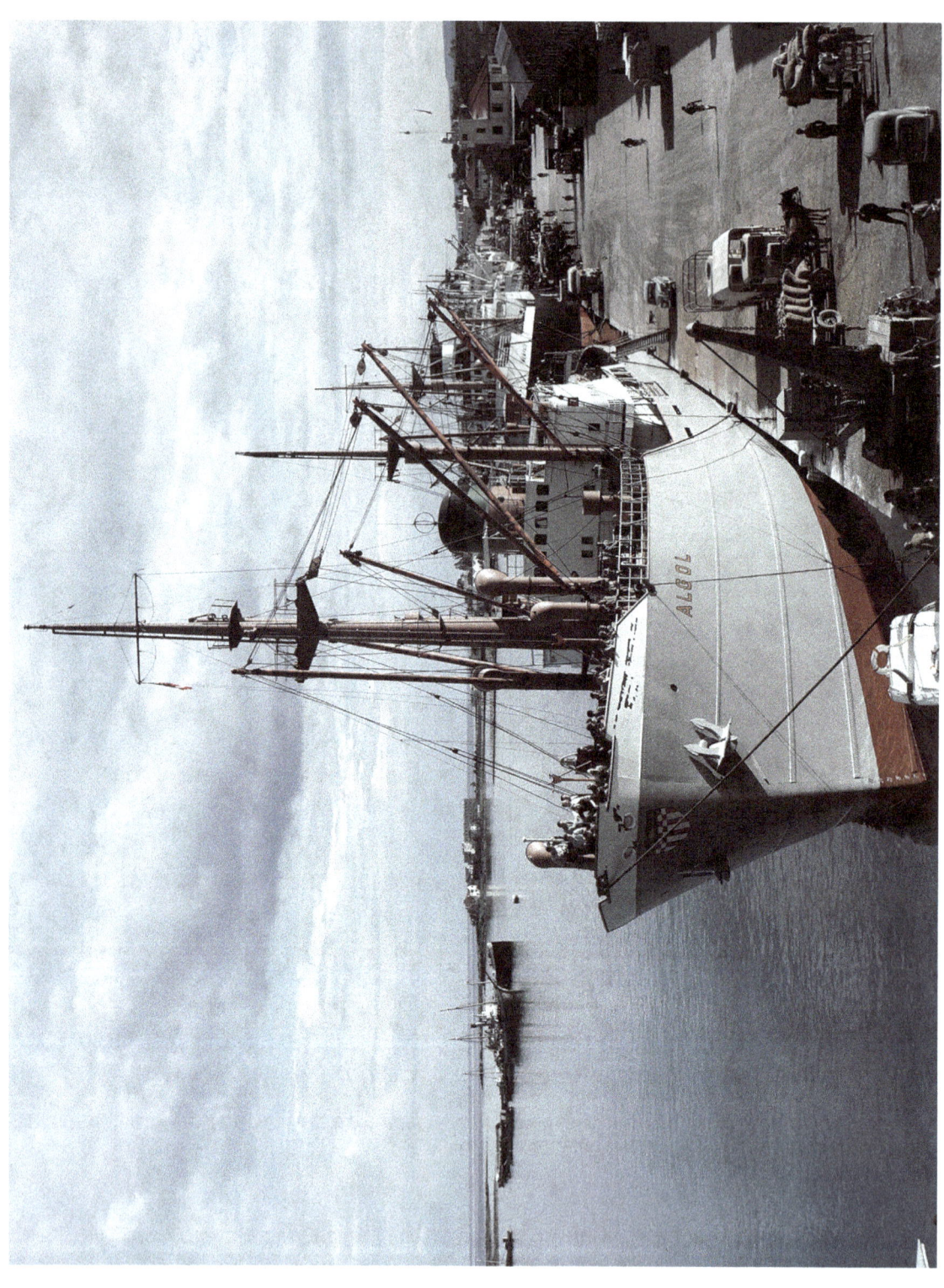

Ships at the dock side in Famagusta harbour, Cyprus, 1953

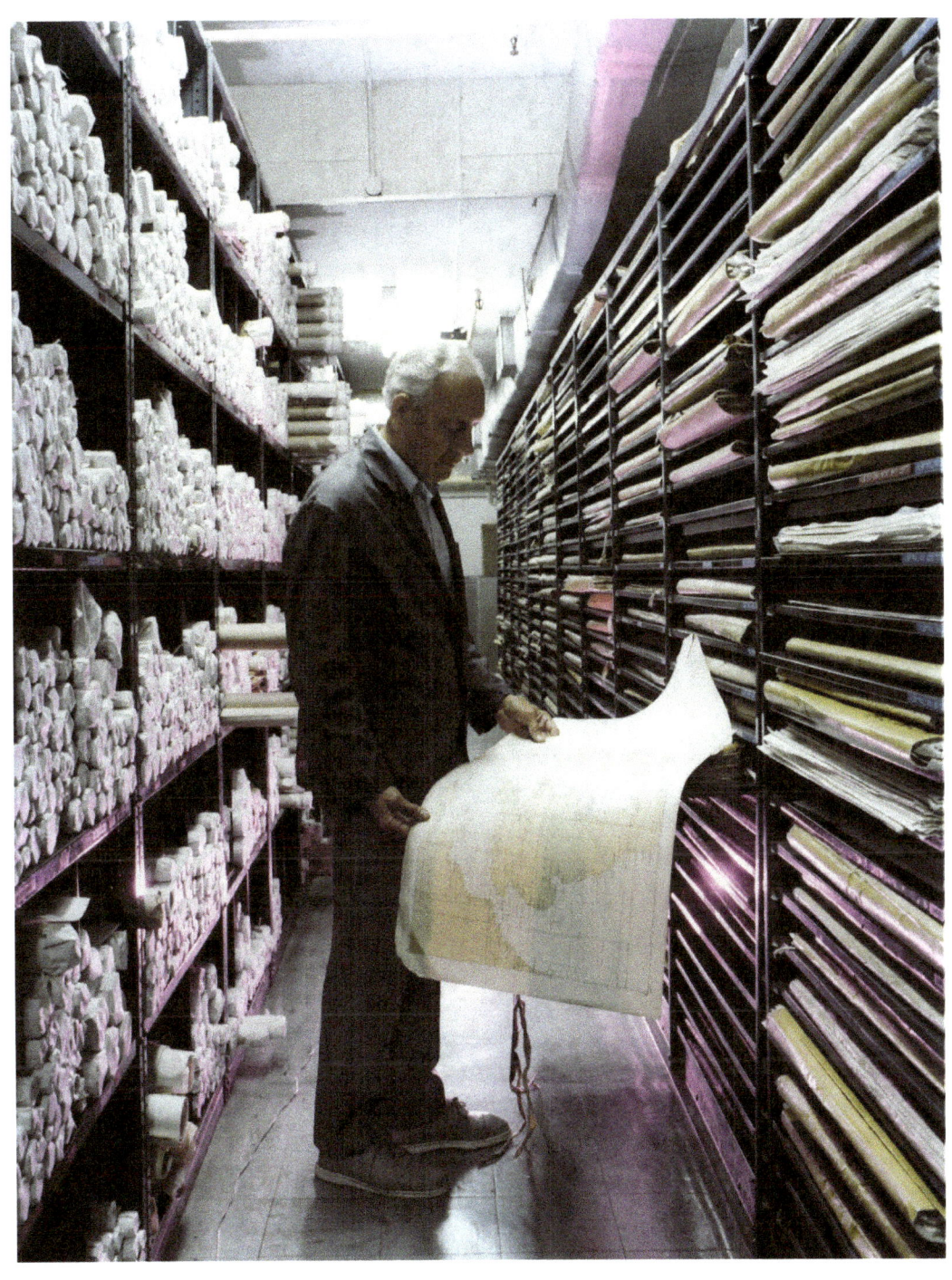

Checking nautical maps from the archive department at the MOD Hydrographic Department, Falmouth

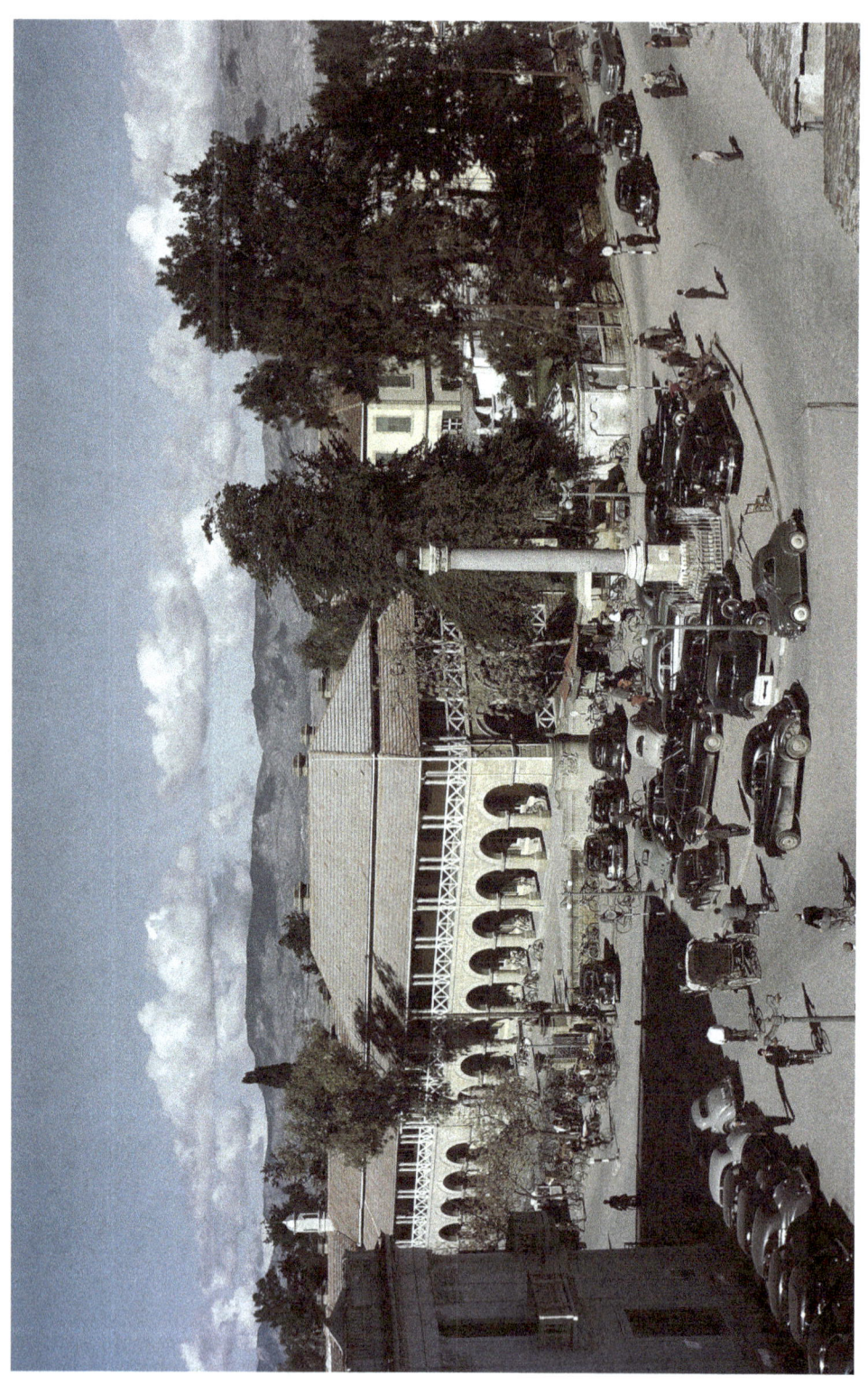

Looking down on Ataturk Square in the centre of Nicosia, Cyprus, 1953

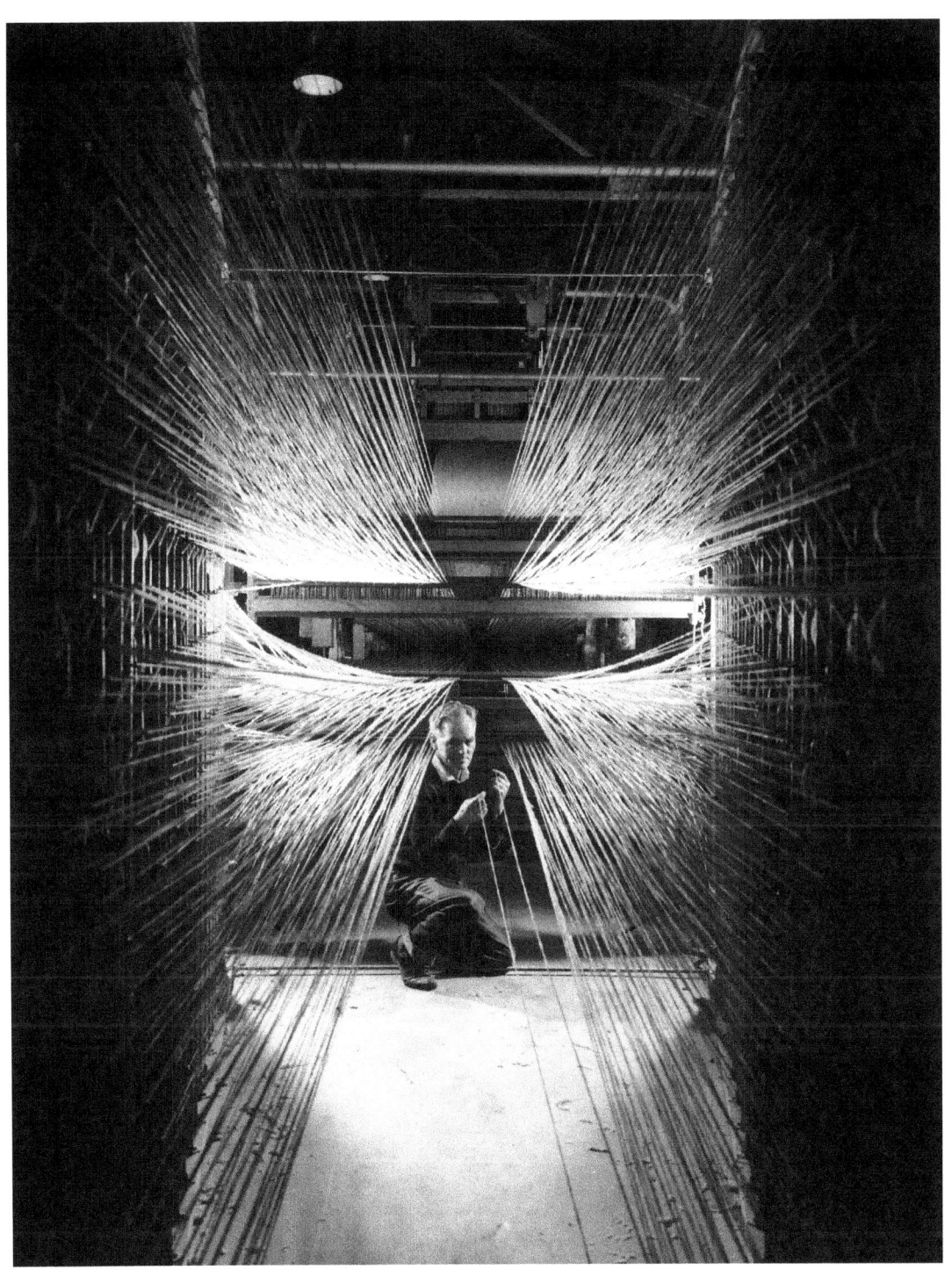

Carpet Making at Wilton, Wiltshire

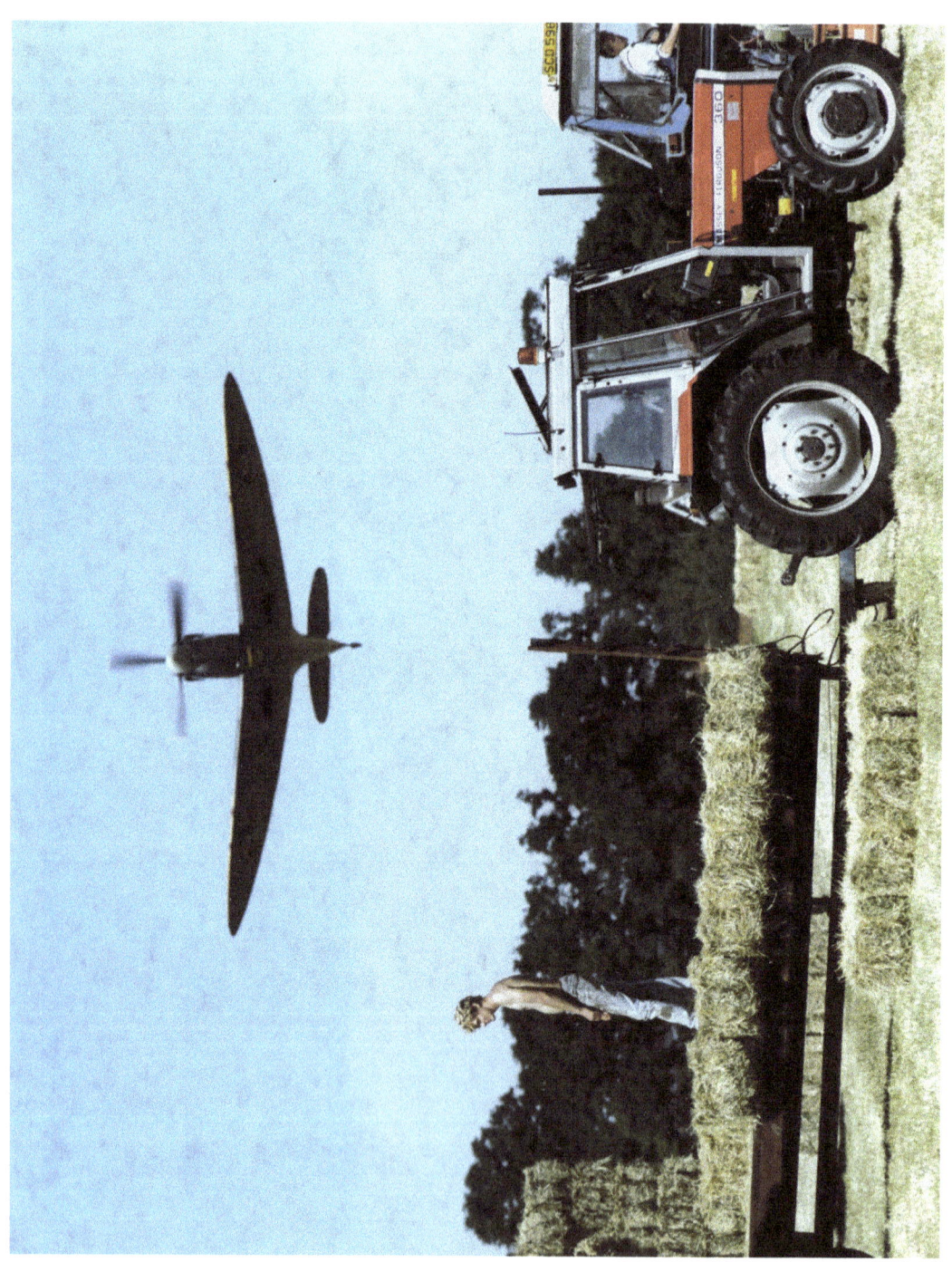

Spitfire flying over the field used as alternative runway during WW2, Coolham, West Sussex, in celebration of the 50th Anniversary of the Battle of Britain.

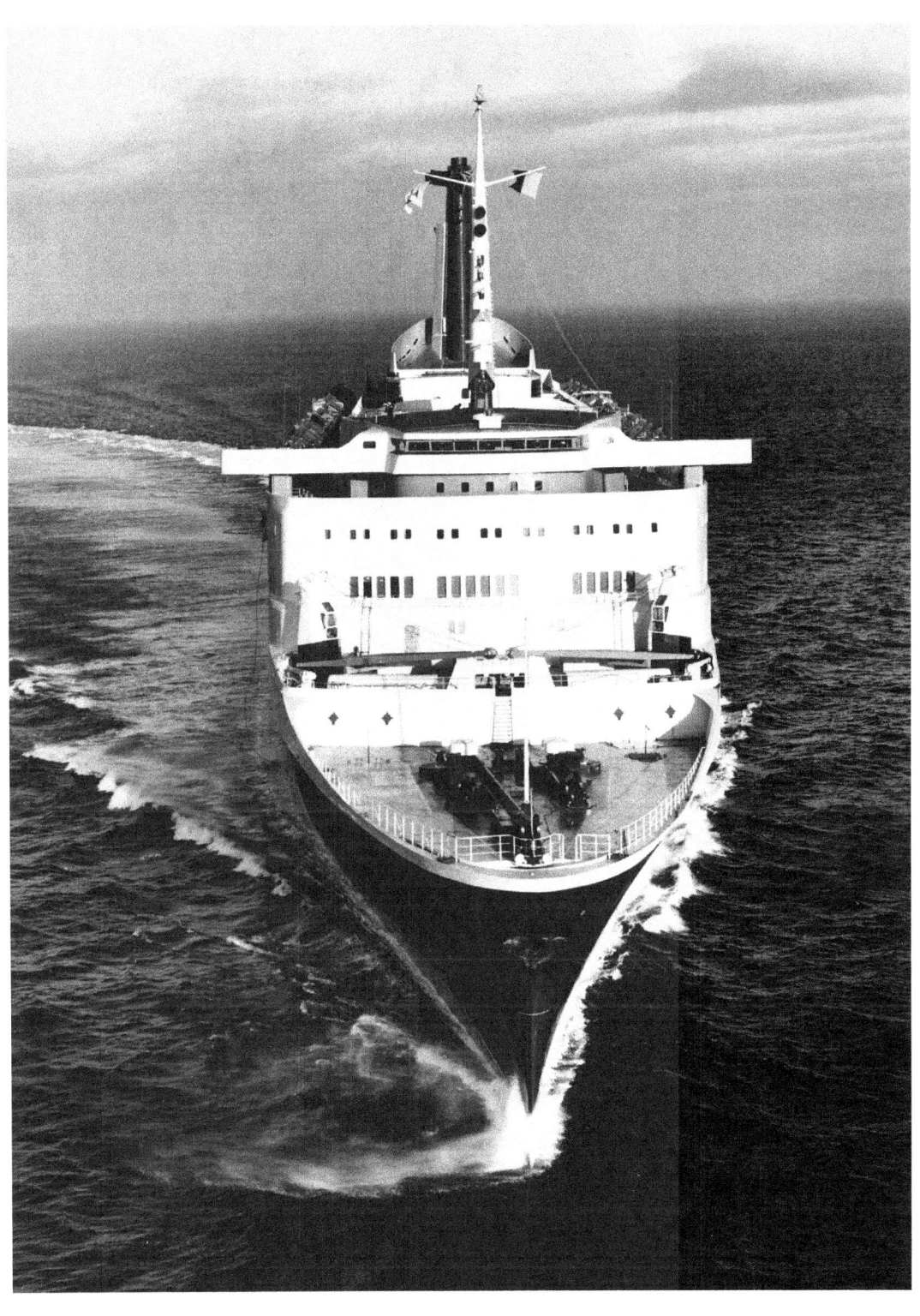

The QE2 during her speed trials off the Isle of Arun

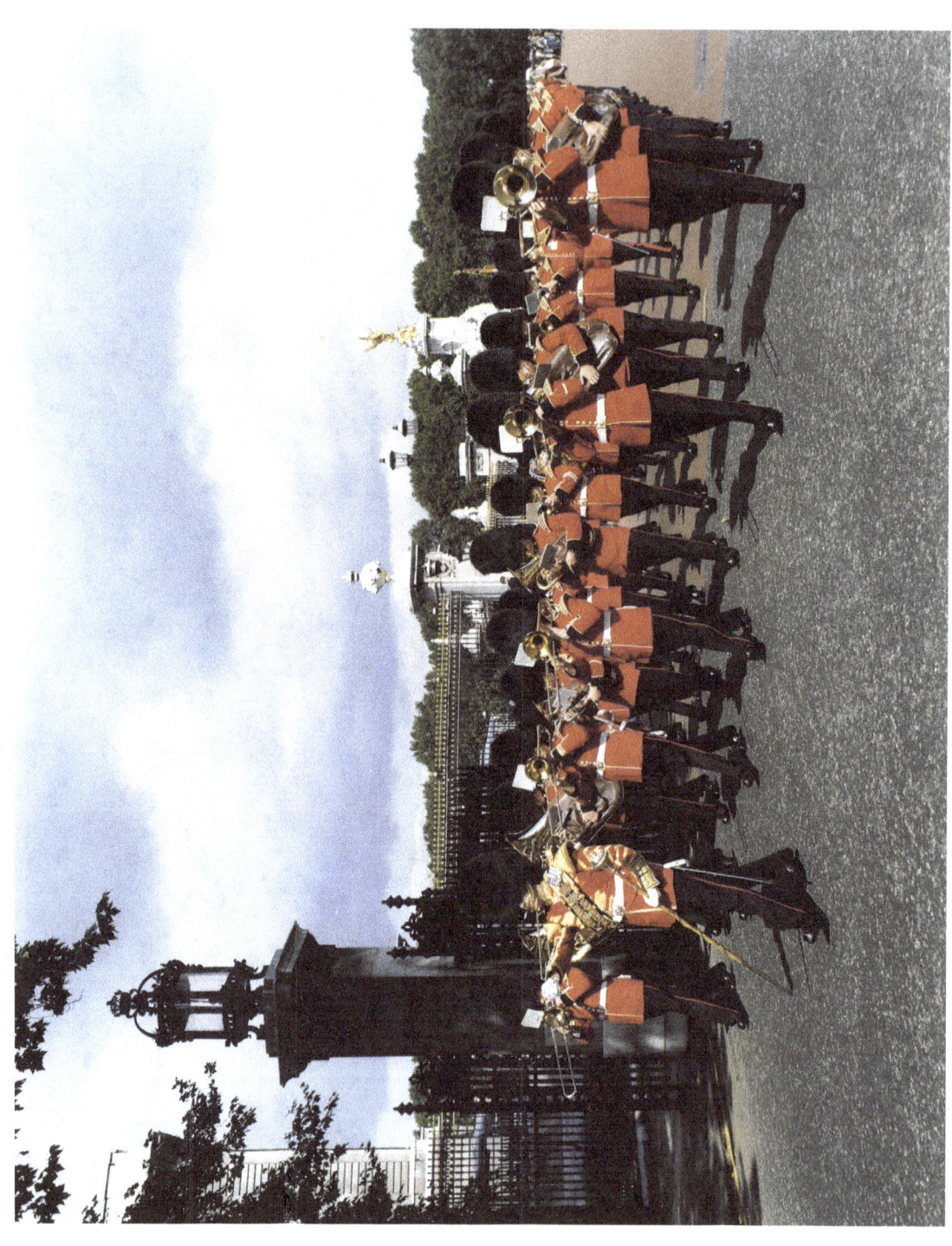

The band of the Irish Guards playing as they march away from Buckingham Palace

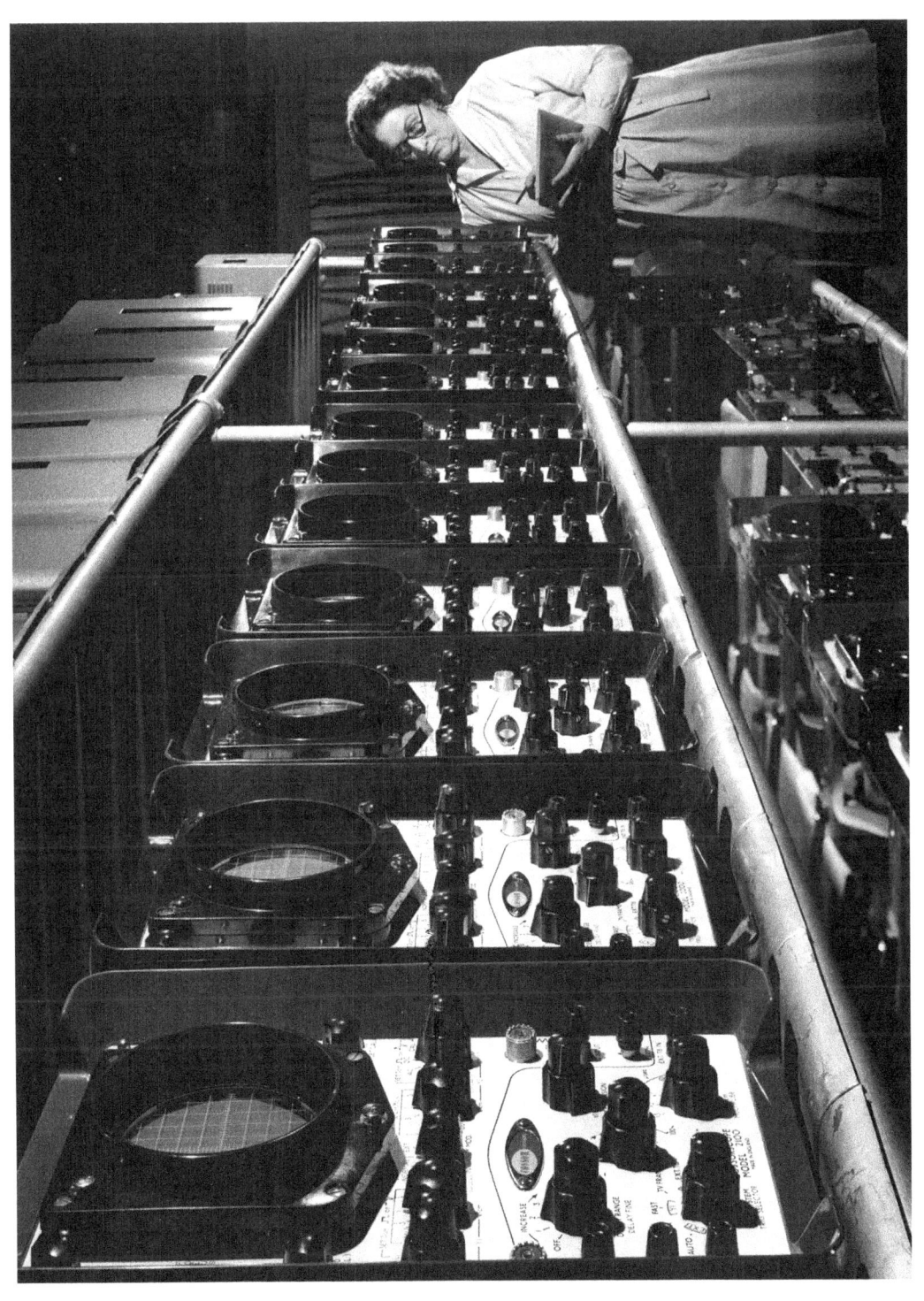

Checking scopes that were made at Cossor, Harlow in the 80's

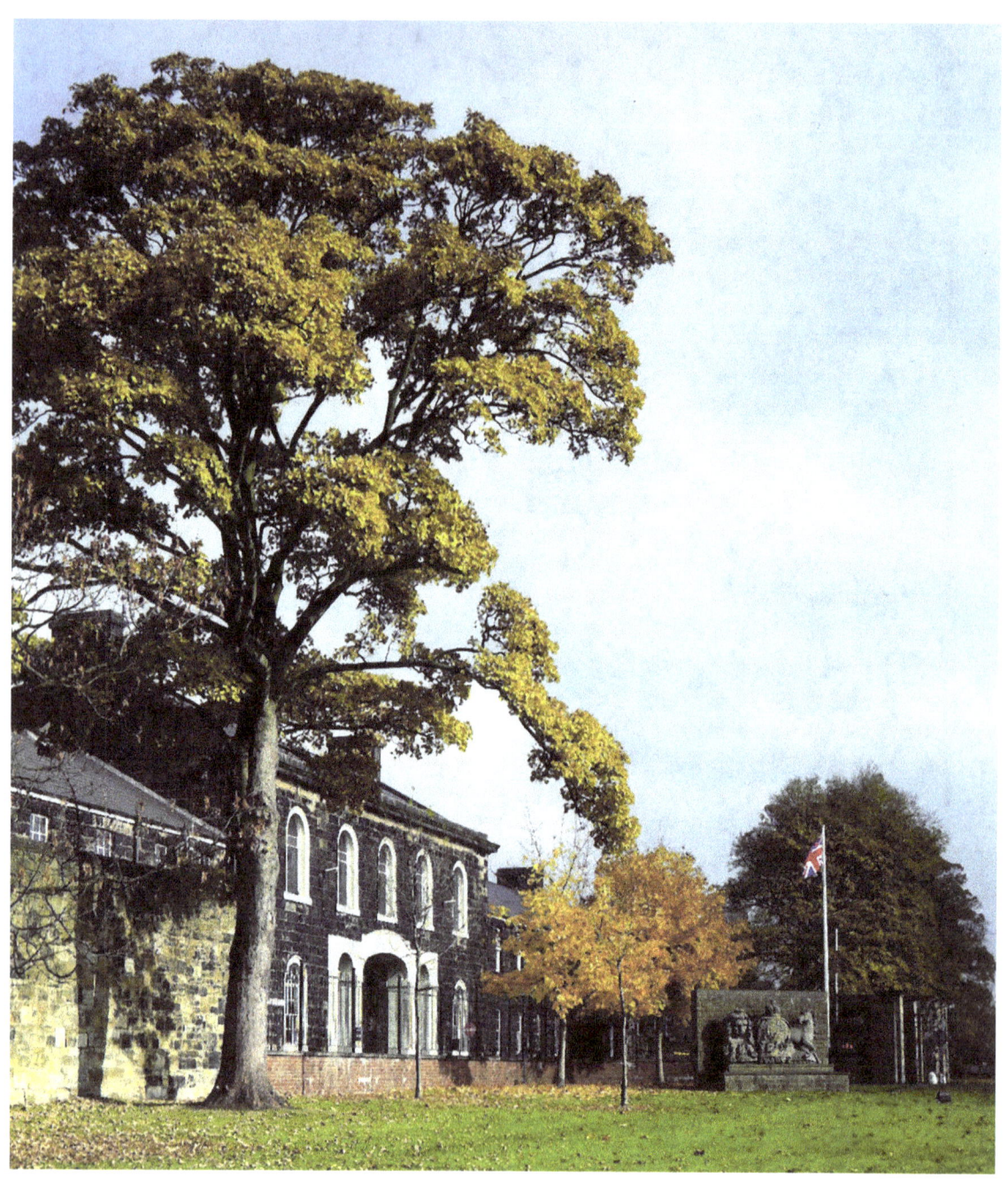

Preston Barracks in the autumn

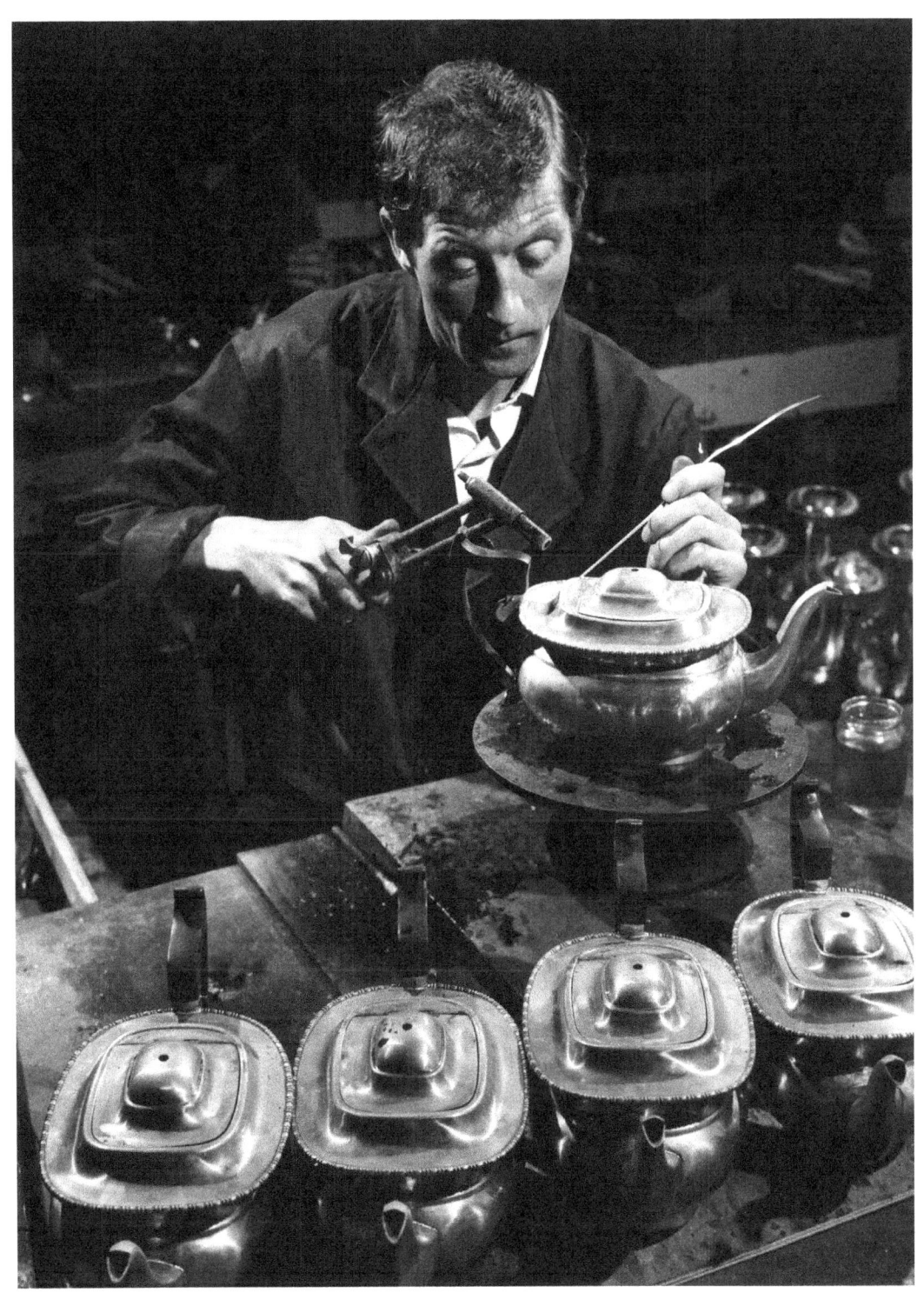

A silver smith at work making tea pots at Viners, Sheffield

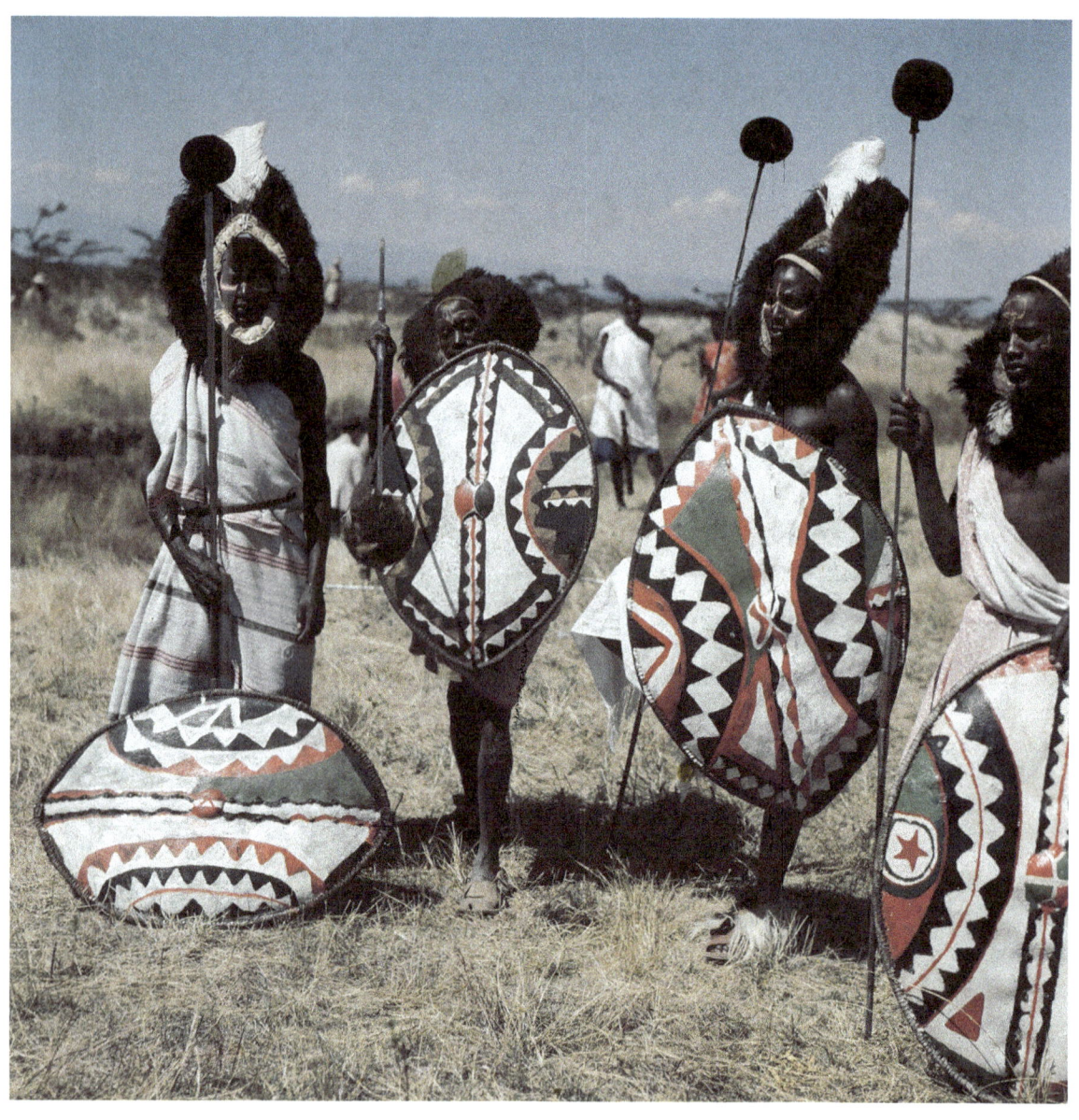

Four Nandi recruits wearing tribal dress from the 4th Battalion, Kings African Rifles, Nairobi, Kenya 1952

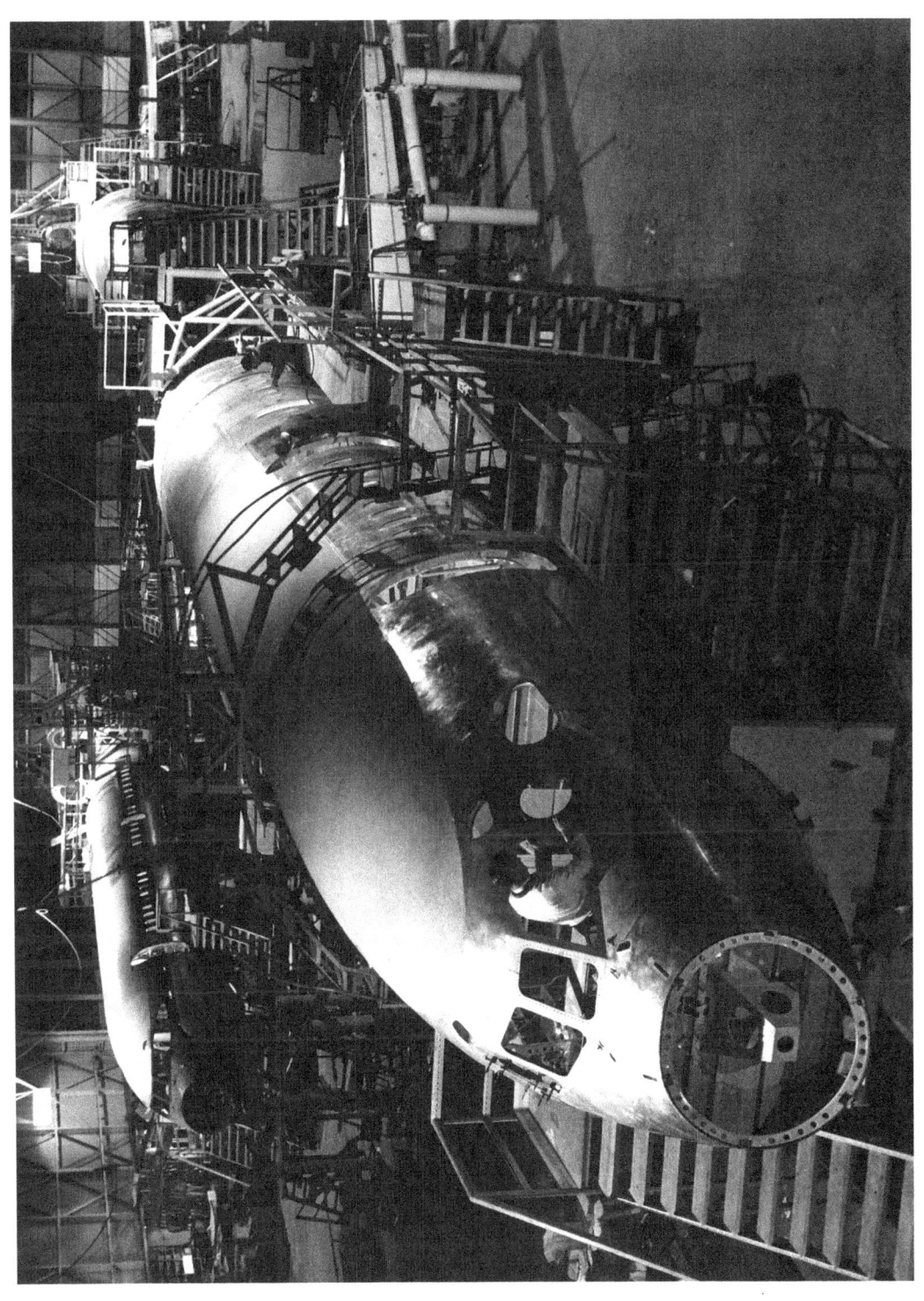

De Havilland Trident aircraft being manufactured at Hatfield works

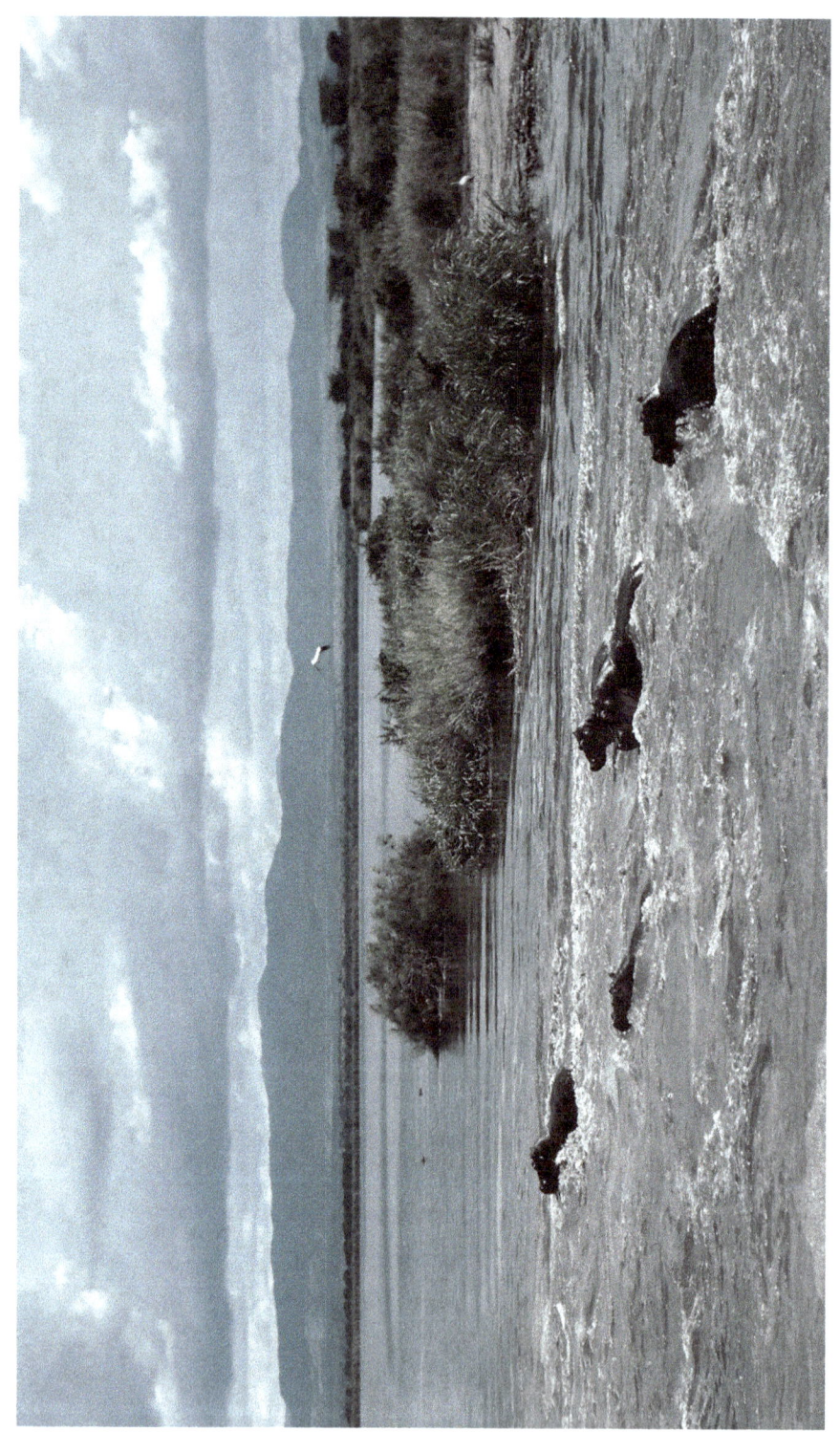

Hippos in Lake George, Western Uganda having been alarmed by a passing ship

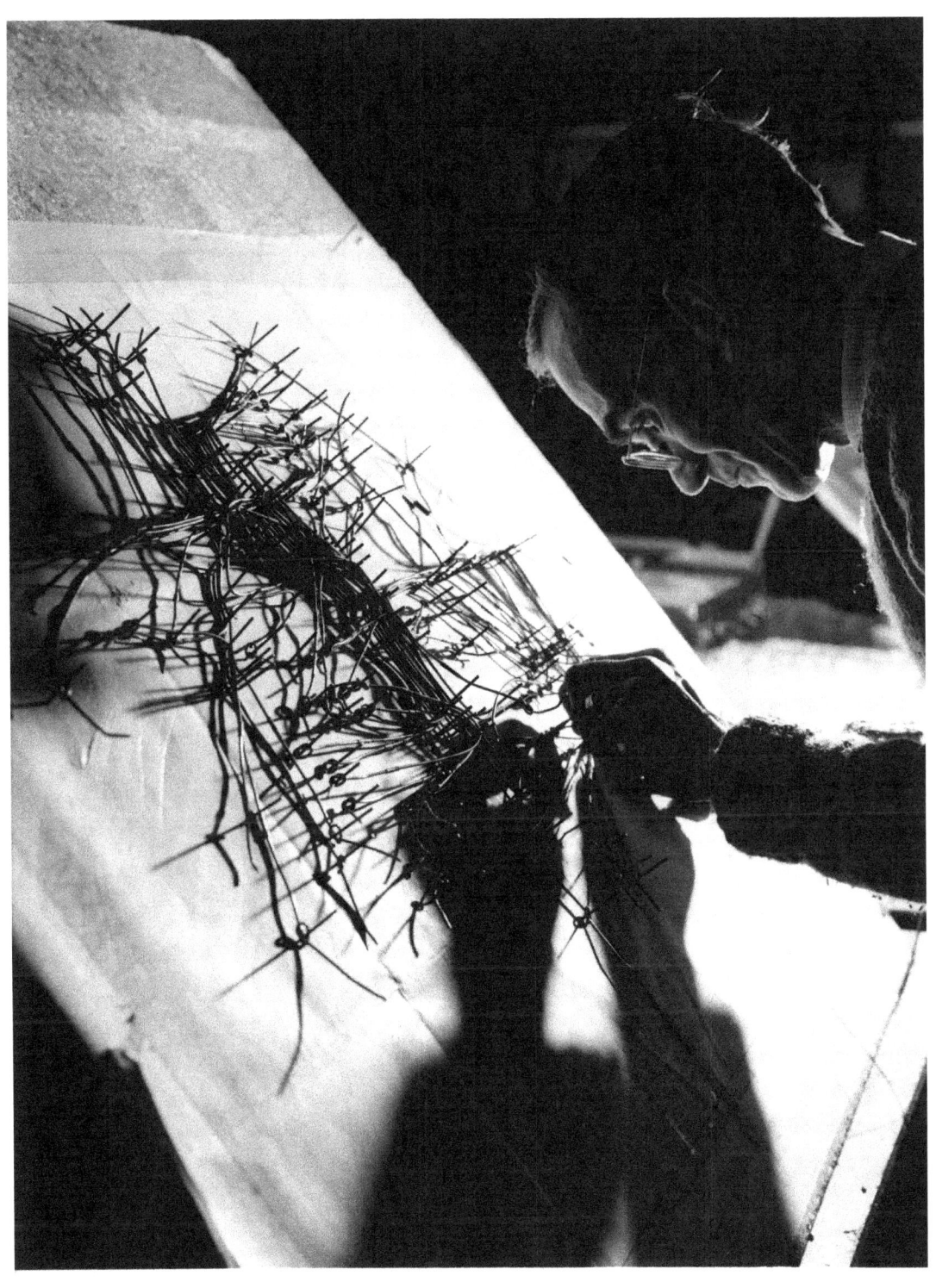

Making a wiring loom at De Havillands, Hatfield

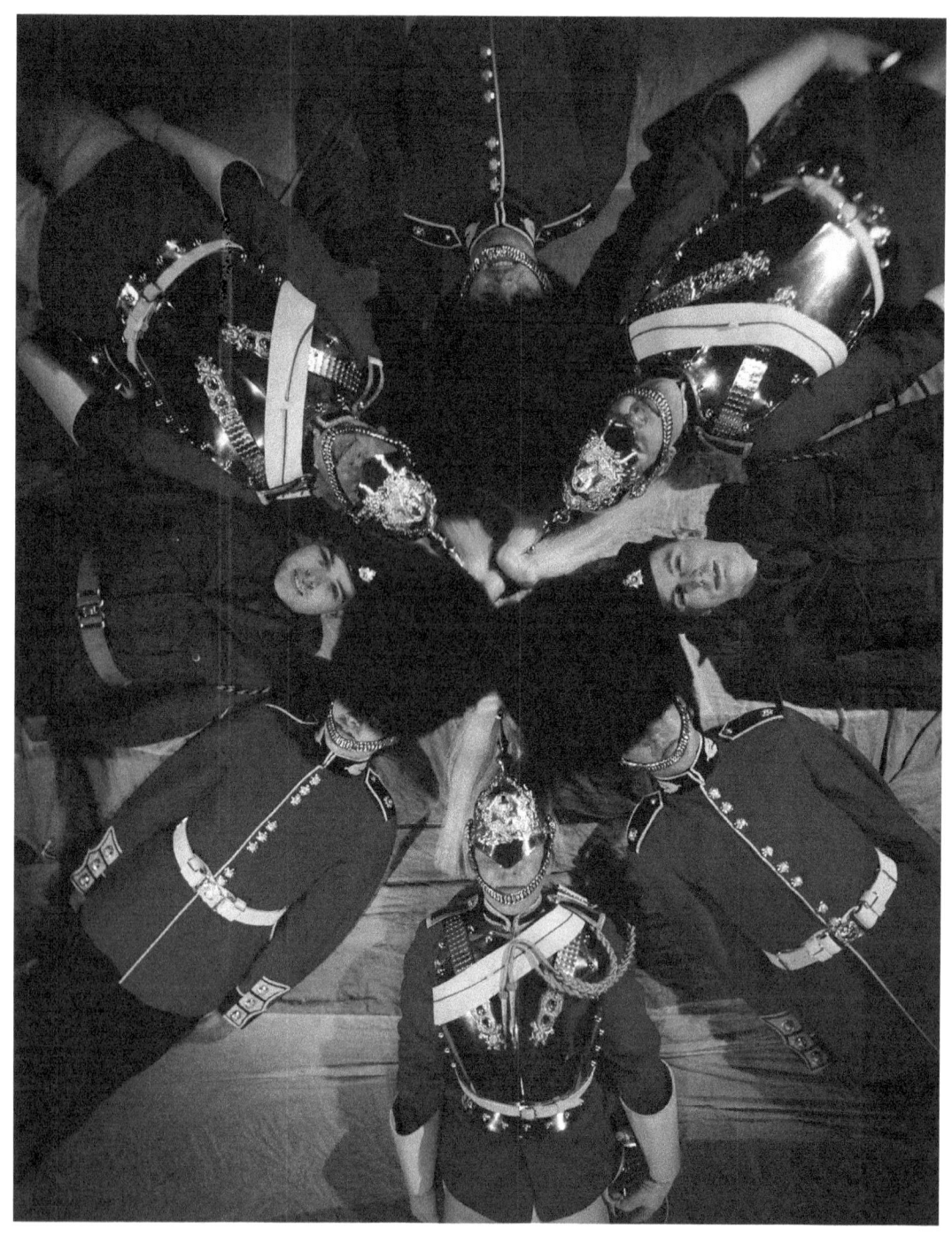

Picture of soldiers in different uniforms for the front cover of 'Today' magazine

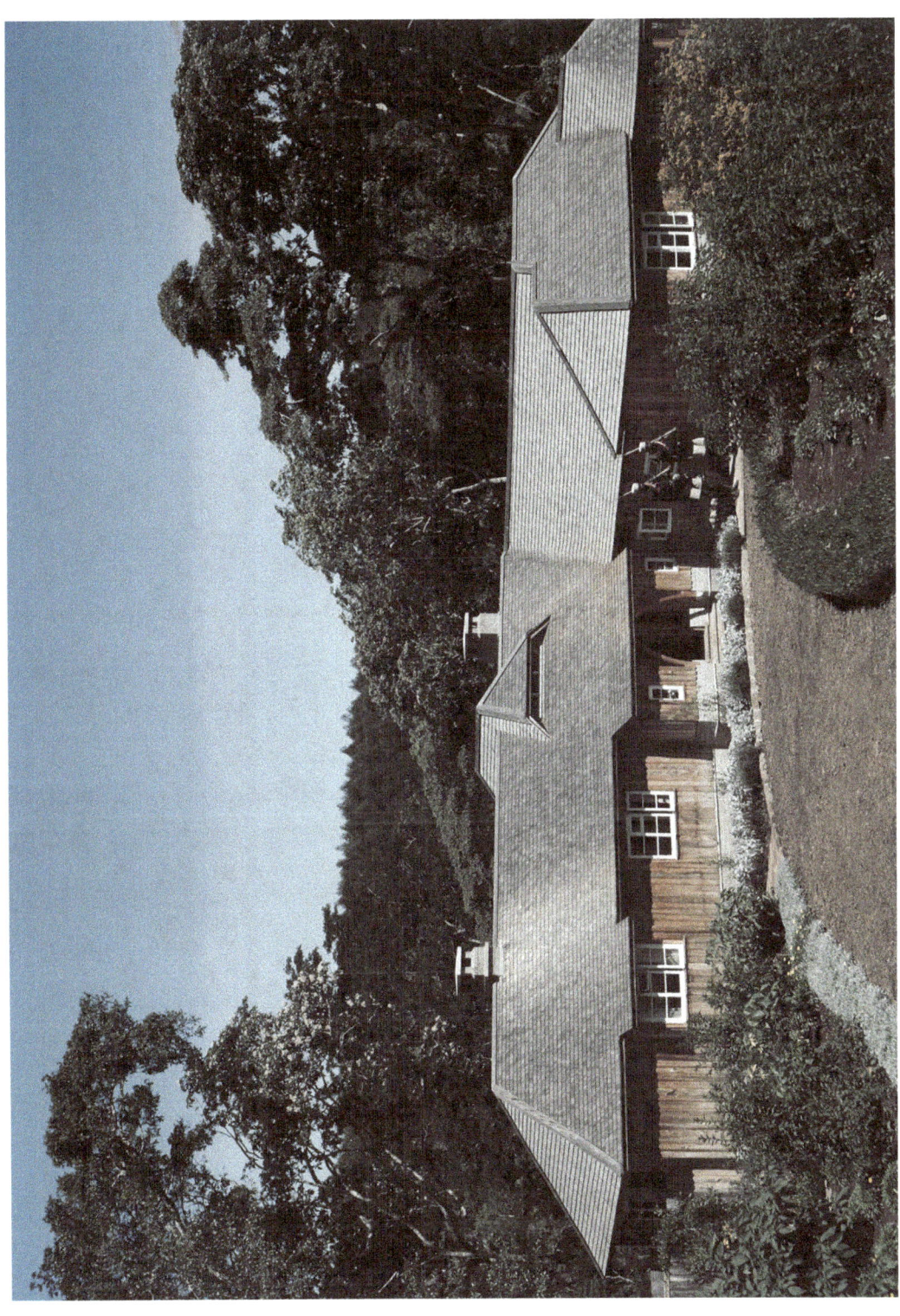

Sangana Lodge, presented to Princess Elizabeth and the Duke of Edinburgh by Kenya as a wedding present

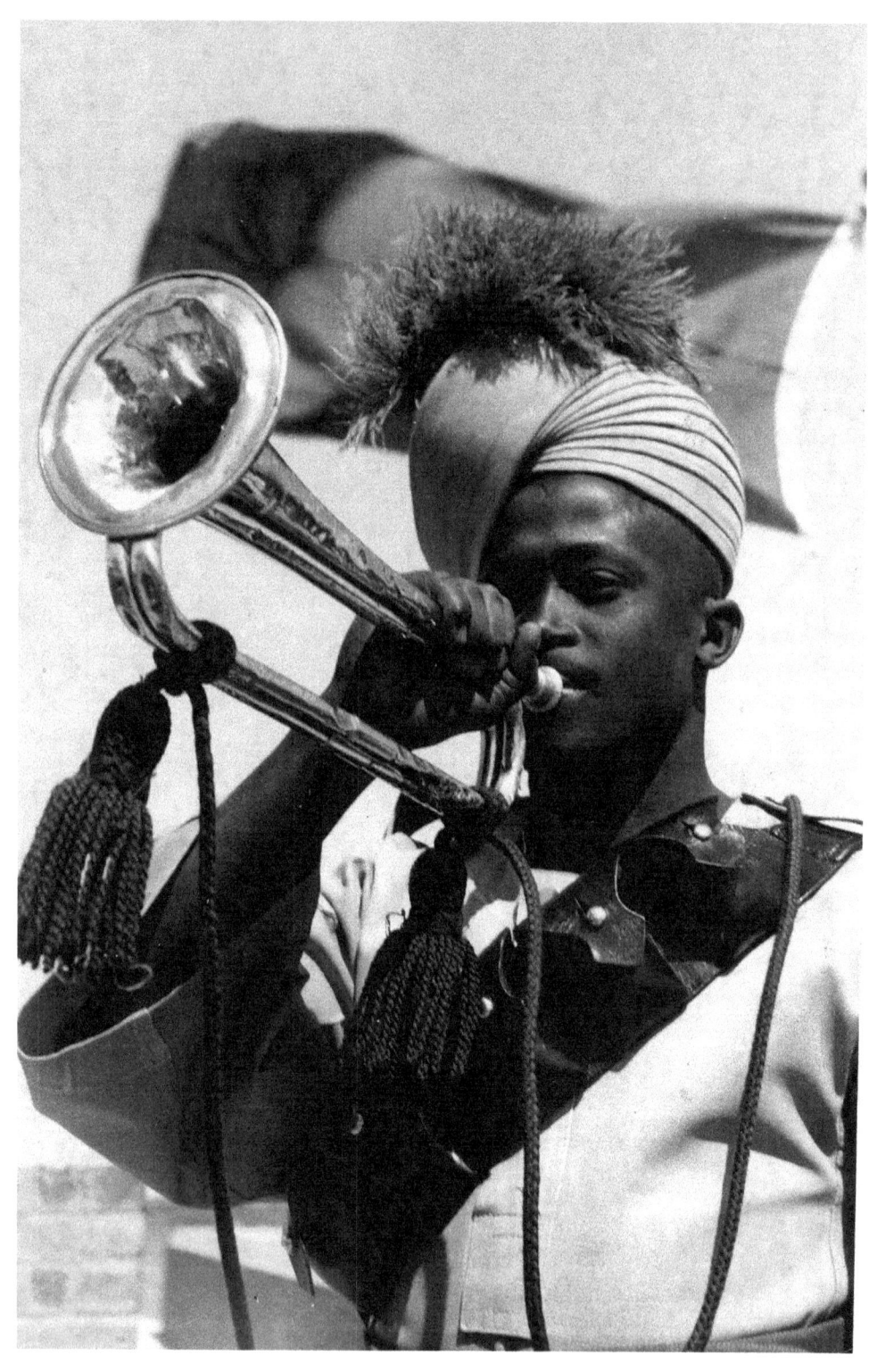

A trumpeter of the Sudan Defence Force, 1952

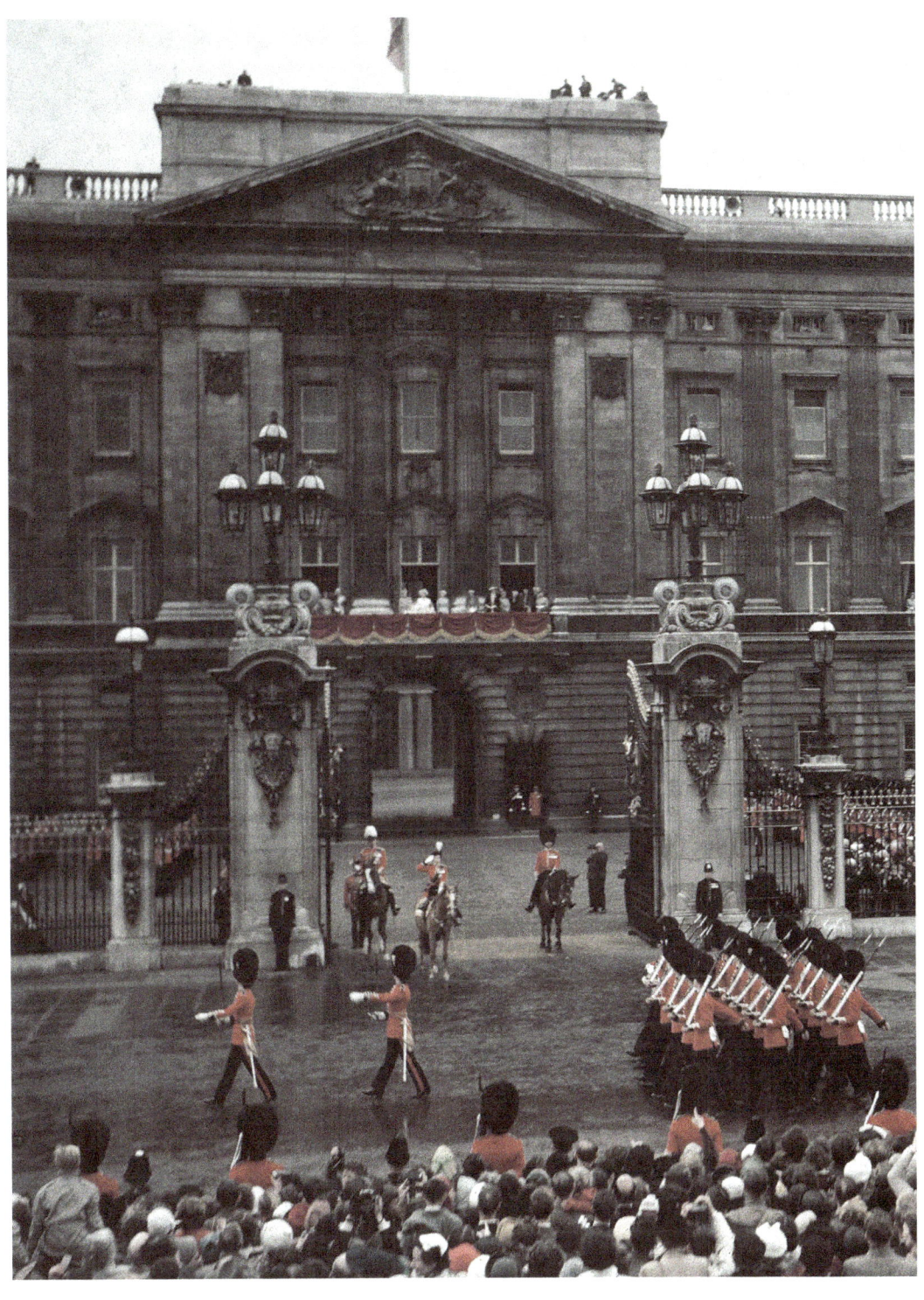

H.M.Queen Elizabeth takes the salute at Buckingham Palace as the Brigade of Guards march past, 1953

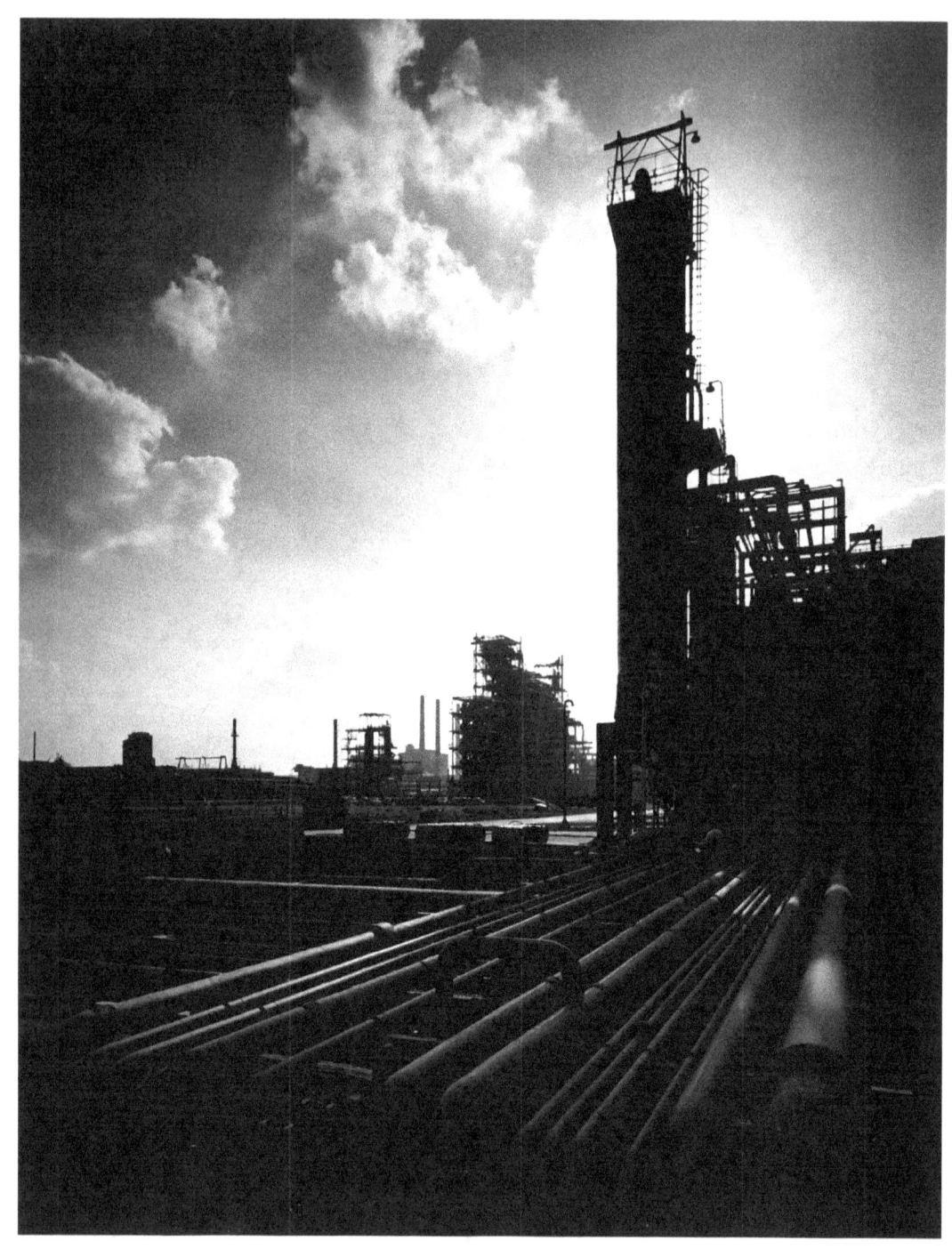

ICI Billingham Works, circa 1980

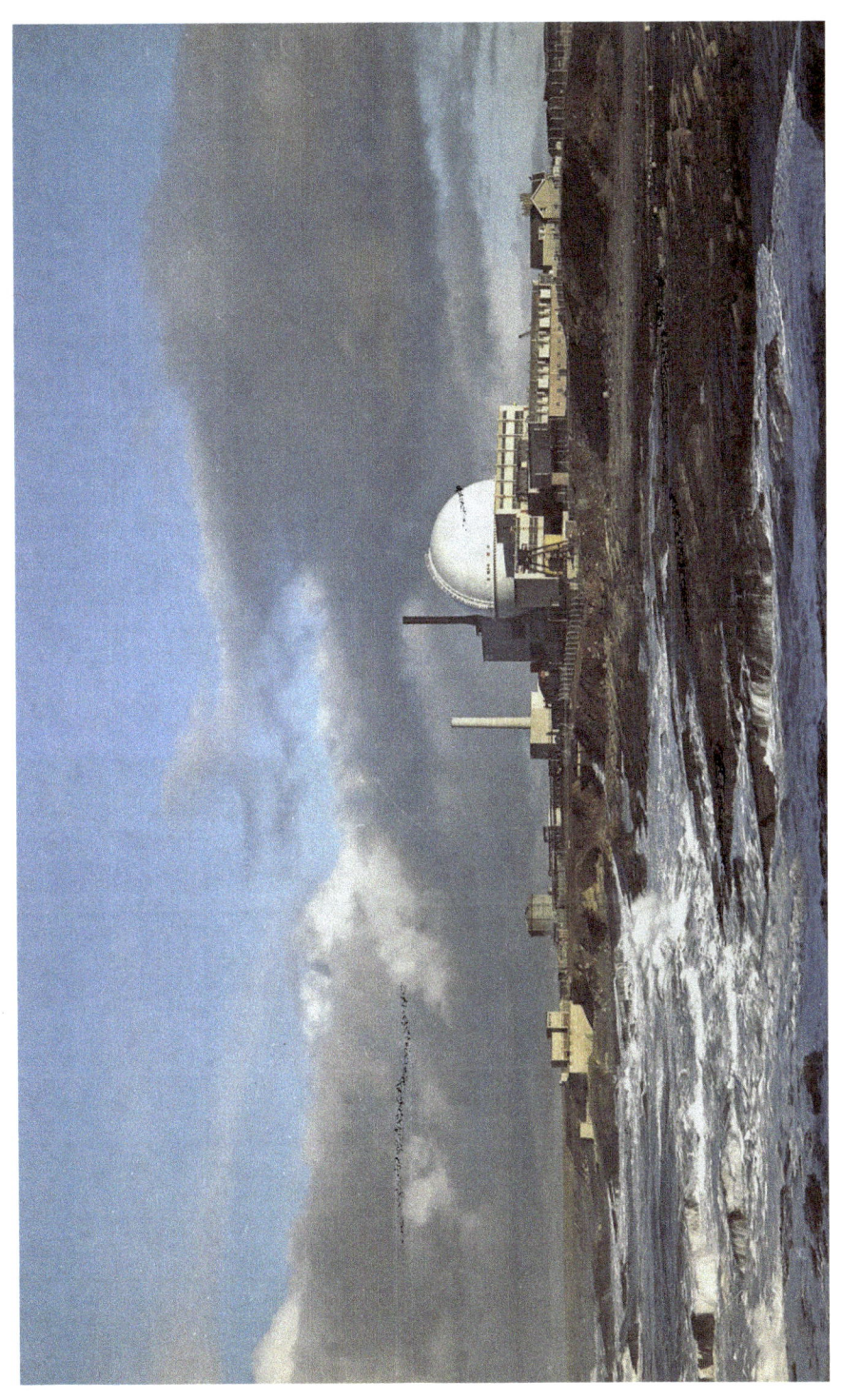

The fast breeder reactor at Dounreay facing Pentland Firth, 1958

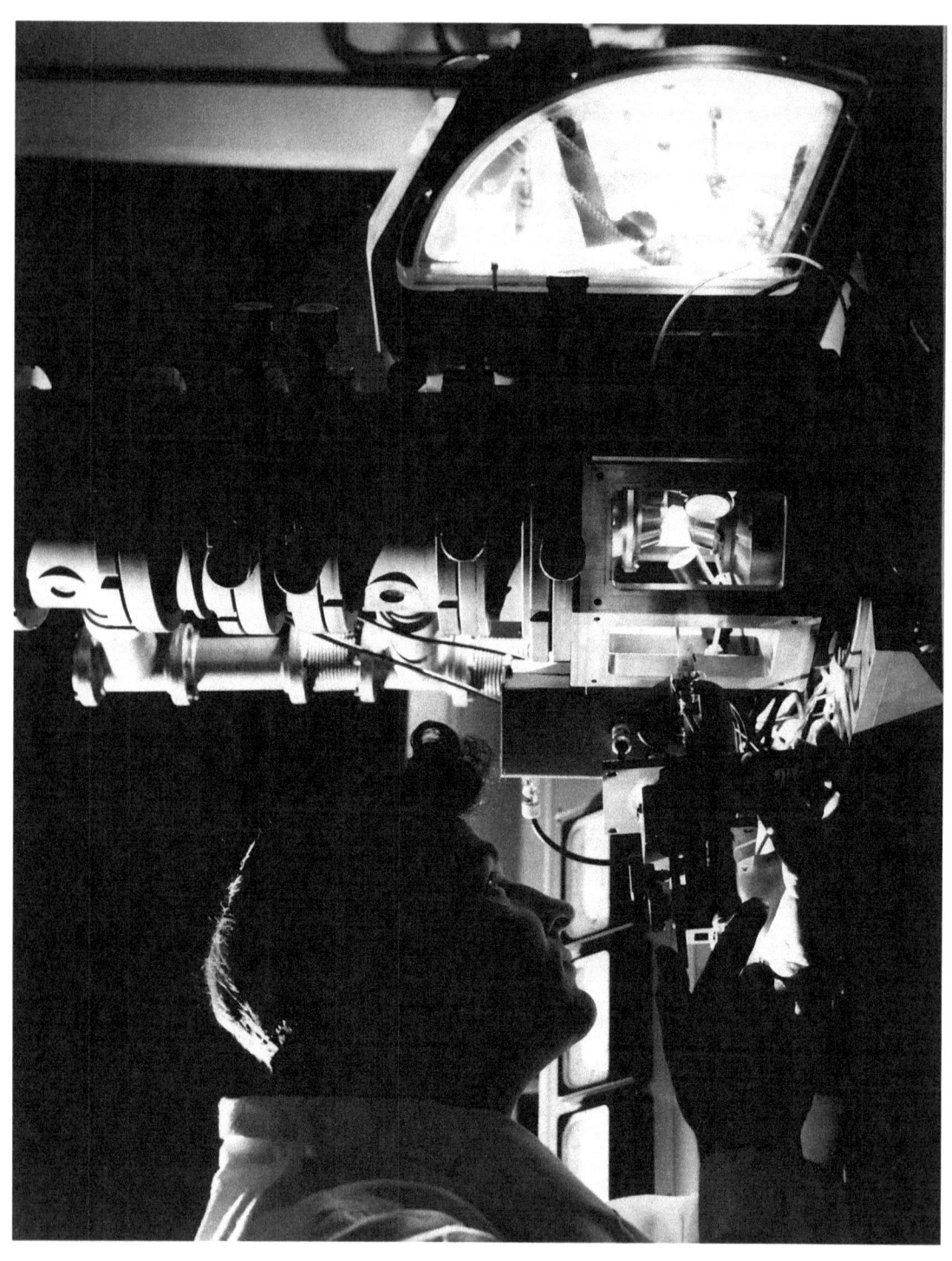

Electron Microscope at Tube Investments

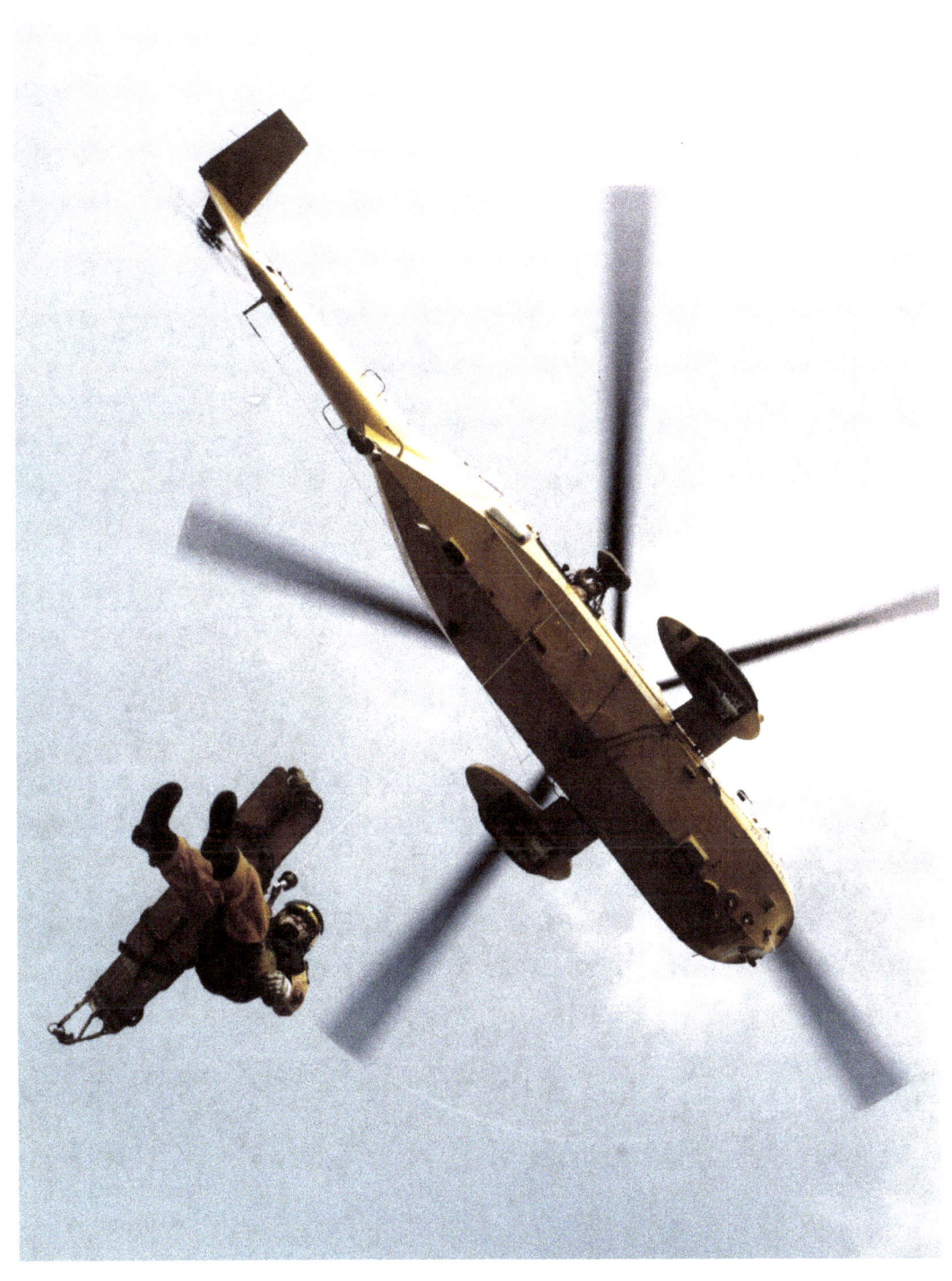

Lowering a man and stretcher from an RAF rescue helicopter

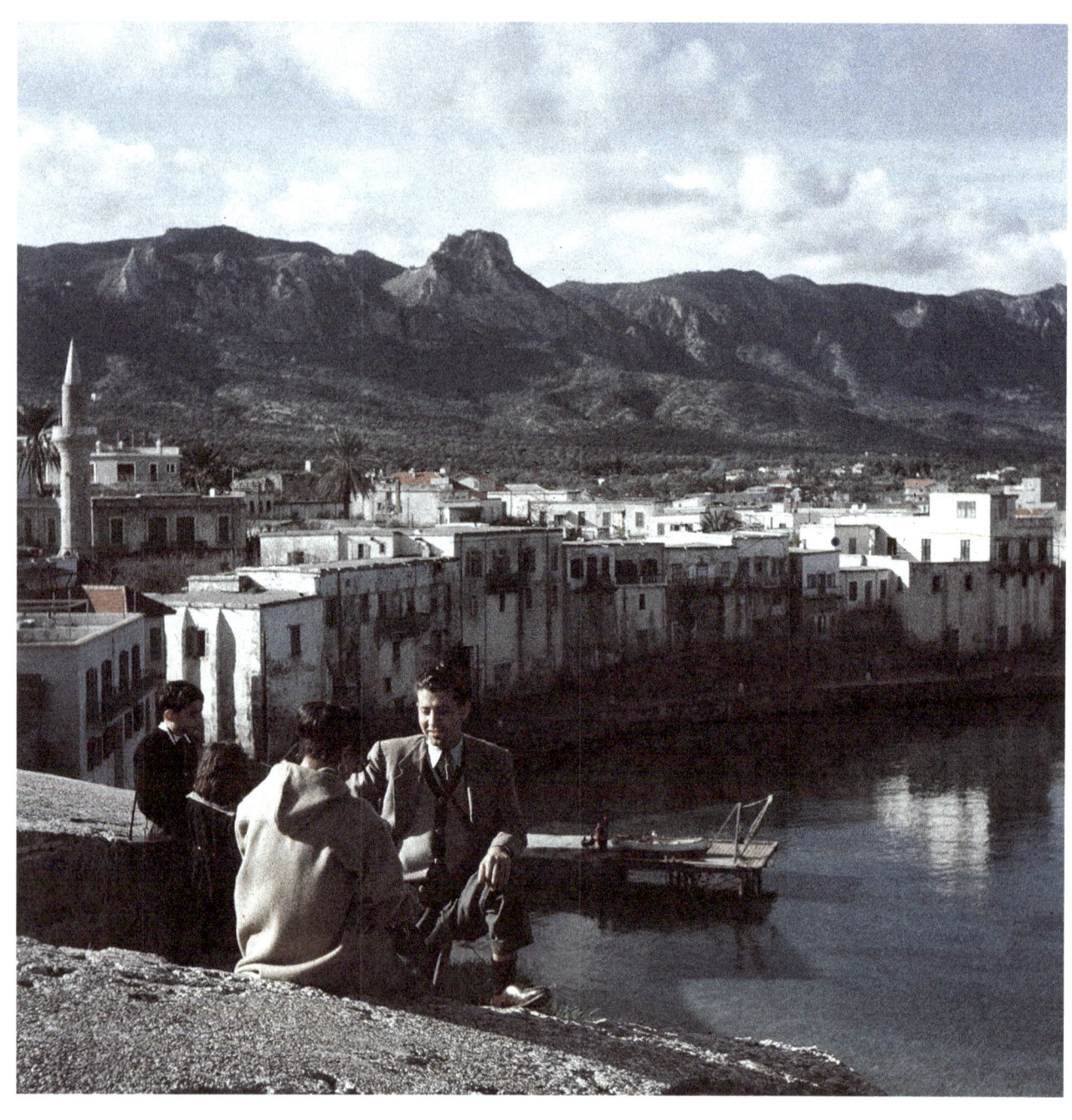

Looking down at Kyrenia Harbour in Cyprus, 1953

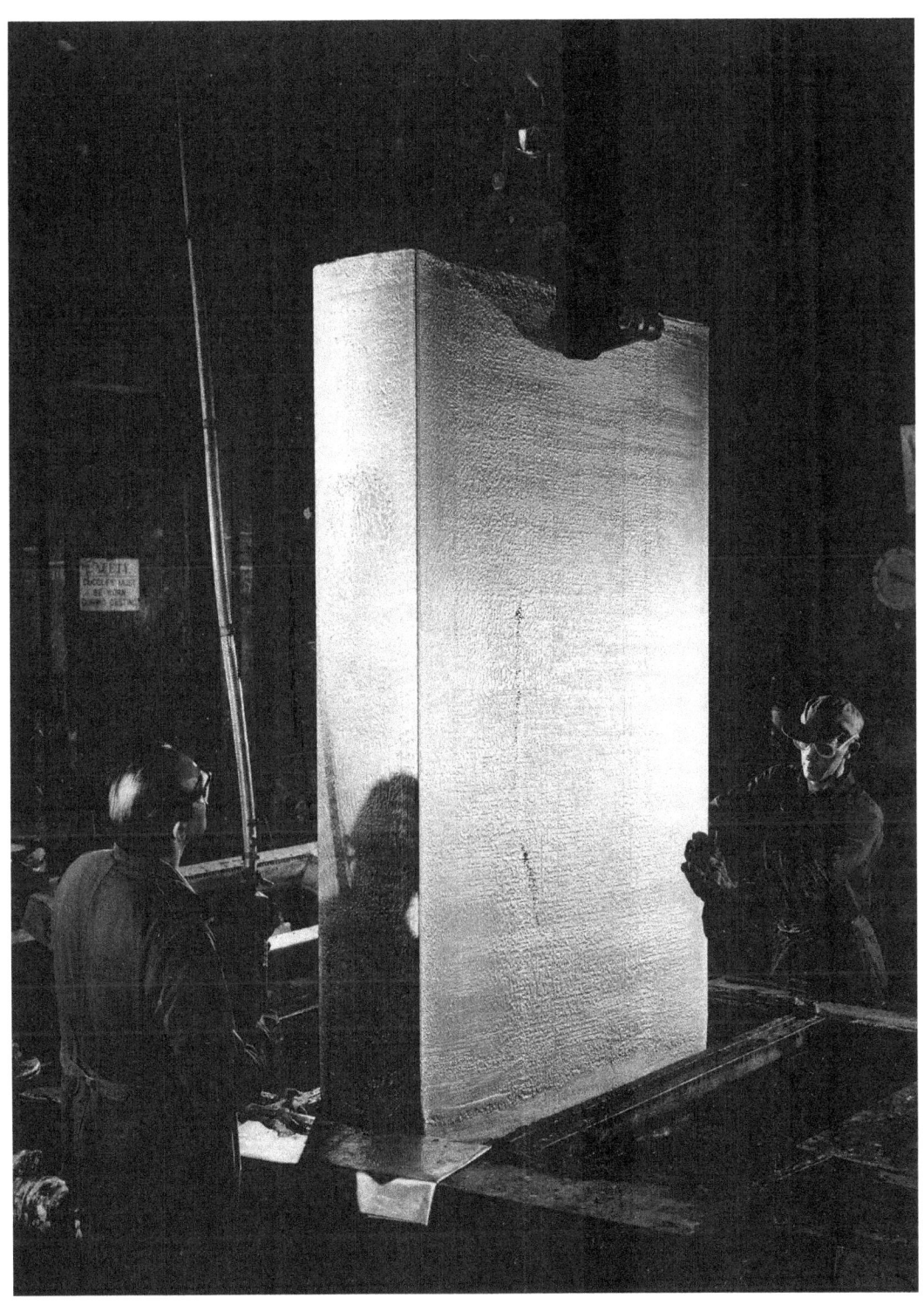

A large aluminium billet being lowered at British Aluminium, Falkirk

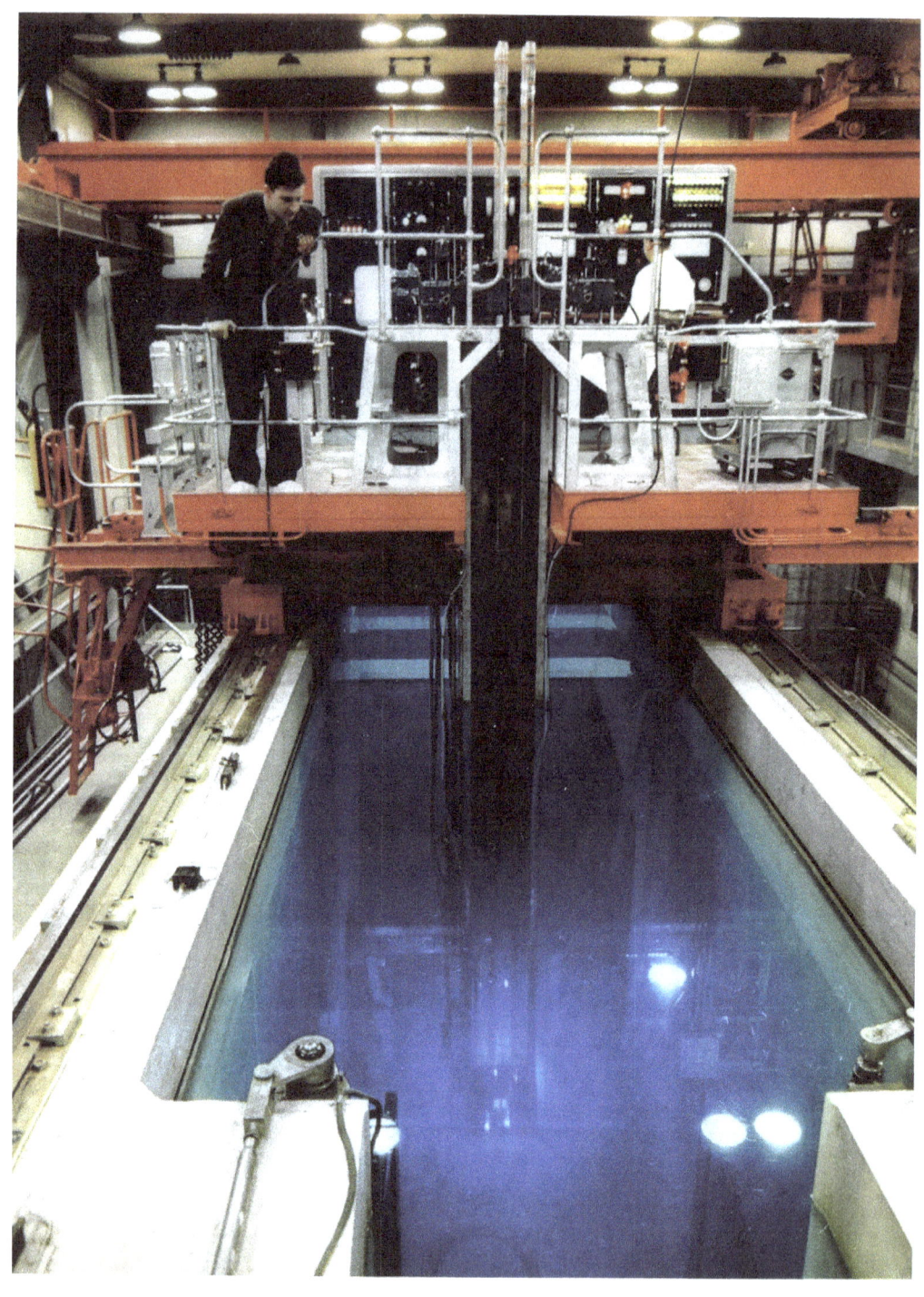

'LIDO'- the enriched uranium thermal swimming pool reactor used for nuclear physics experiments at Harwell

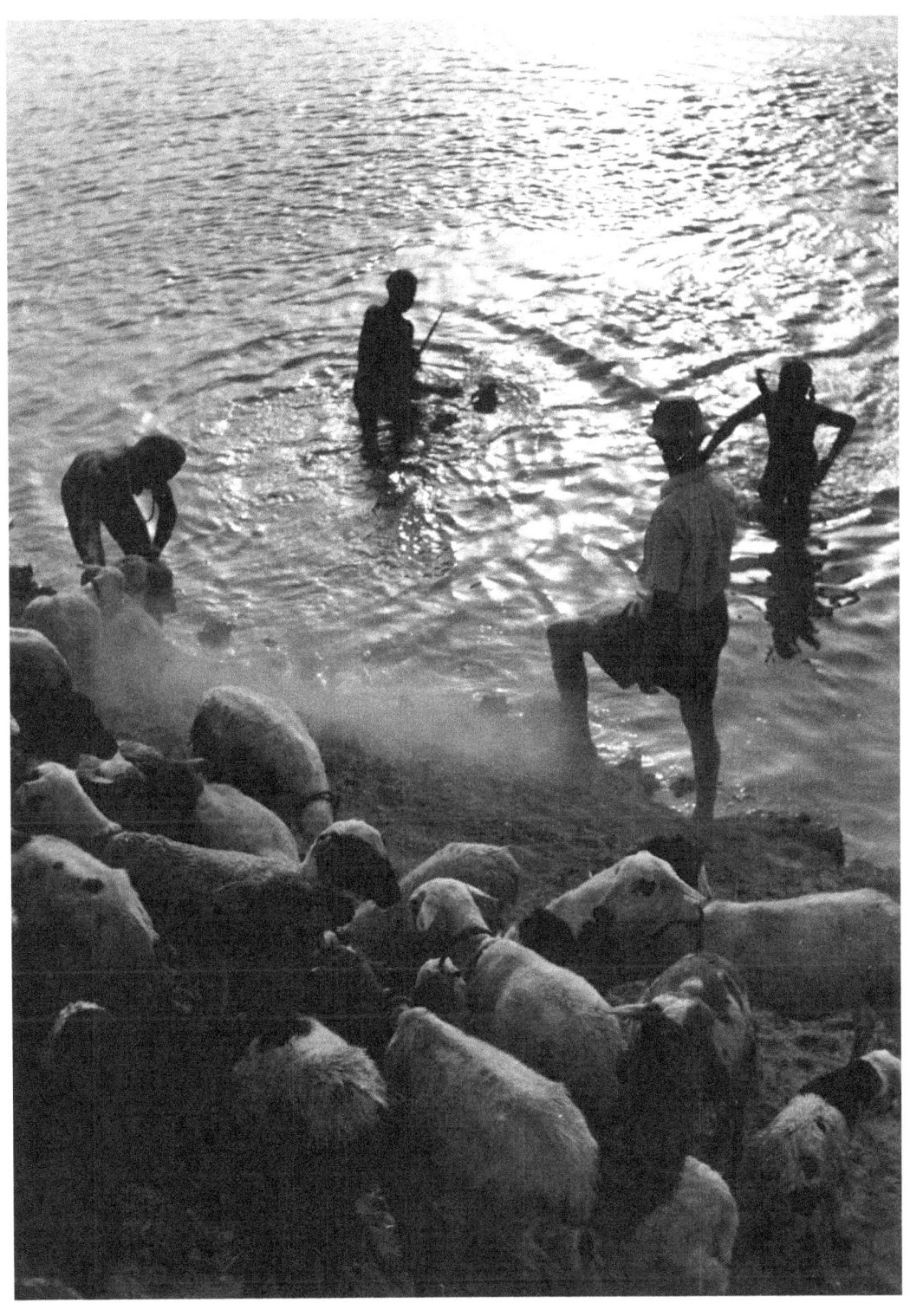

Washing sheep in the Nile at Juba, Southern Sudan

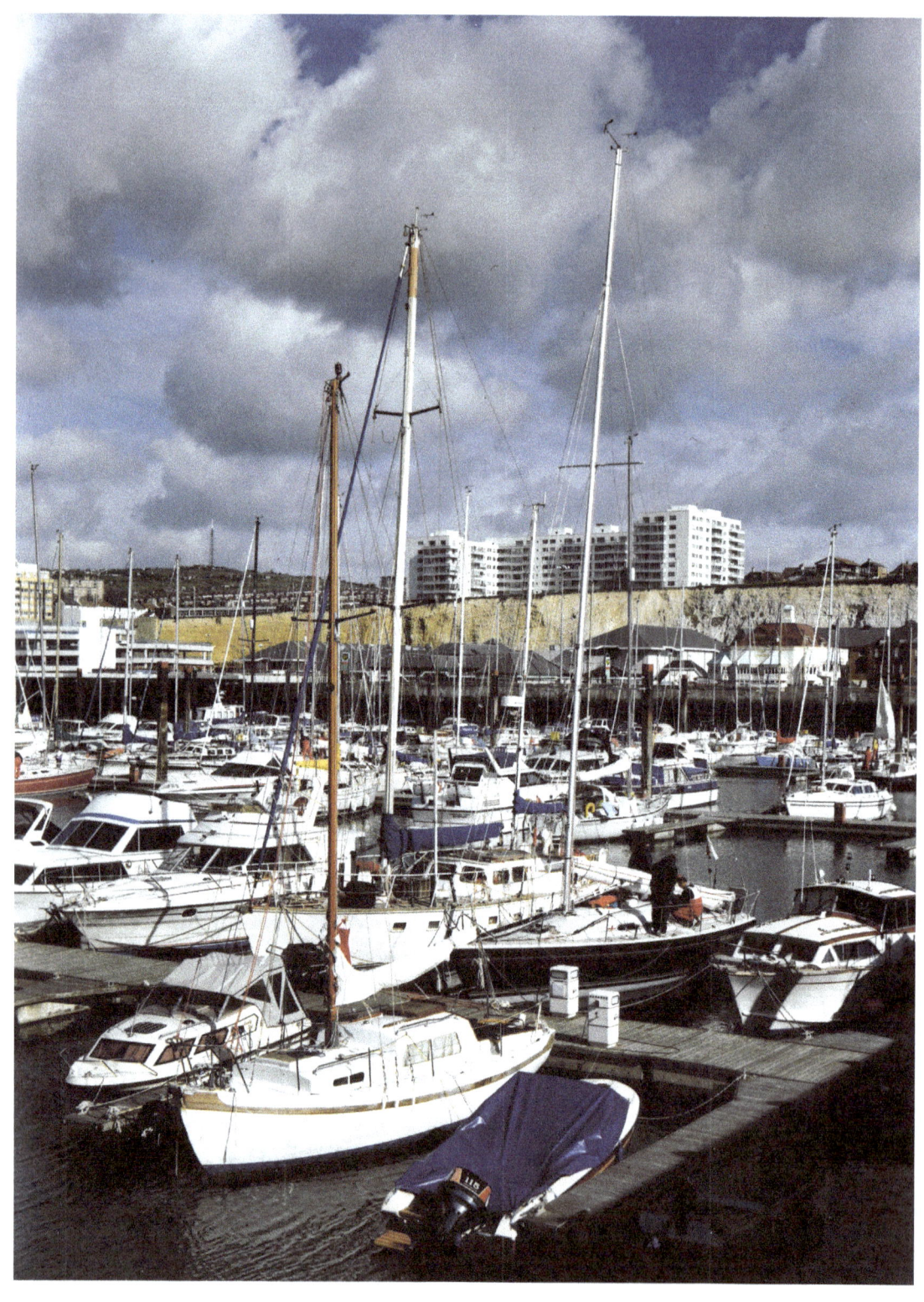

Brighton Marina showing flats on the hills behind

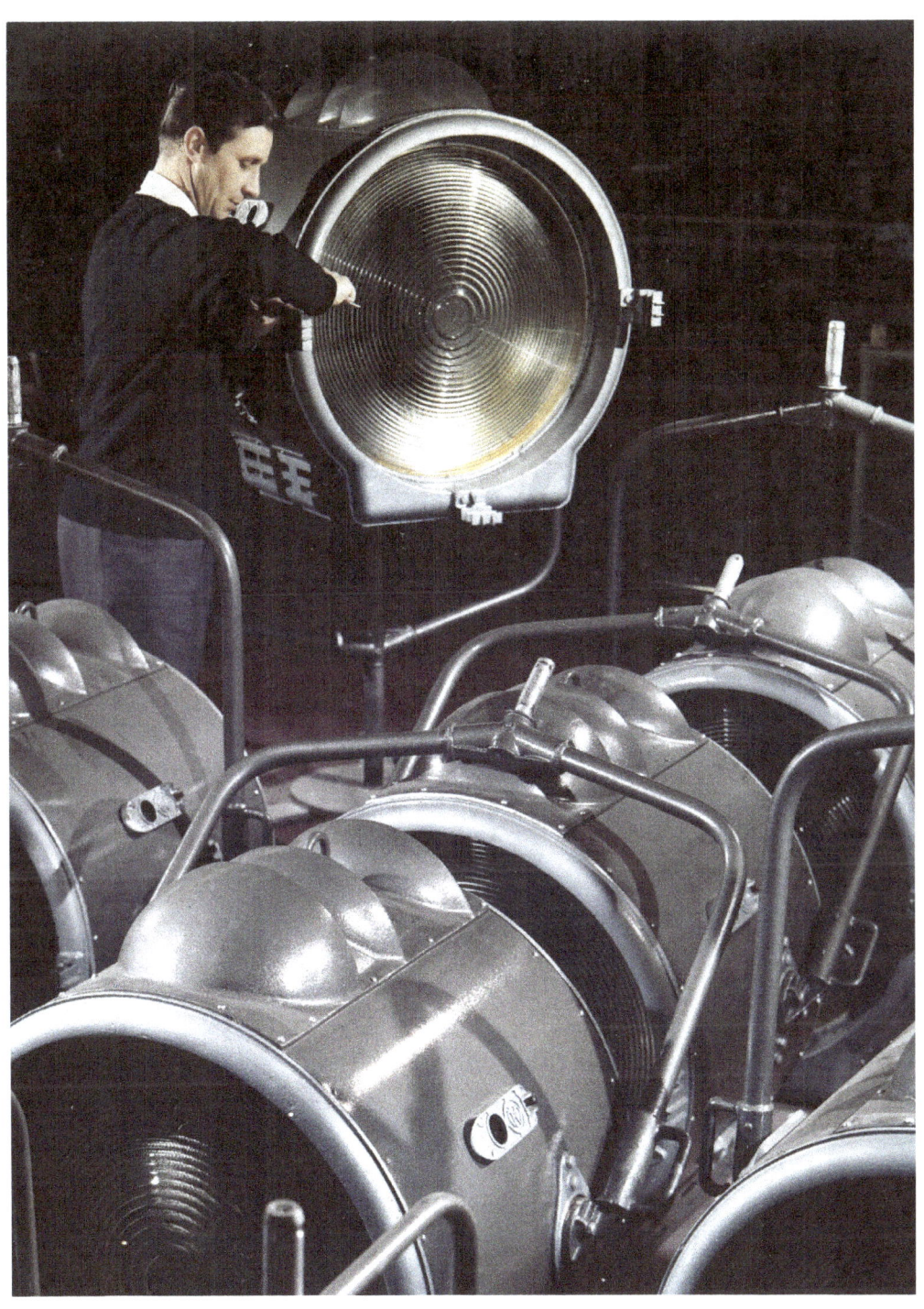

Mole-Richardson film lights being checked before going out on loan

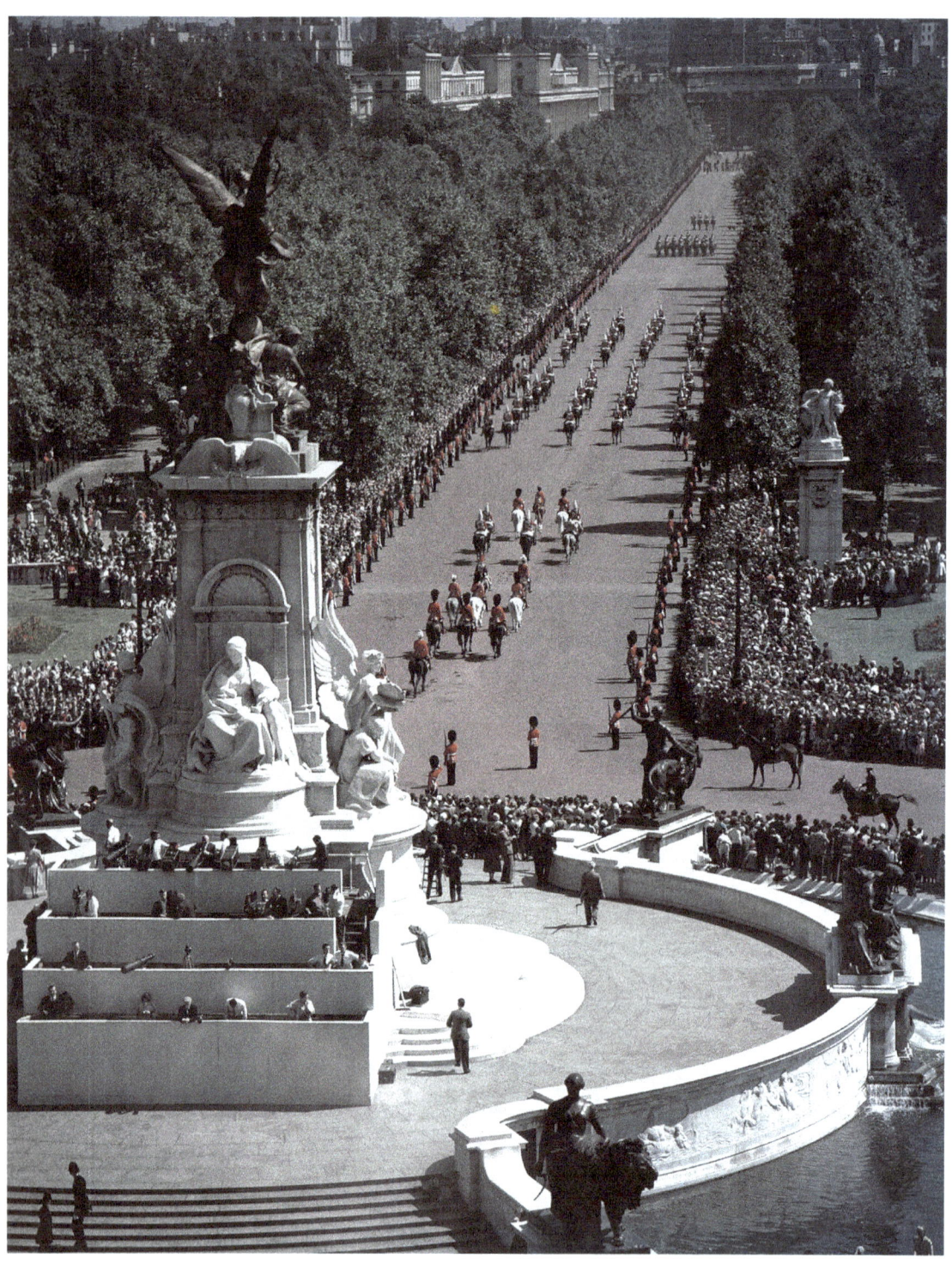

From the roof of Buckingham Palace, the procession of Trooping the Colour as it moves down the Mall

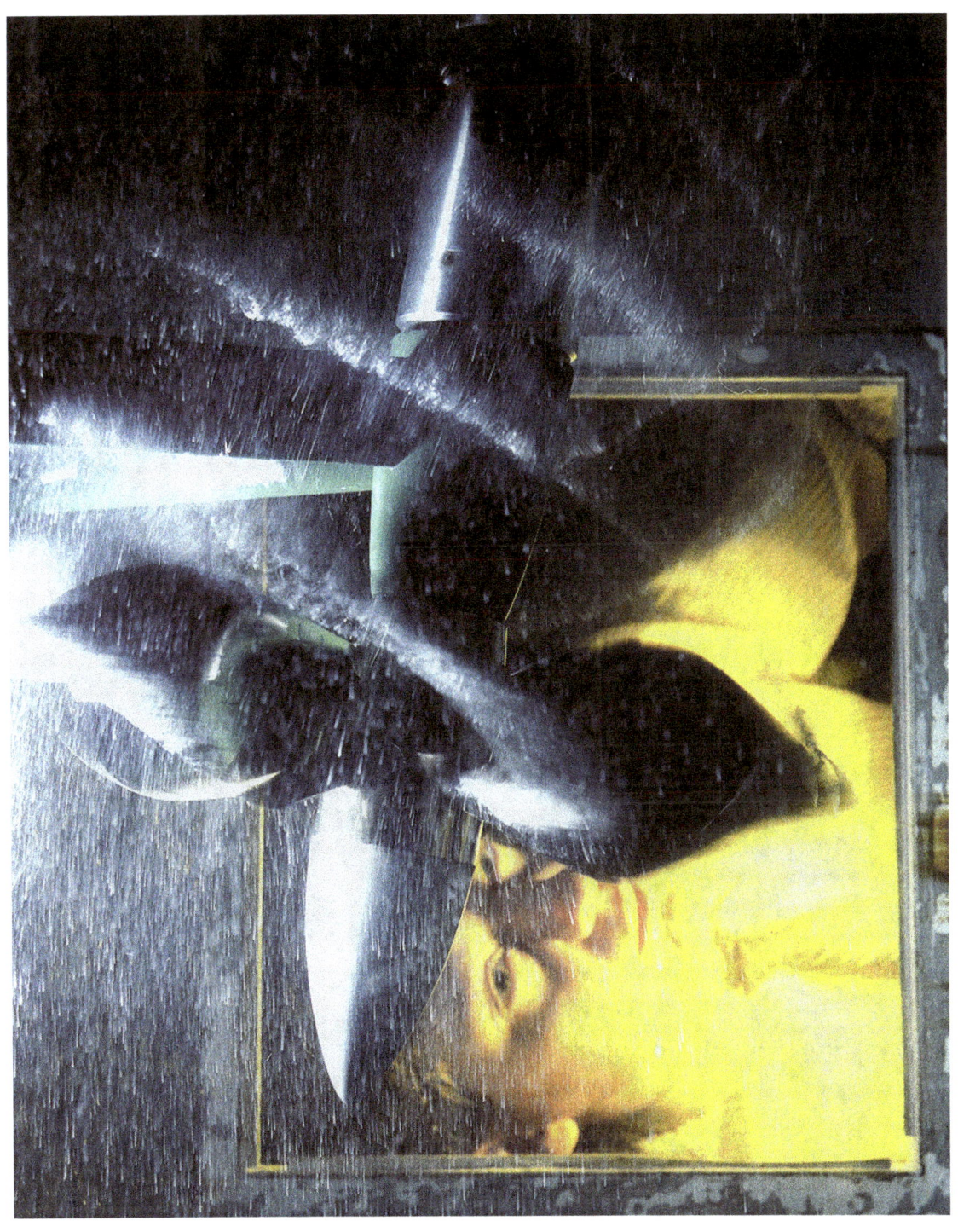

Admiralty Research Establishment, Haslar showing cavitations from a propeller under water

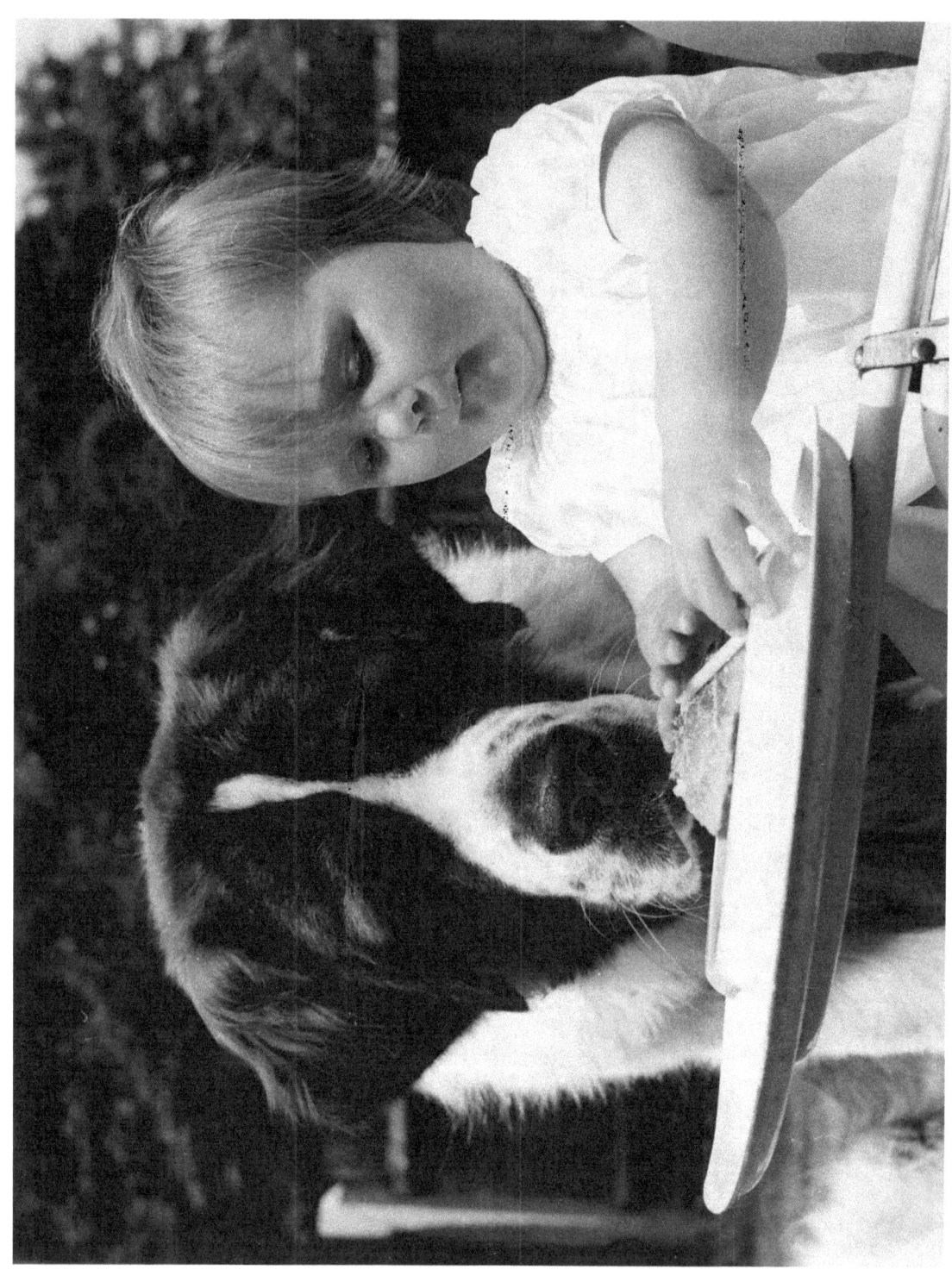

Our dog Hornblower and my daughter Sally on her first birthday

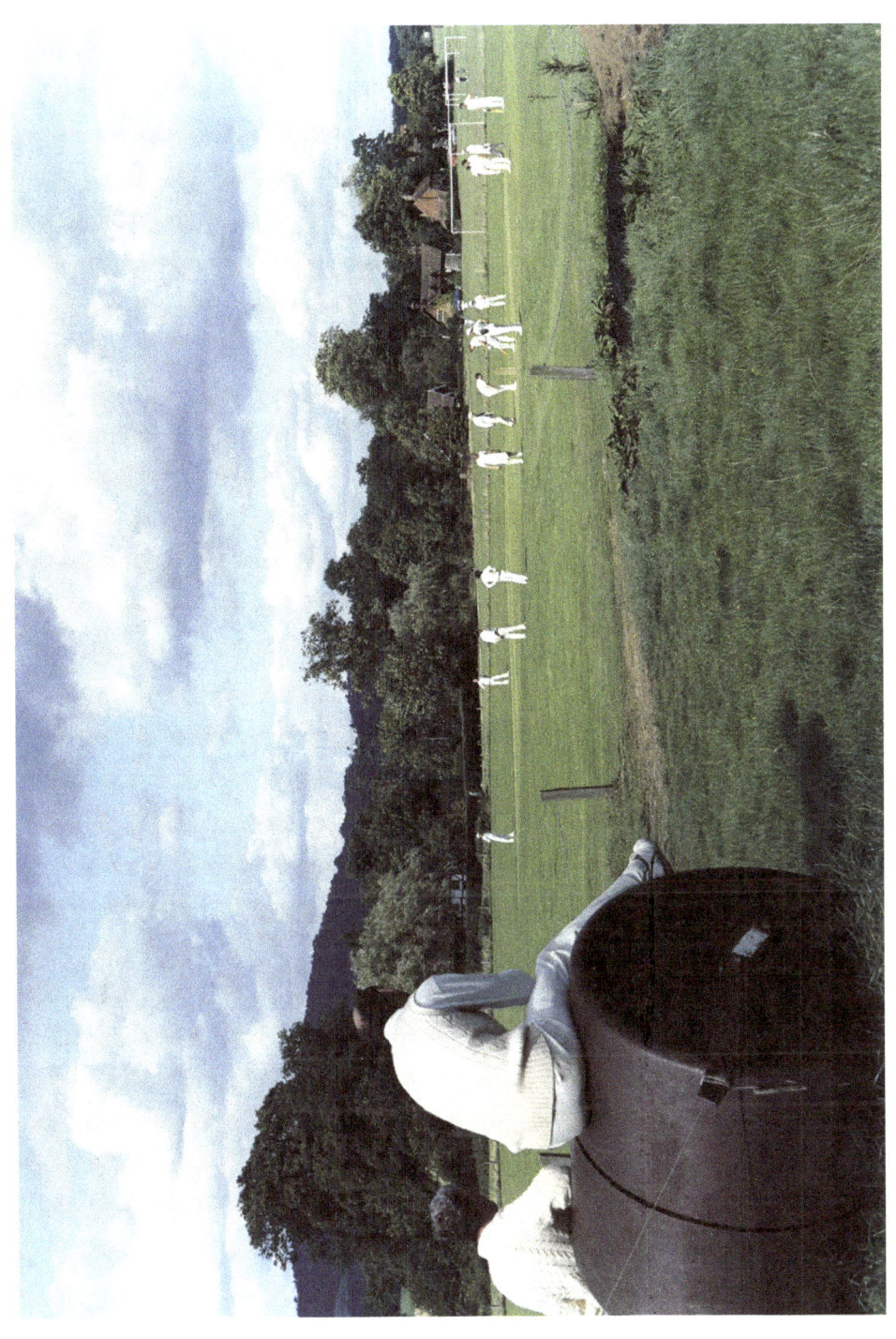

Cricket on the village green at Ockley in Surrey

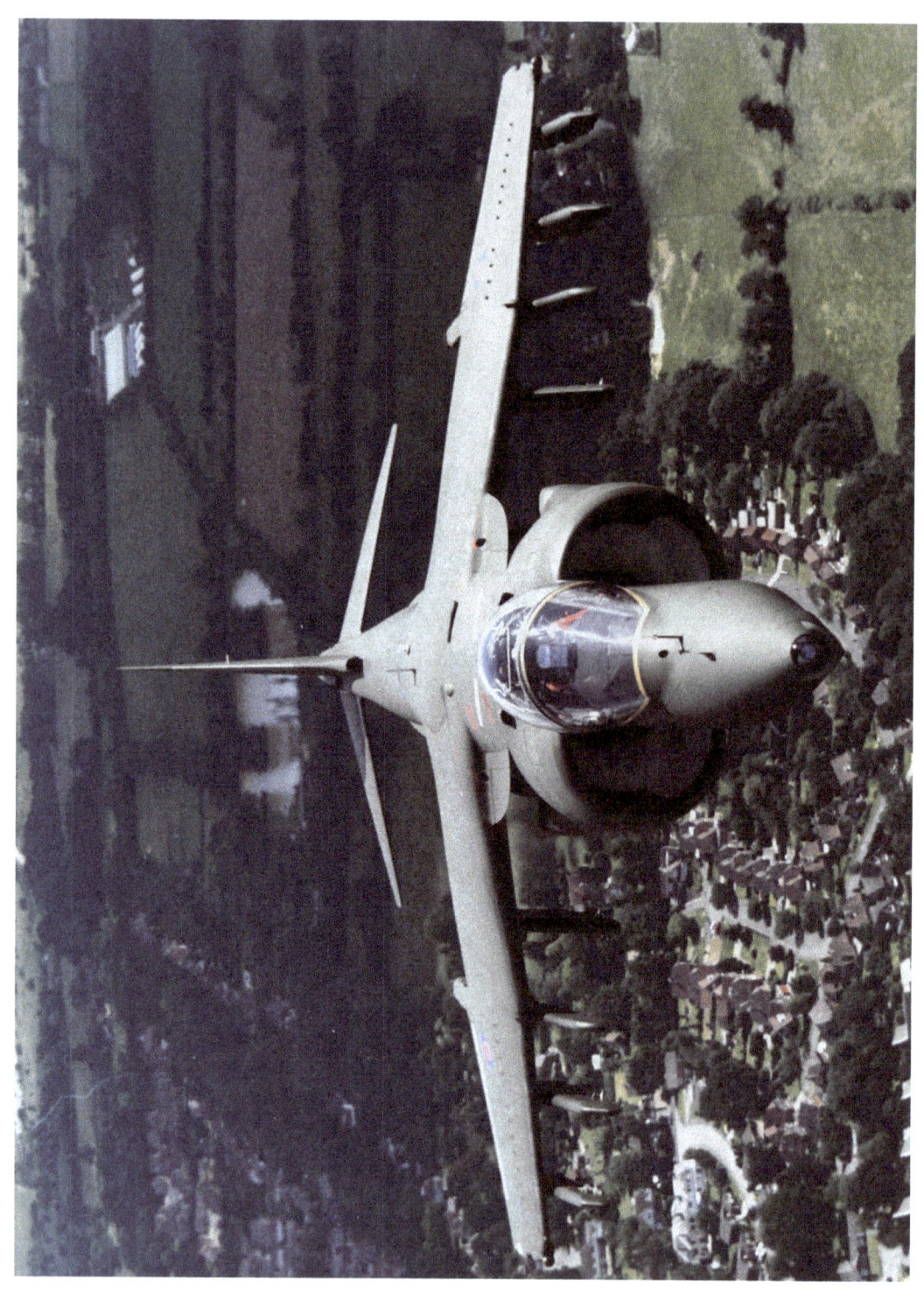

The first GR7 Harrier for the RAF having been manufactured at BAE Dunsfold

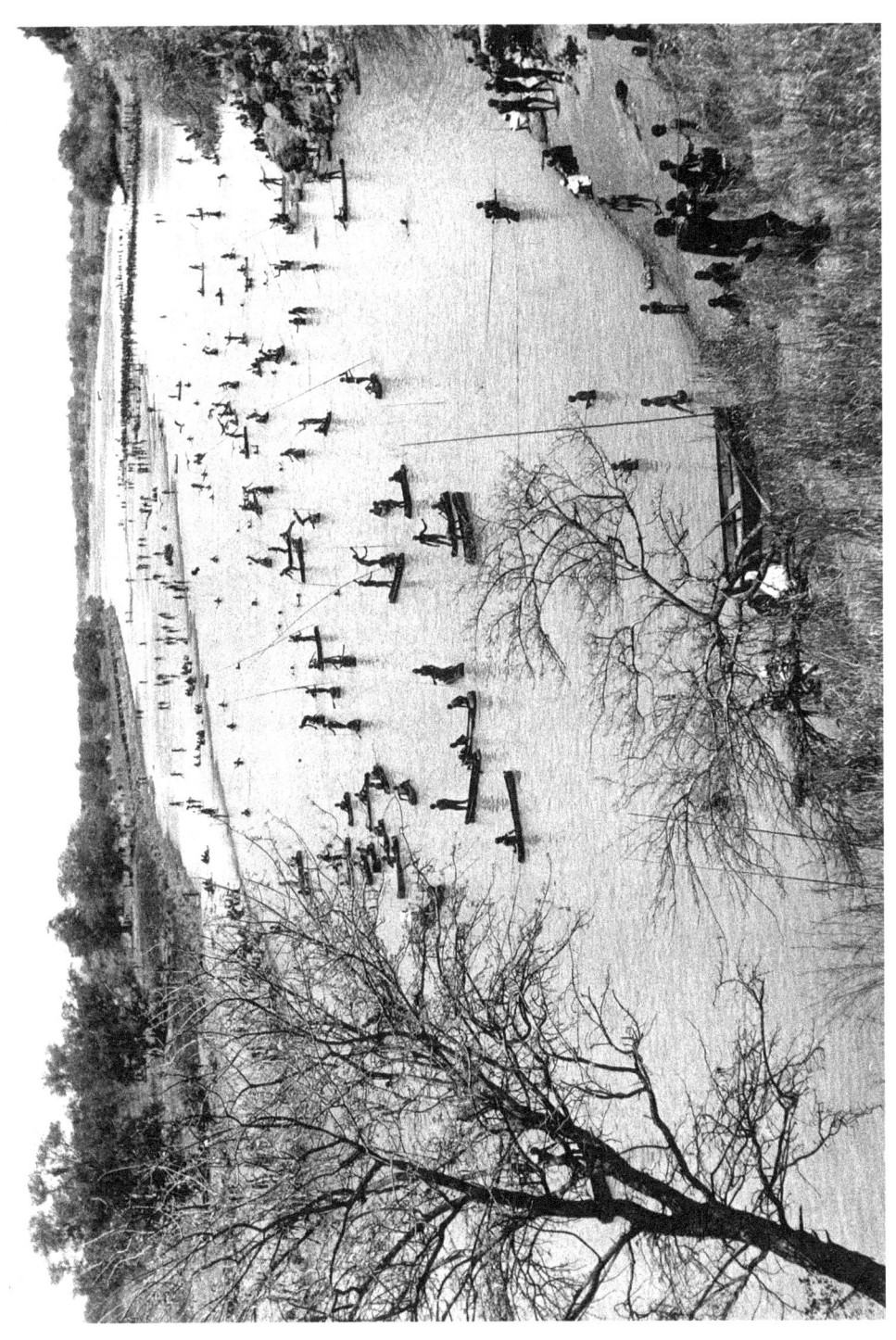

The Dinkas of Juba, Southern Sudan catching fish in the Nile, an annual event

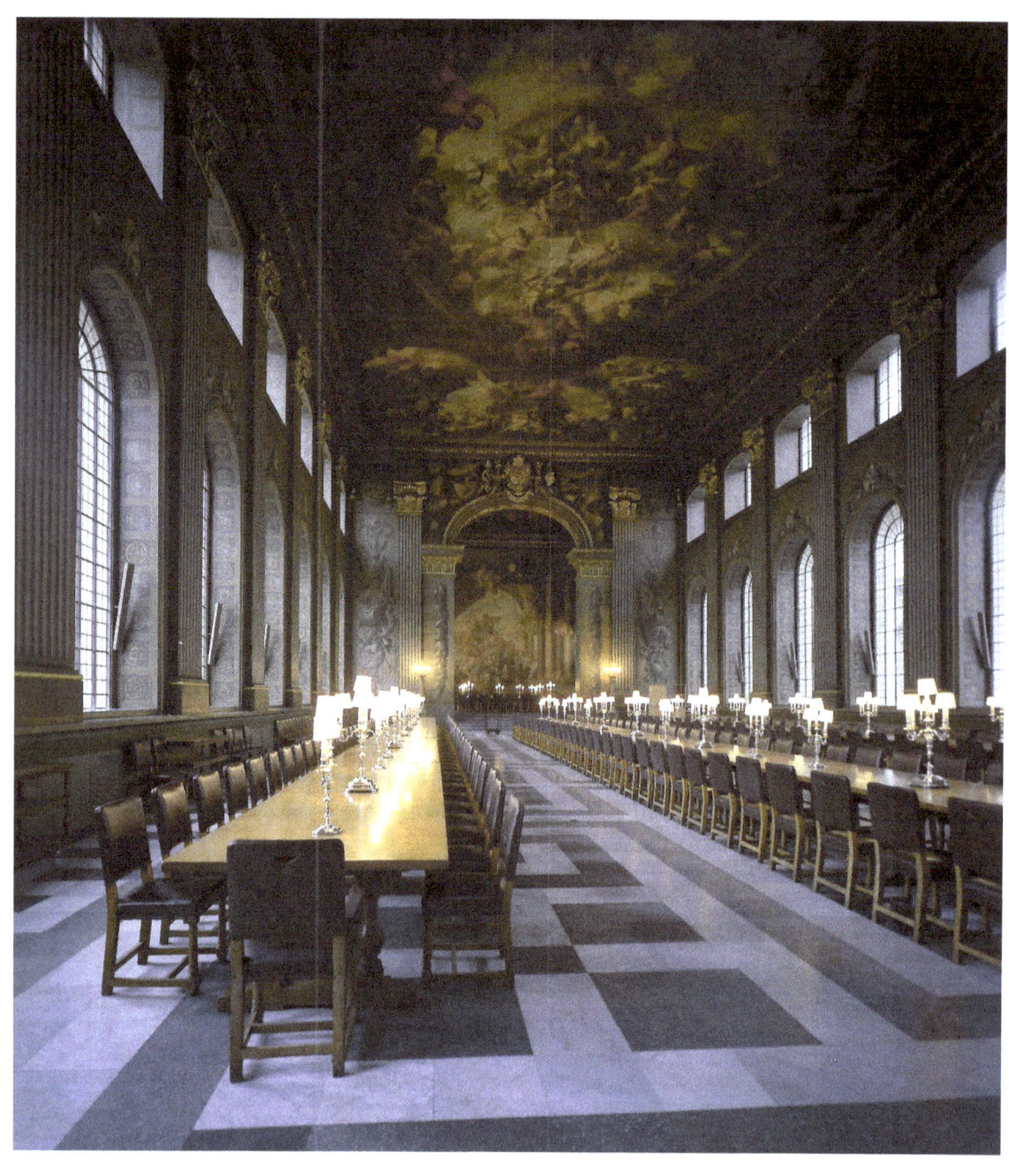

Royal Naval College, Greenwich showing the long room with painted ceiling

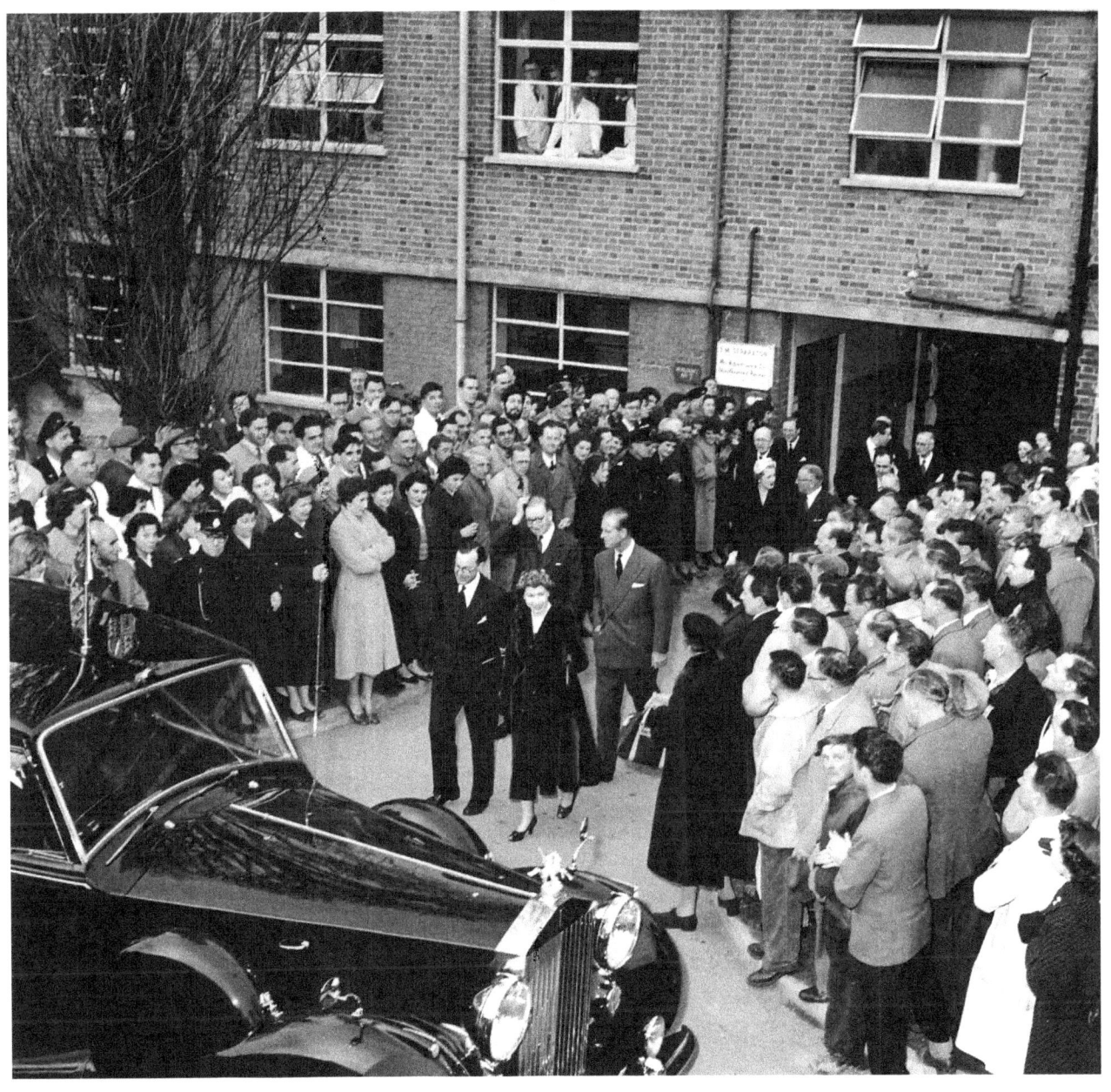

The Queen and the Duke of Edinburgh leaving AERE Harwell after looking round the laboratories

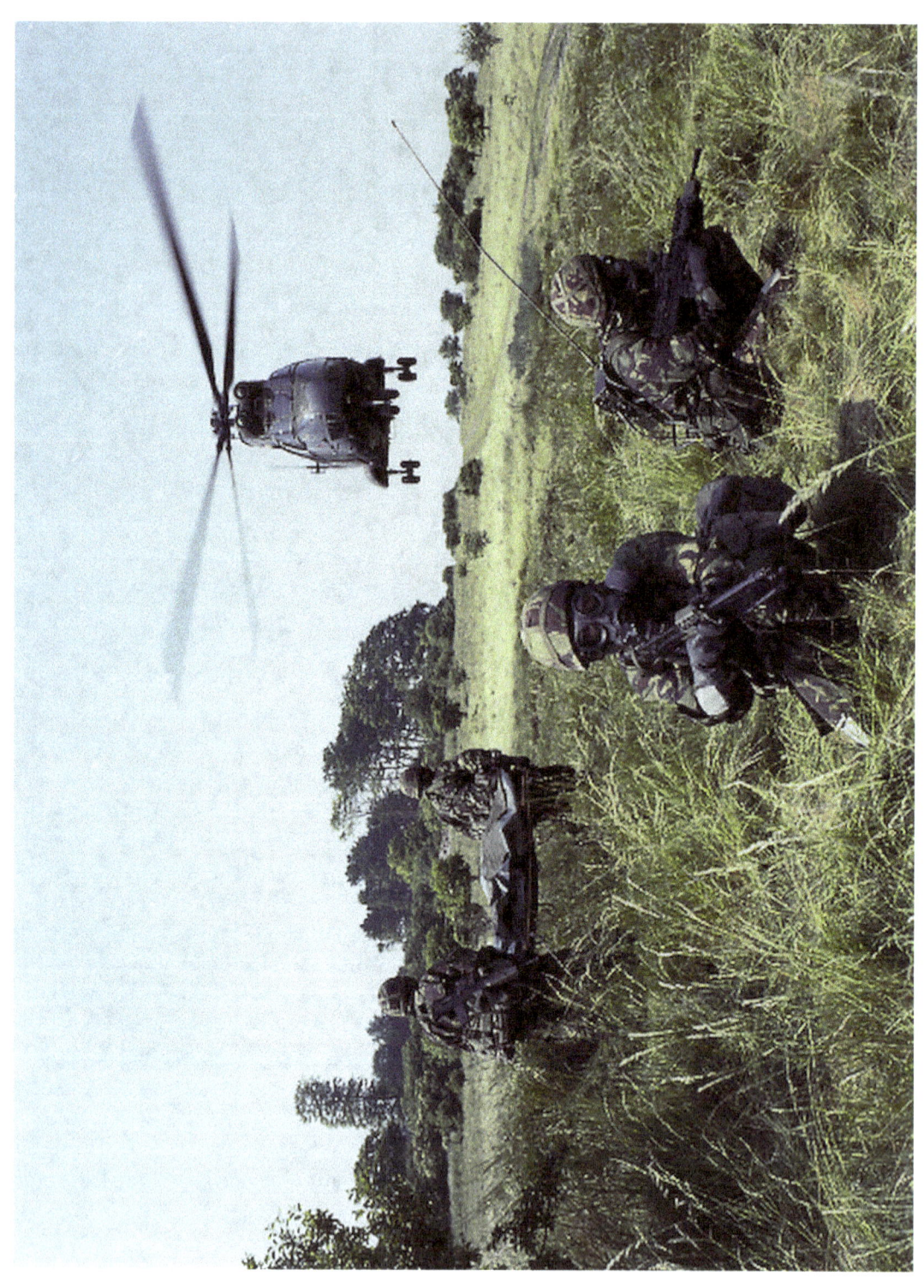

MOD Porton Down. Troops in NBC suits get ready to load a casualty onto the incoming helicopter

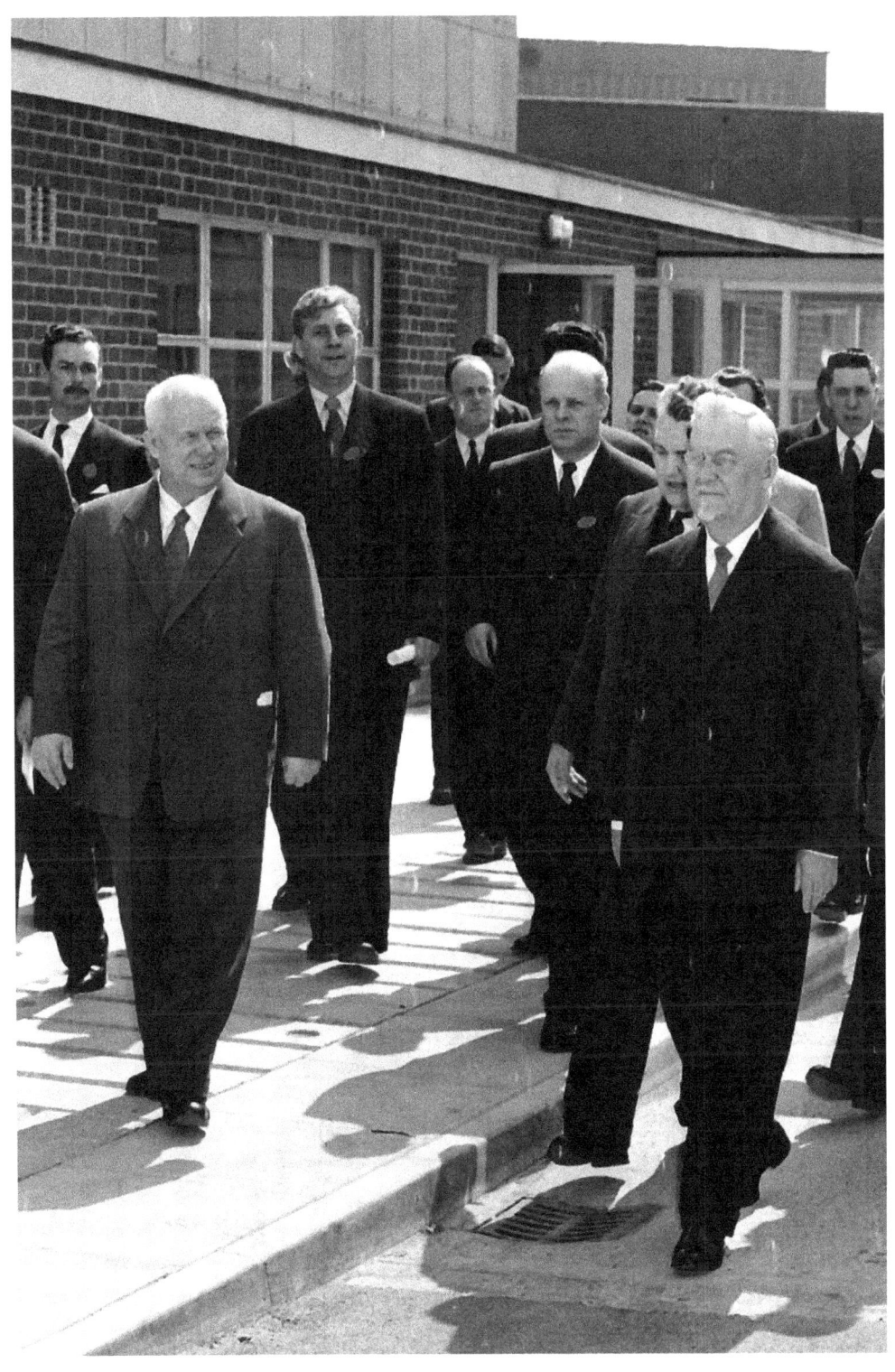

Khrushchev and Bulganin visit Harwell Atomic Energy Research Centre, 1956

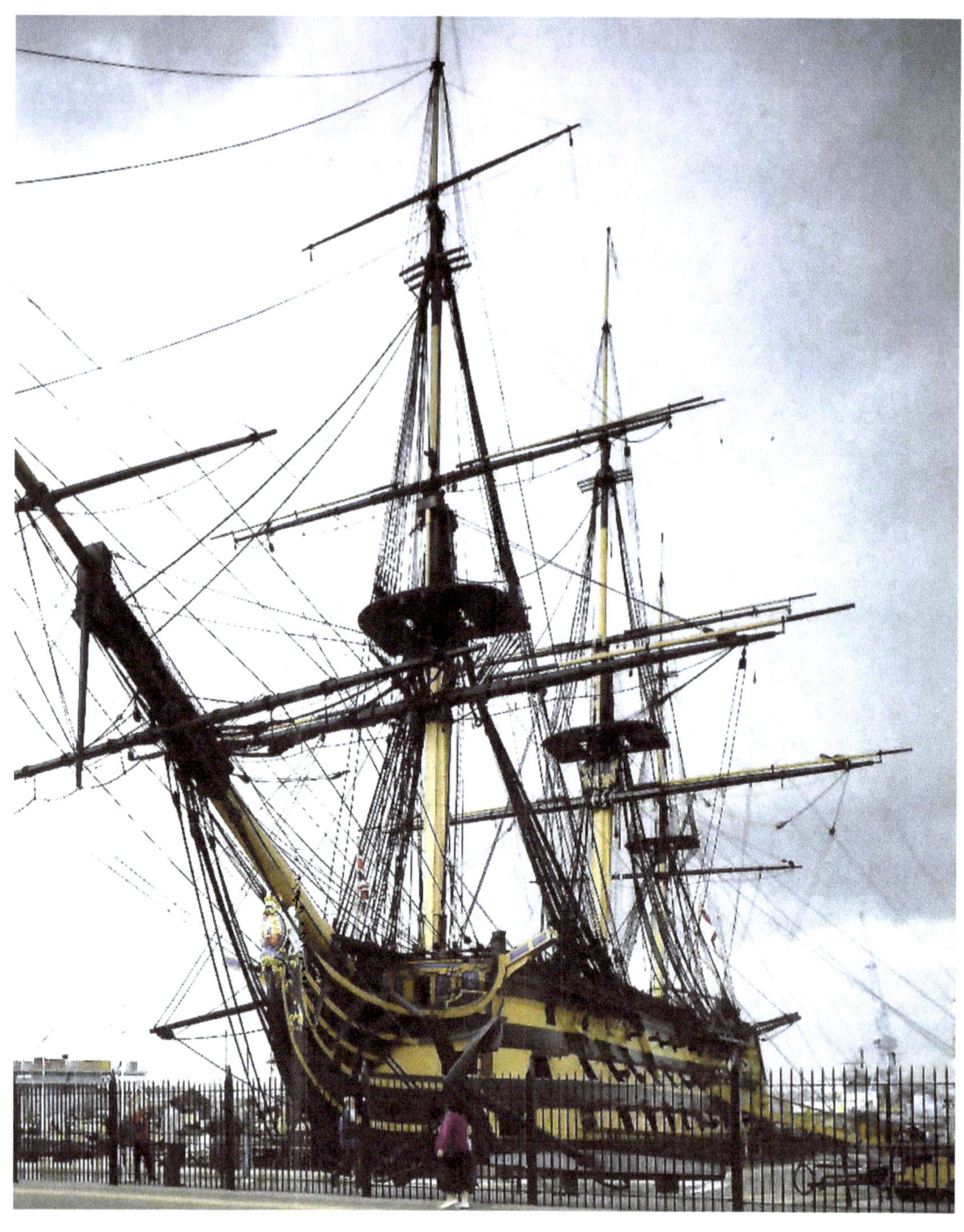

HMS Victory in dry dock at Portsmouth

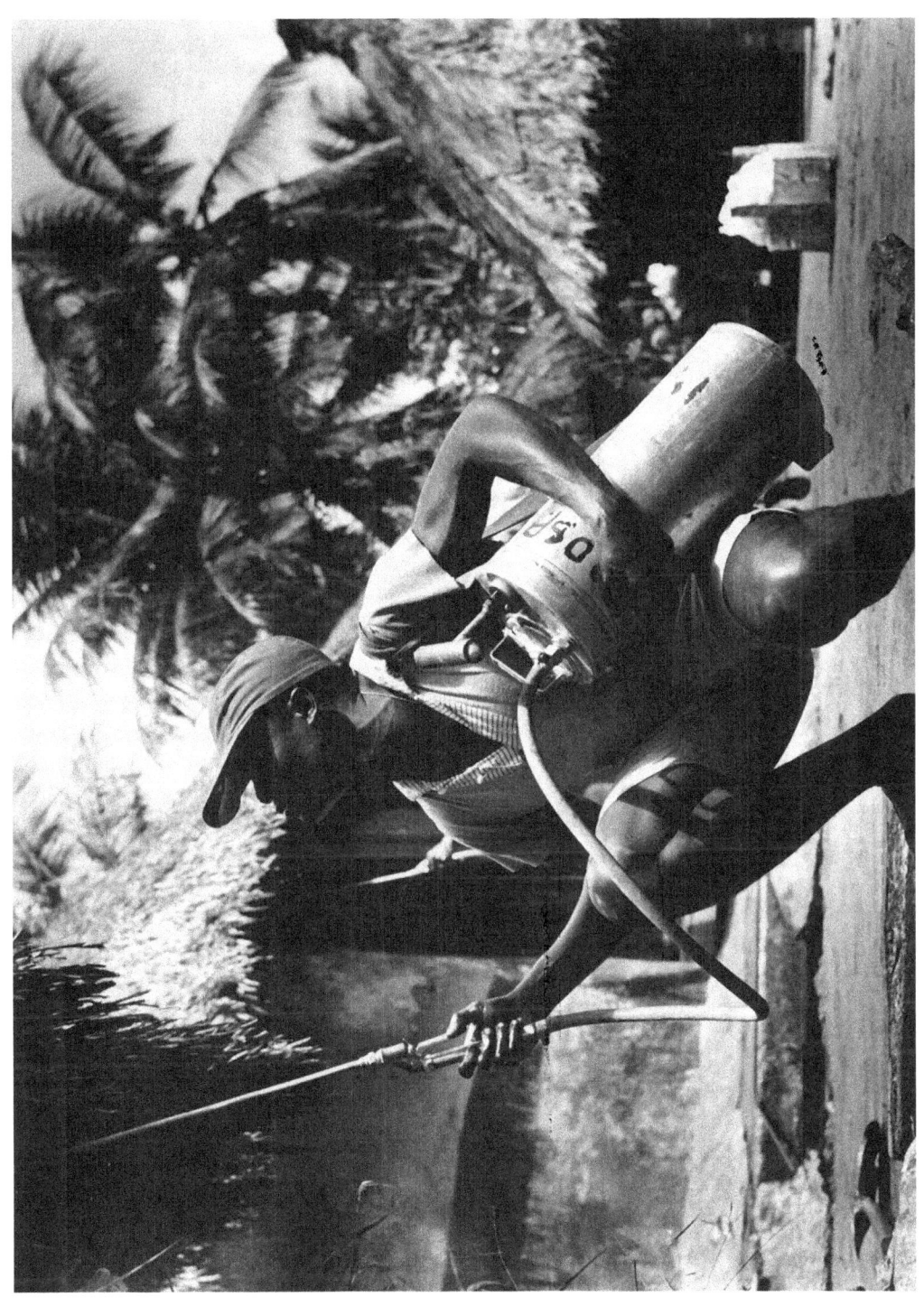

Spraying houses in Monrovia, Liberia to stop the spread of malaria

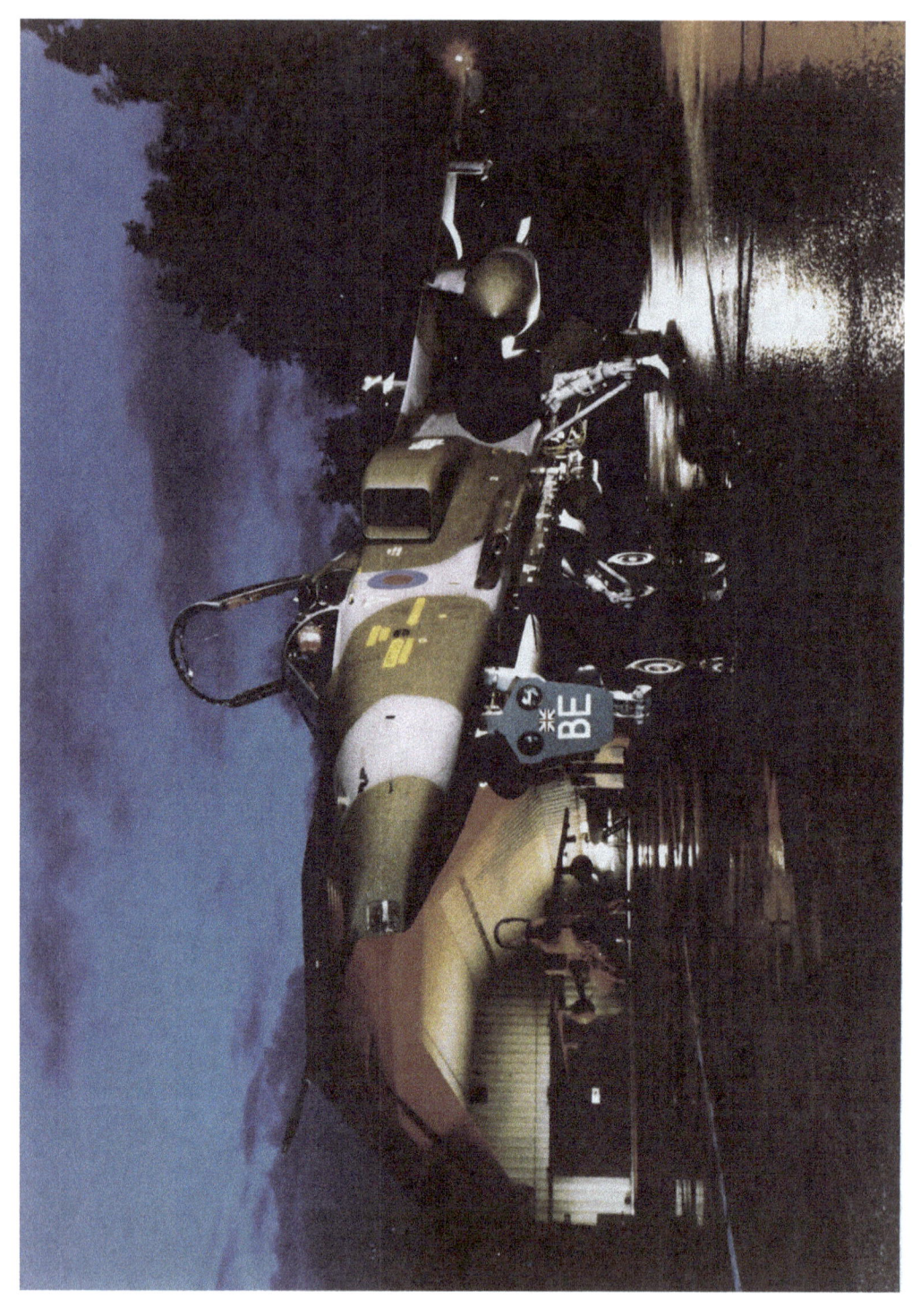

A Jaguar fighter prepares for a night sortie at RAF Bruggen

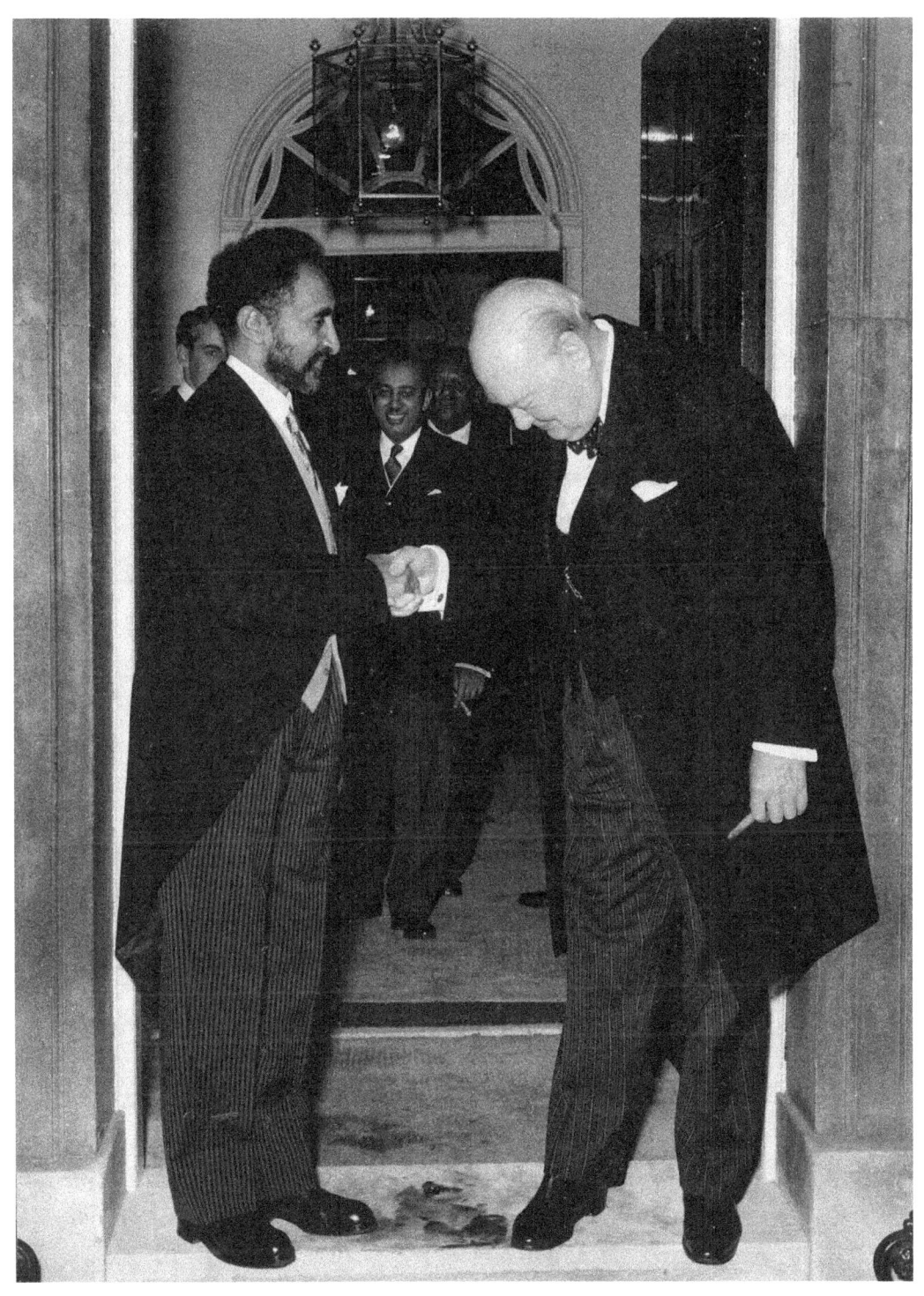

Winston Churchill and Haile Selassie on the steps of No10, 1954

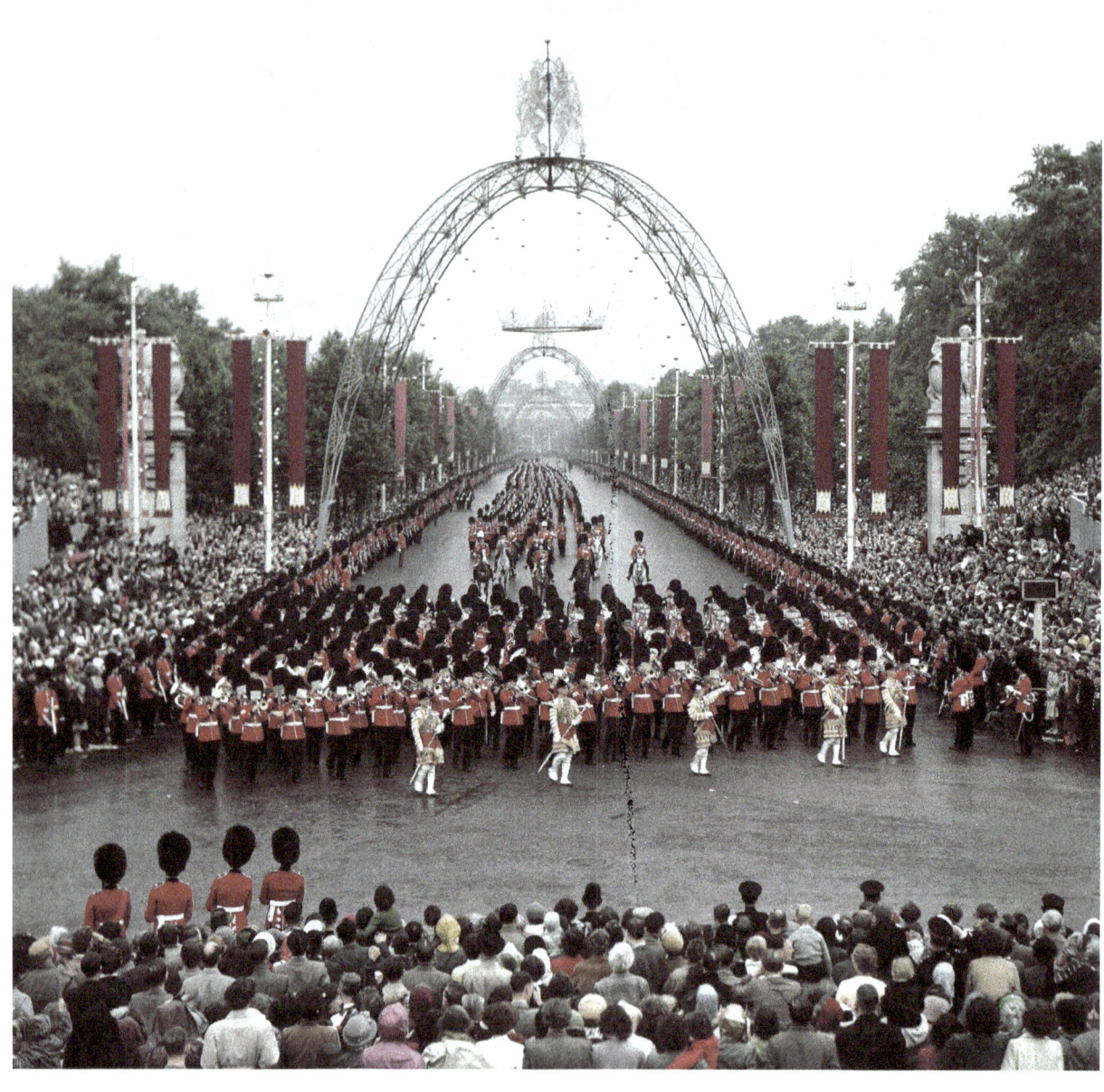

Trooping the Colour on the 11th June 1953, showing the parade on its way back to the Palace from Horse Guards

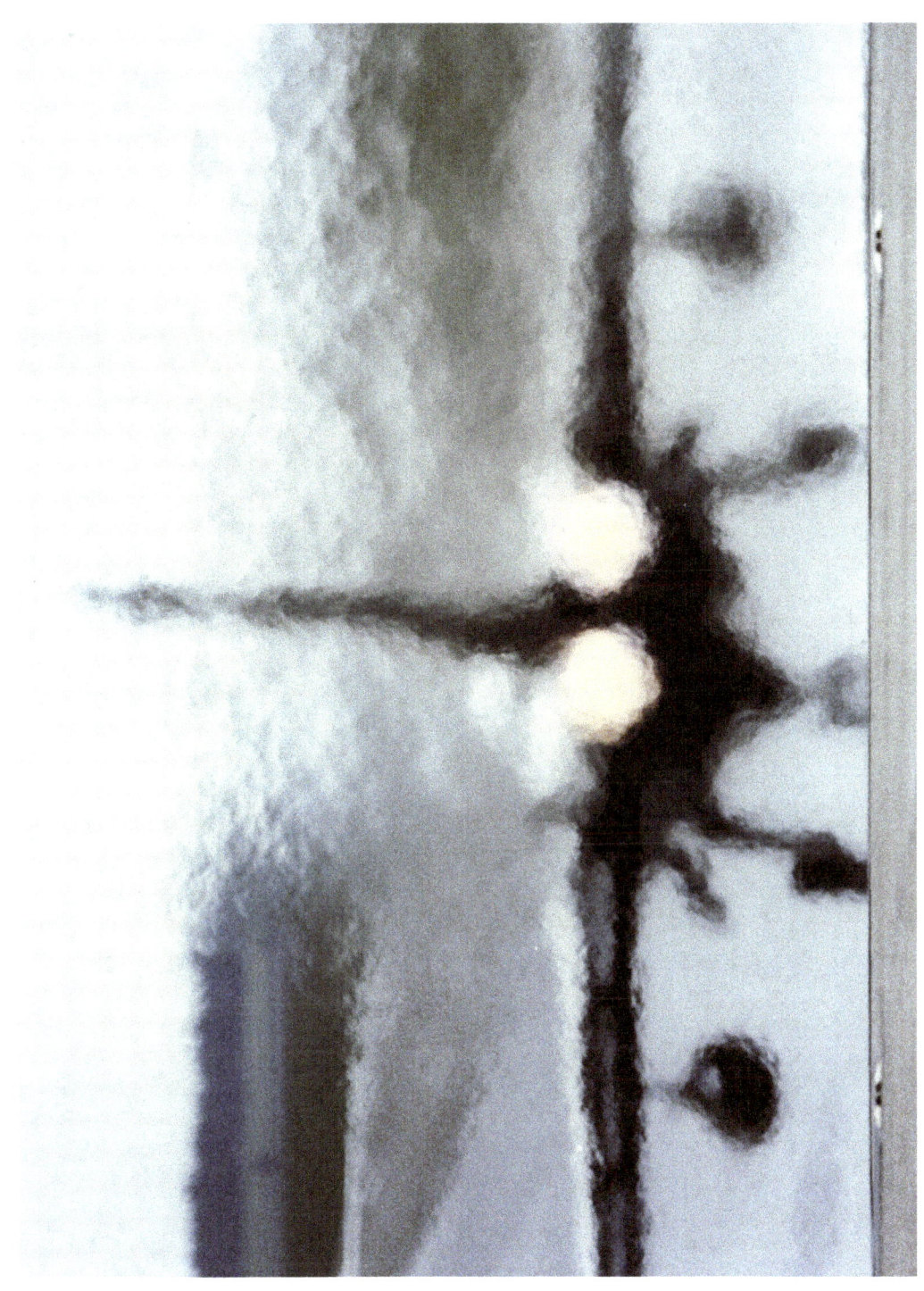

A Tornado with reheat takes off from Boscombe Down

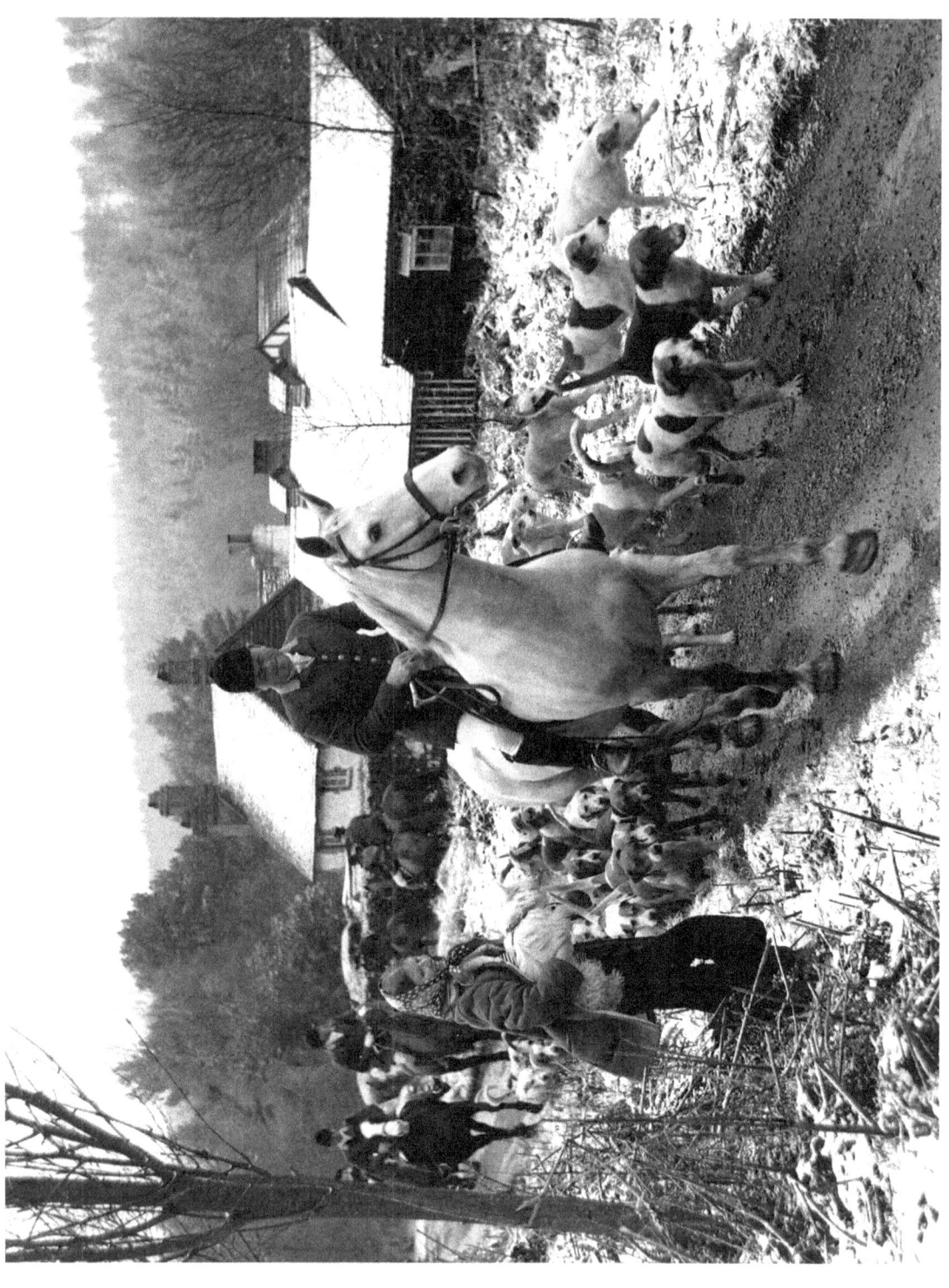

The Surrey Union Hunt in the snow on Leith Hill, Surrey

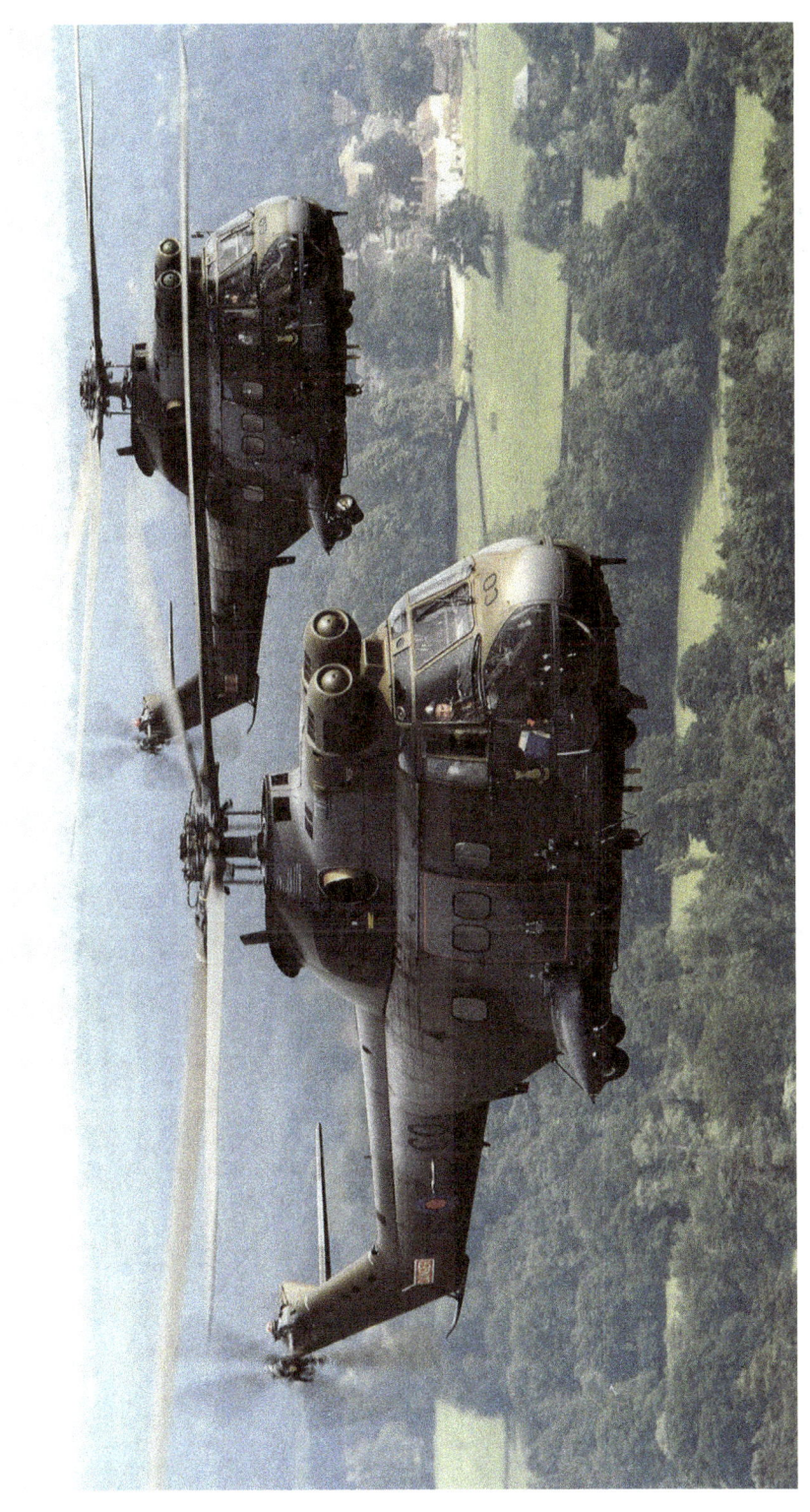

Two RAF Pumas of 33 Squadron, Odiham on patrol

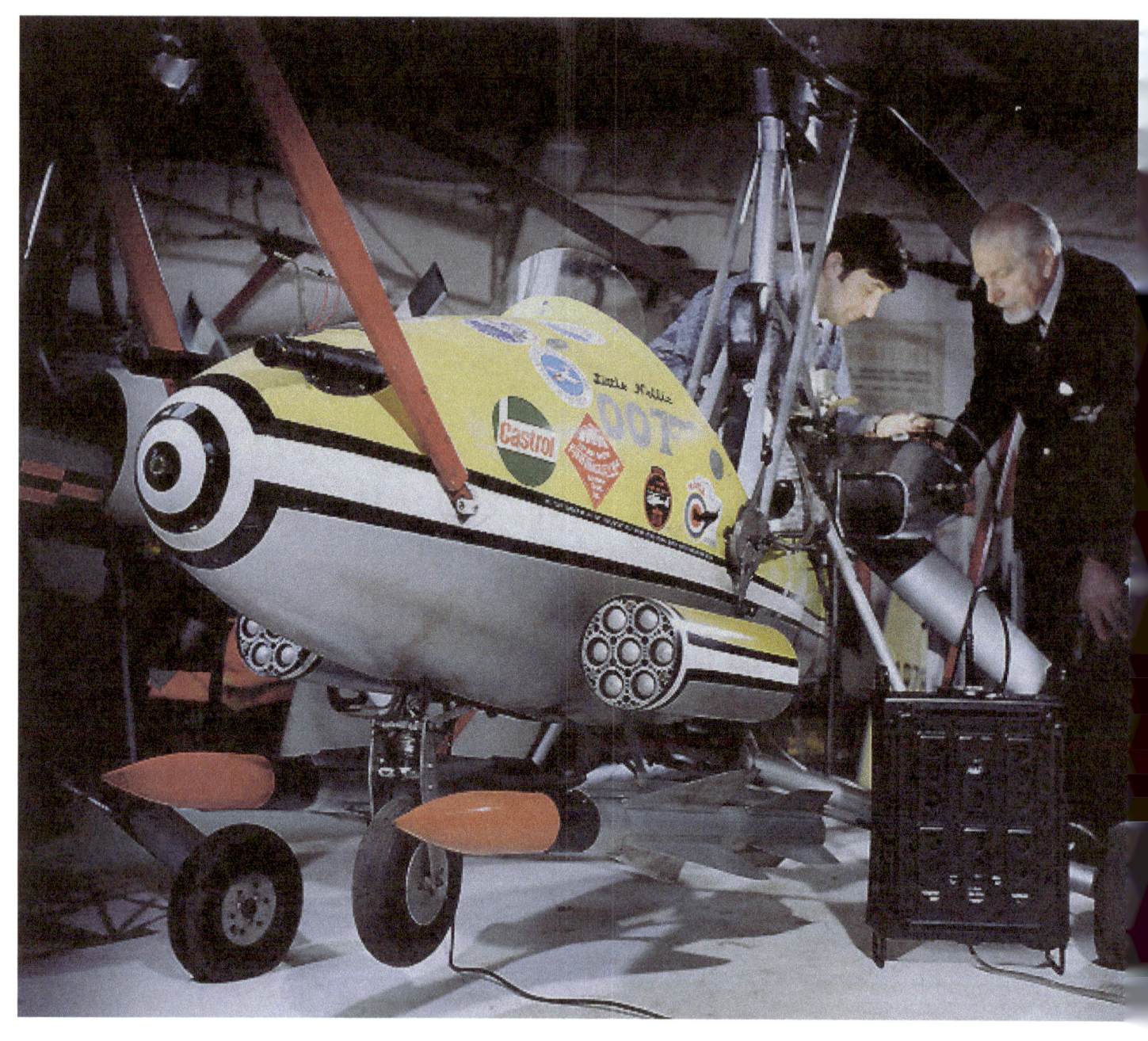

'Little Nellie' of 007 fame with her designer and builder Wing Commander Ken Wallis (retired)

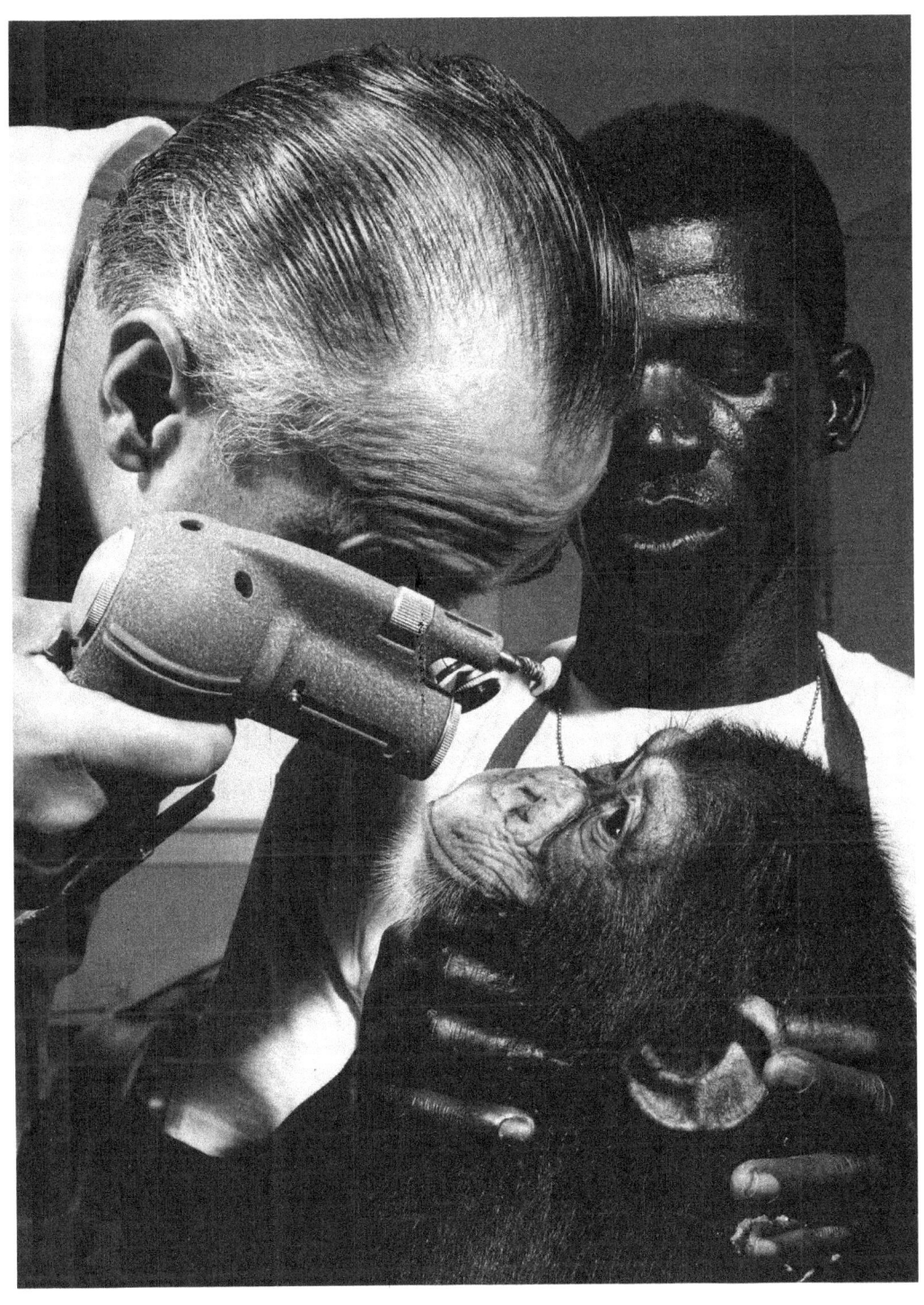

The veterinary department of Monrovia examining a monkey for diseases

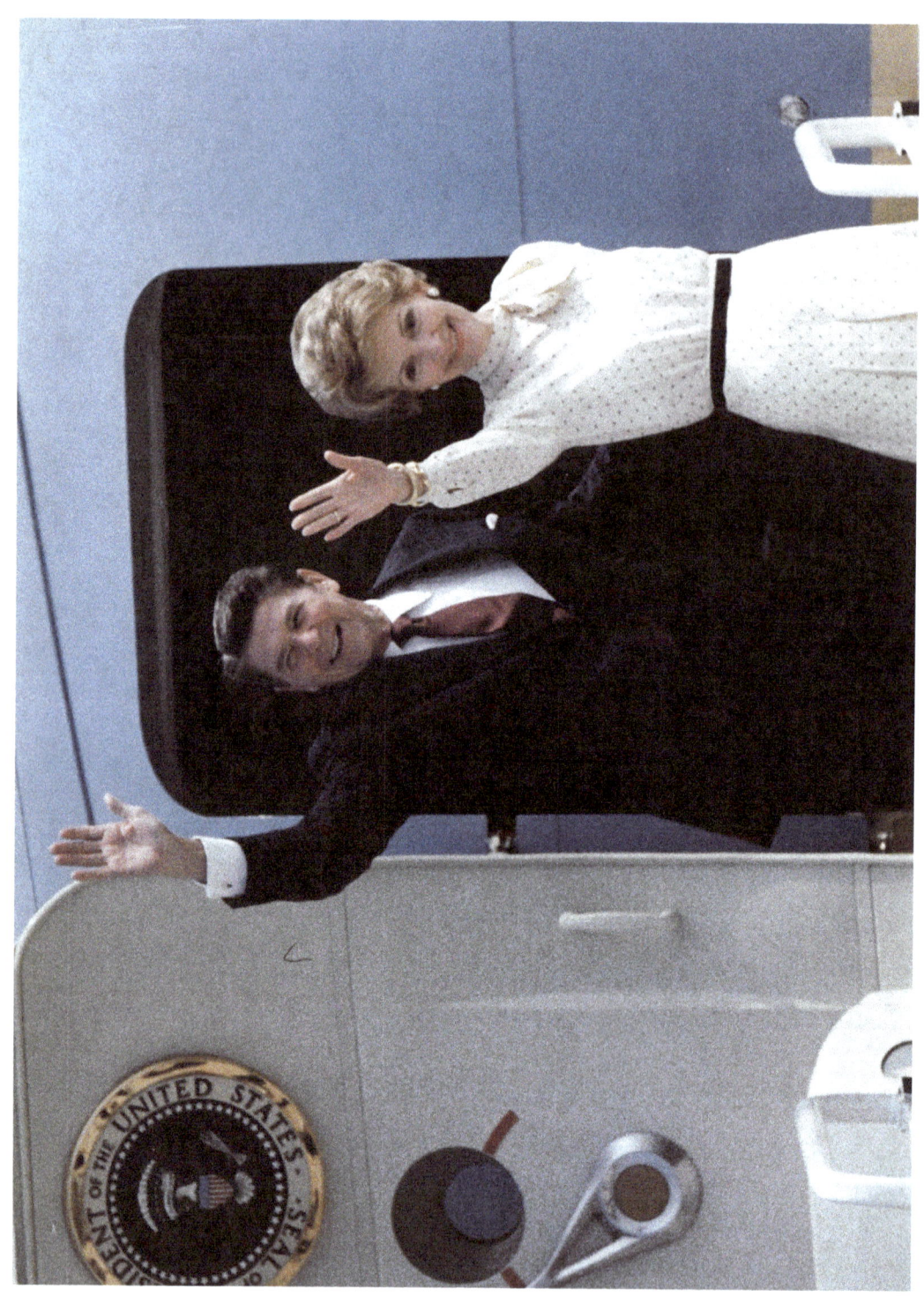

Ronald and Nancy Reagan wave goodbye from the steps of Air Force One

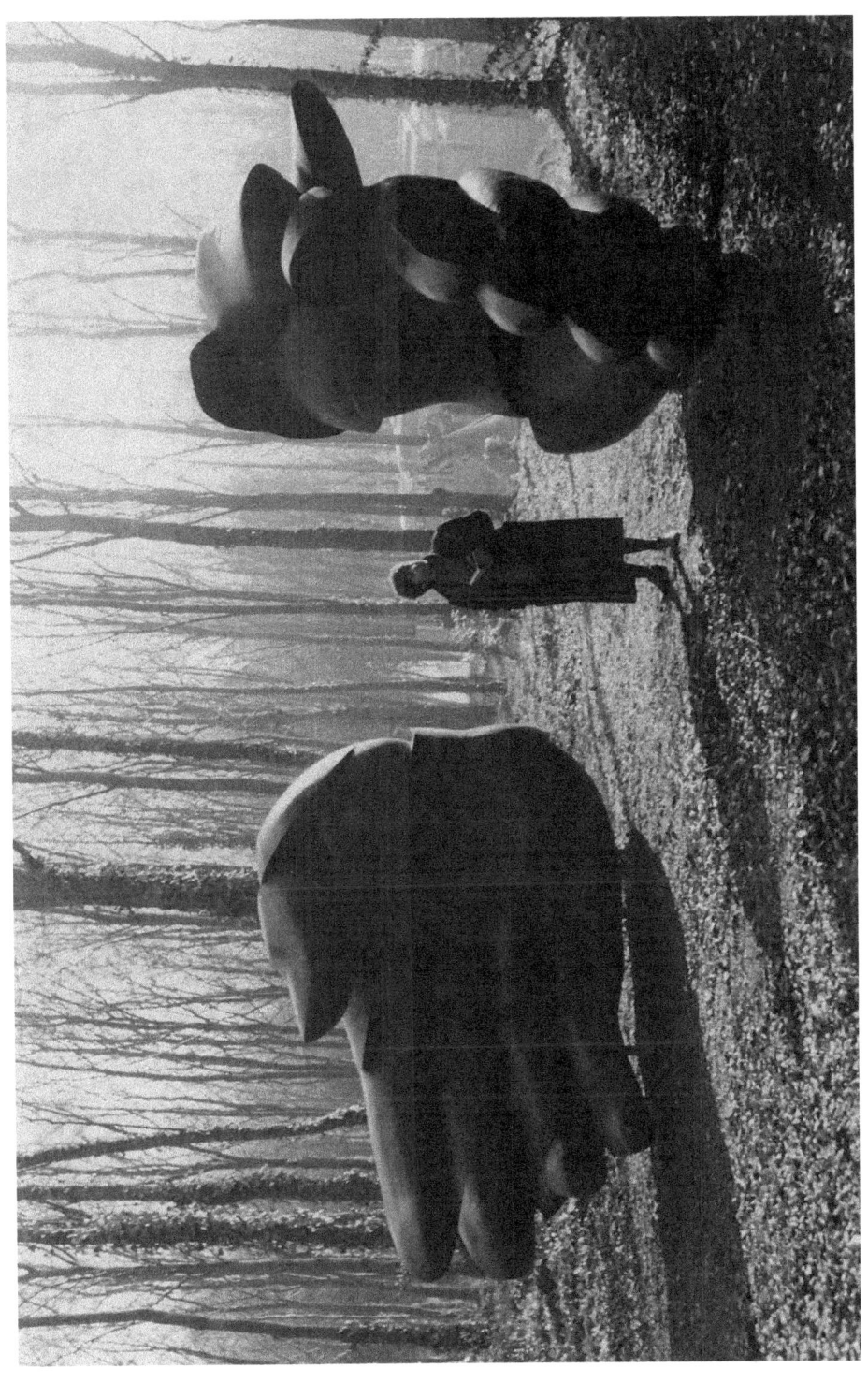

Two welcoming hands – large sculptures at Goodwood, West Sussex

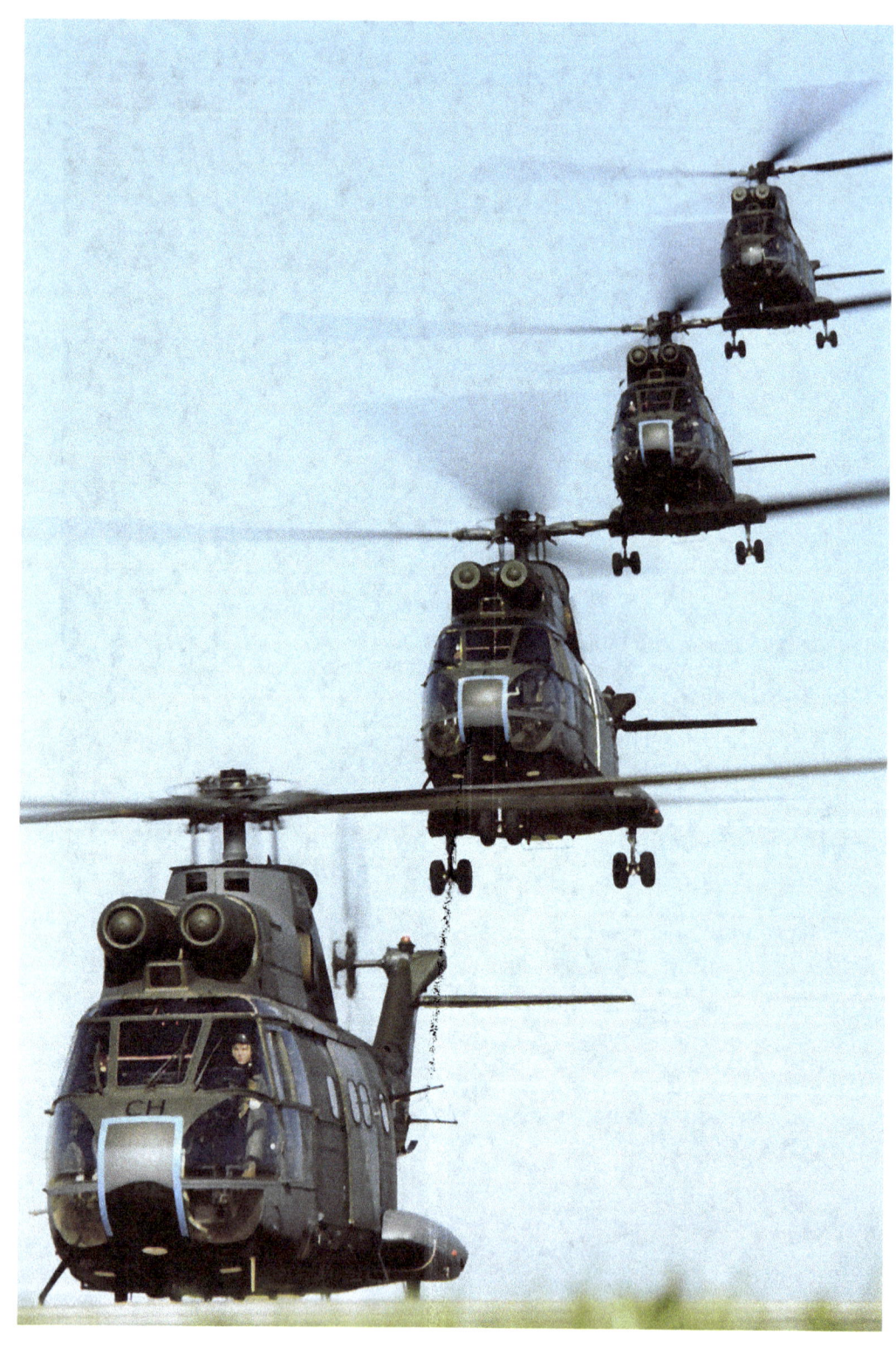

A stack of Puma's of 33 Squadron, RAF Odiham

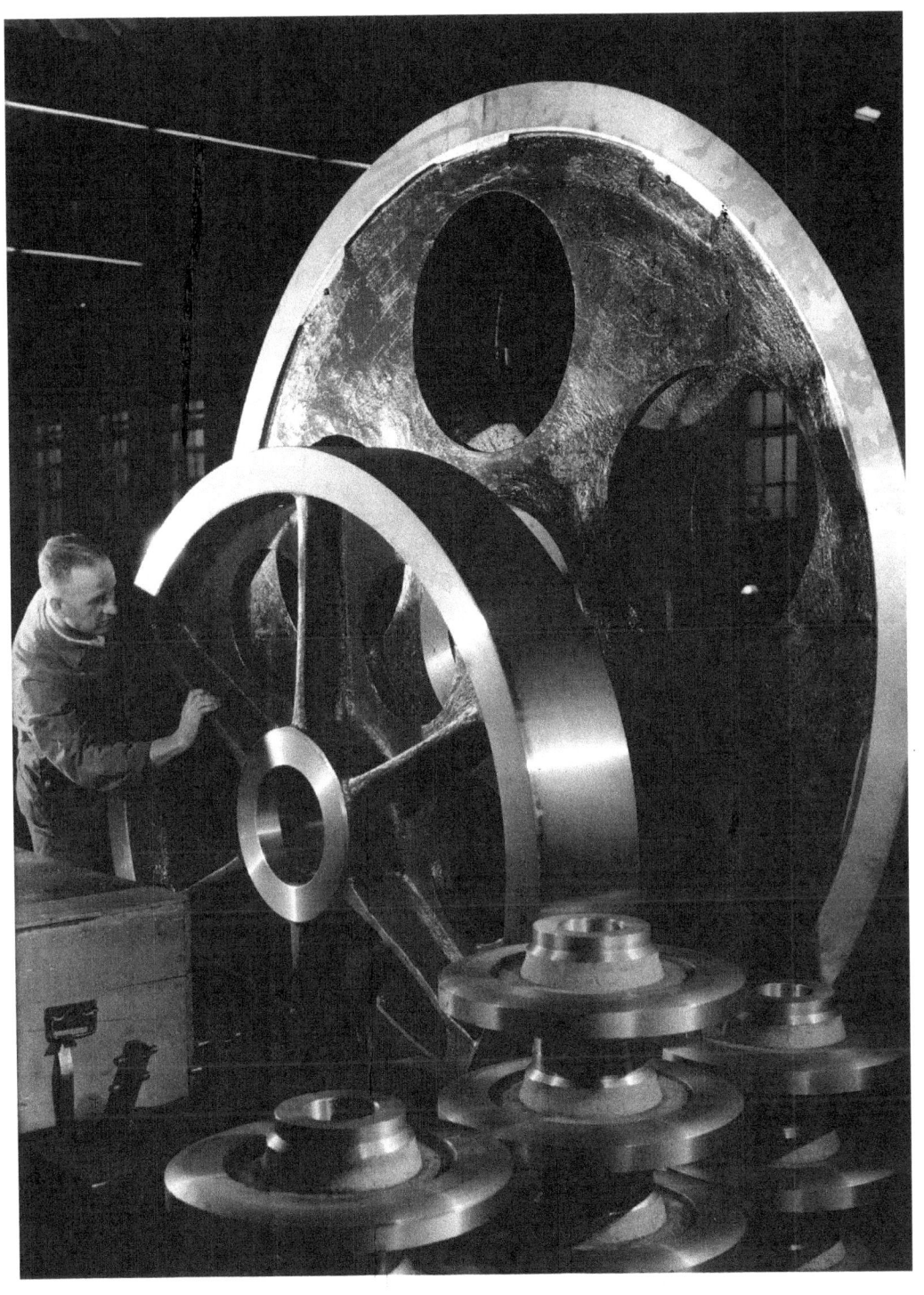

Large machinery being manufactured at Tube Investments, Germany

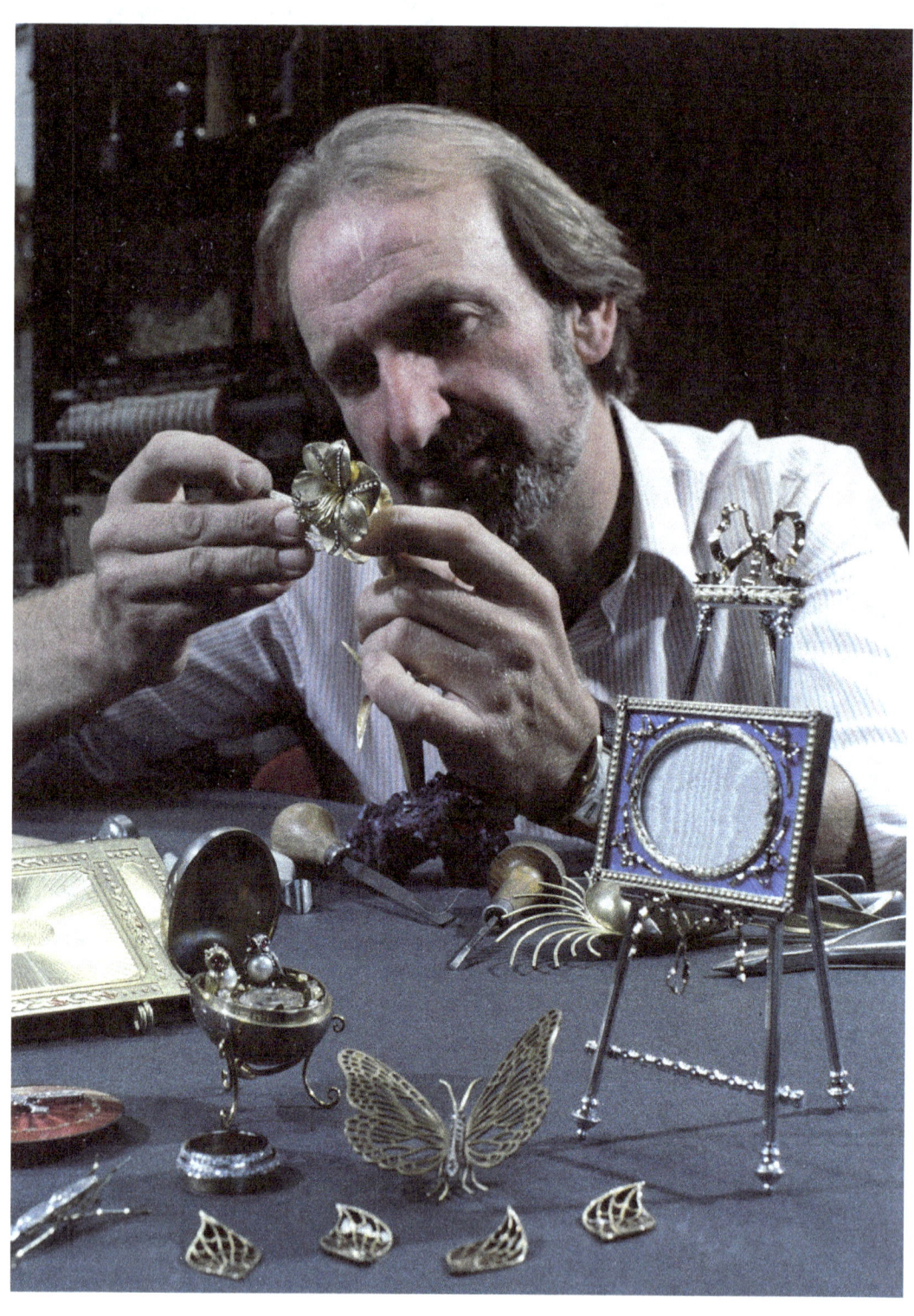

A silver smith at work on jewellery and small trinkets

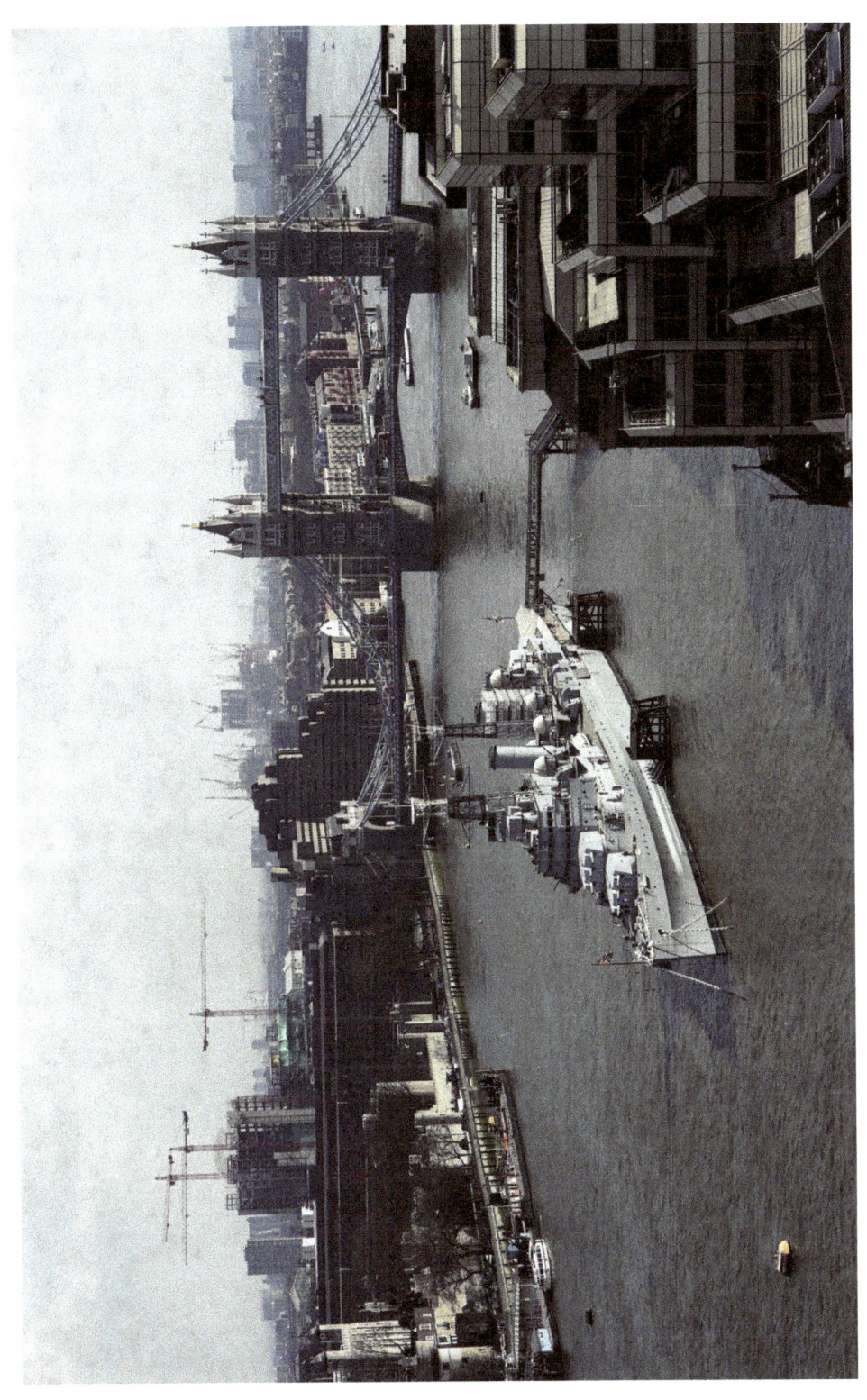

HMS Belfast moored in the Thames with a backdrop of Tower Bridge

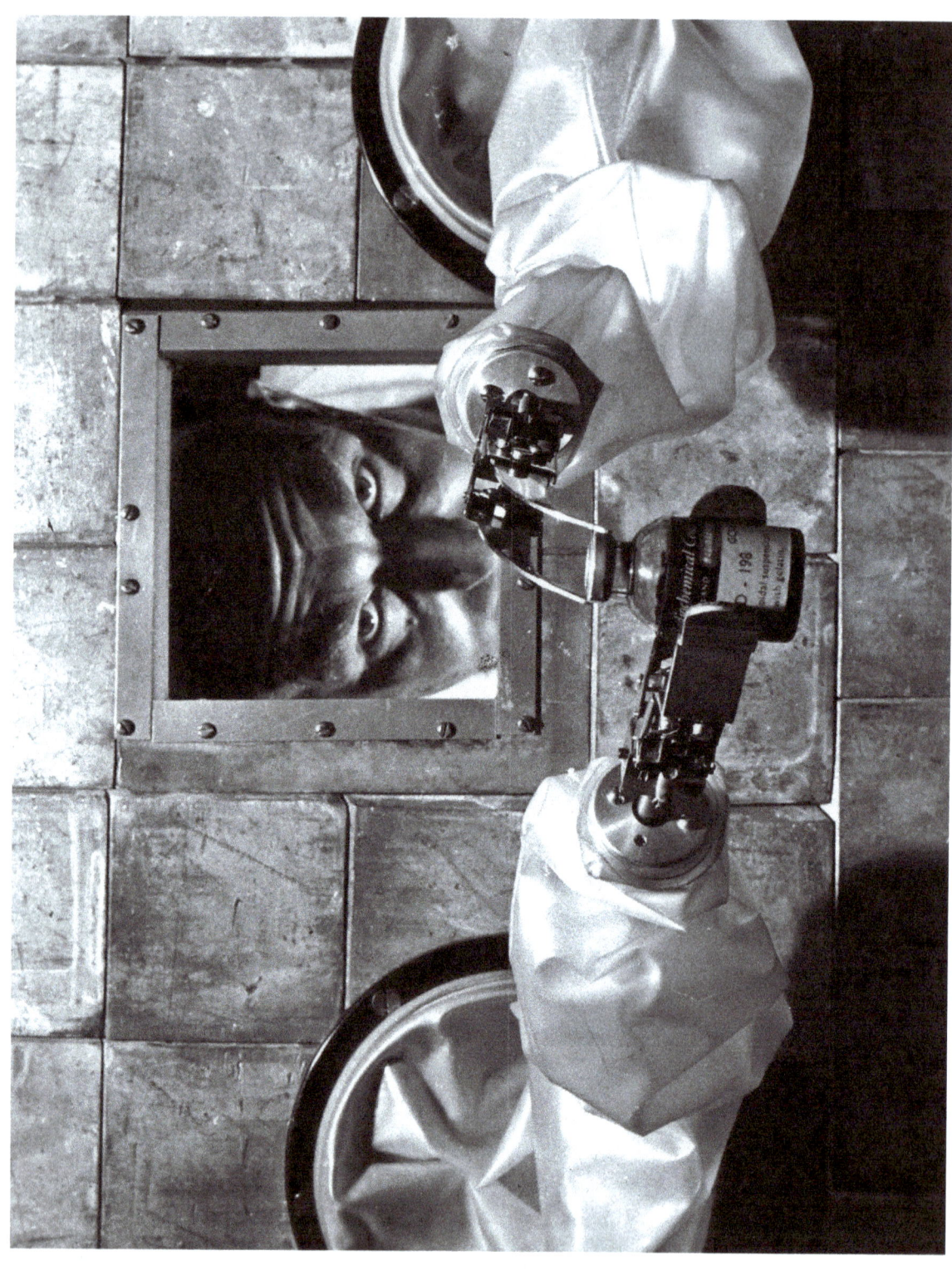

Working in a glove box with nuclear isotopes to protect against radiation

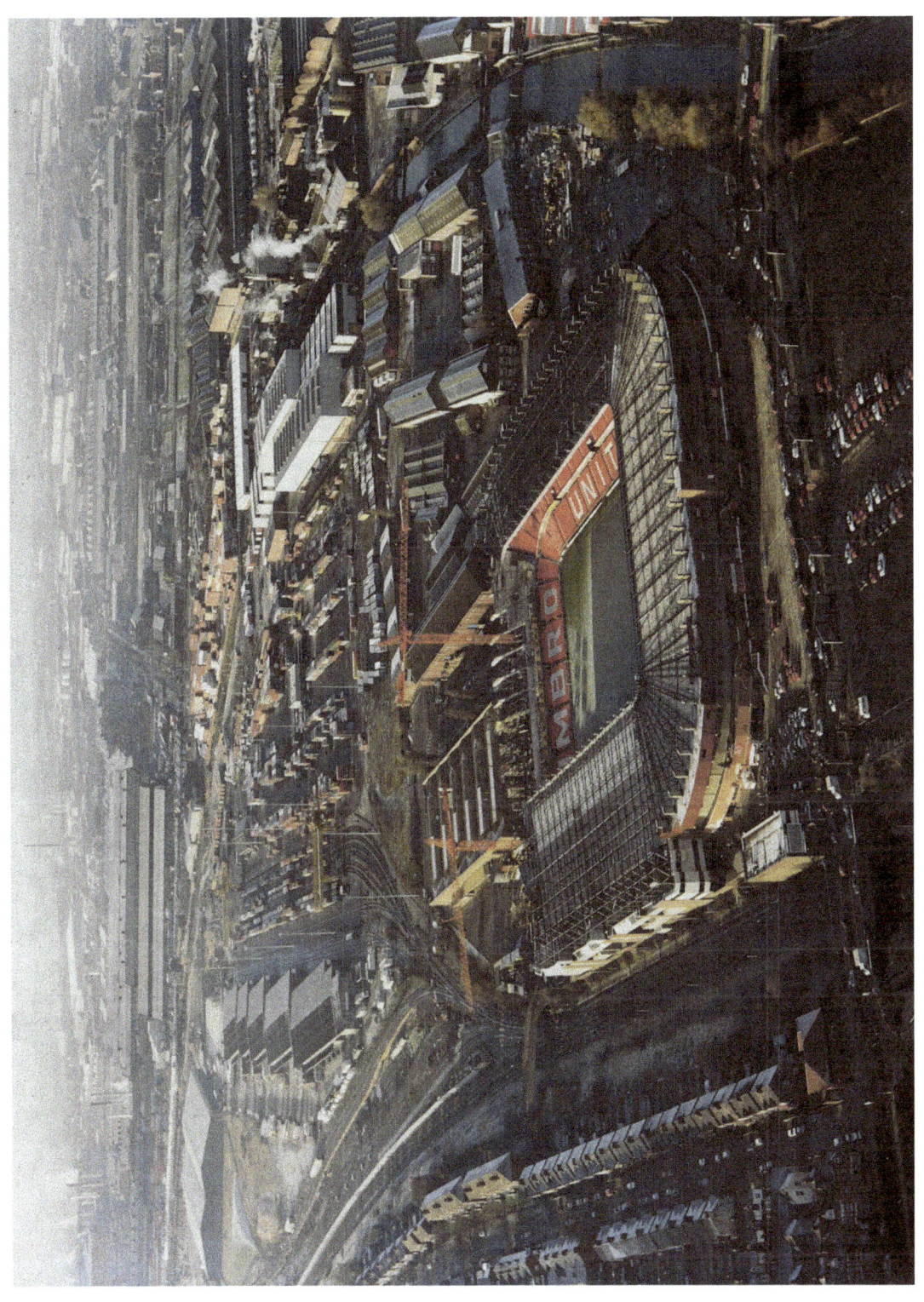

Manchester United football ground from the air

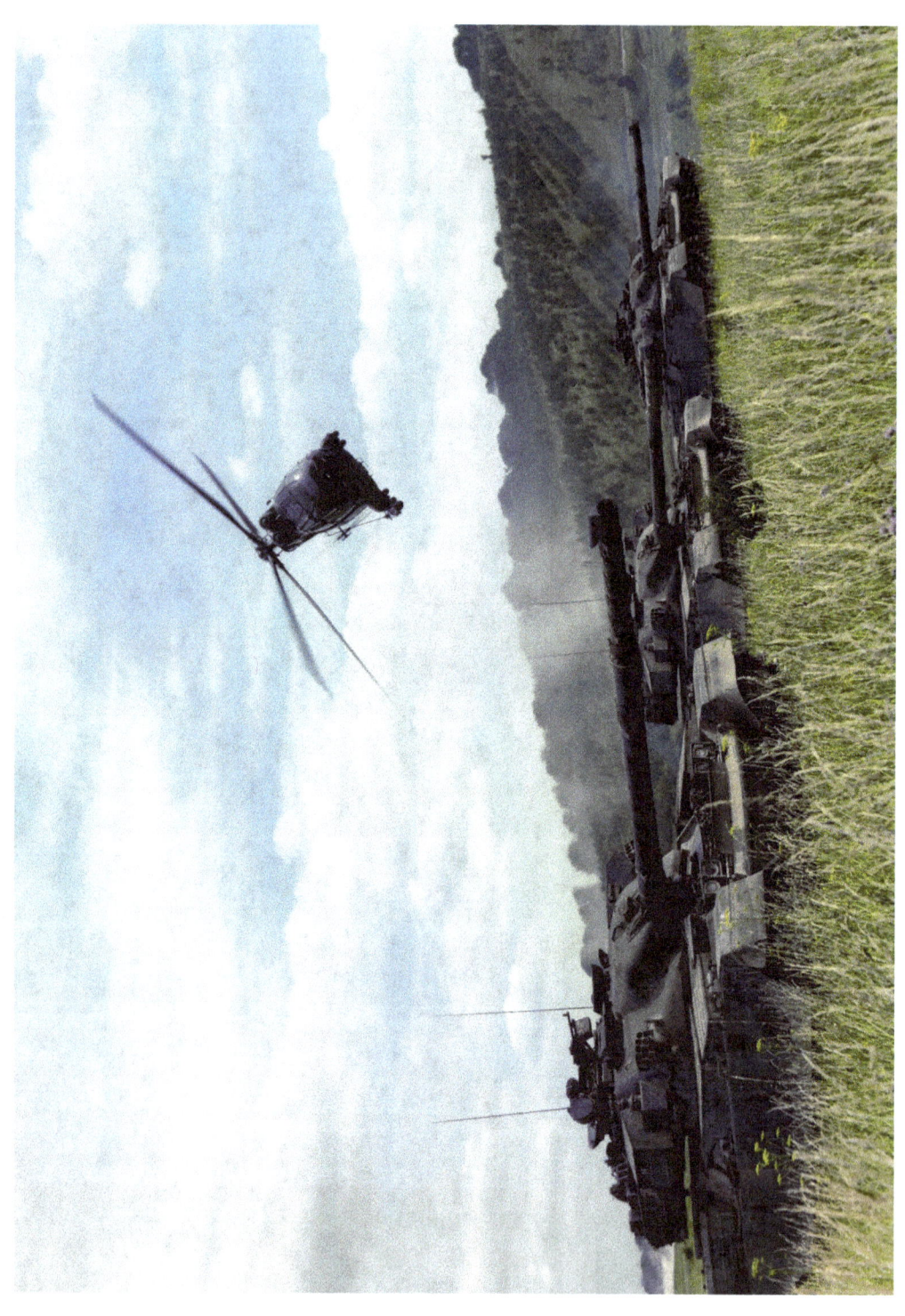

A Puma helicopter flying over tanks on Salisbury Planes

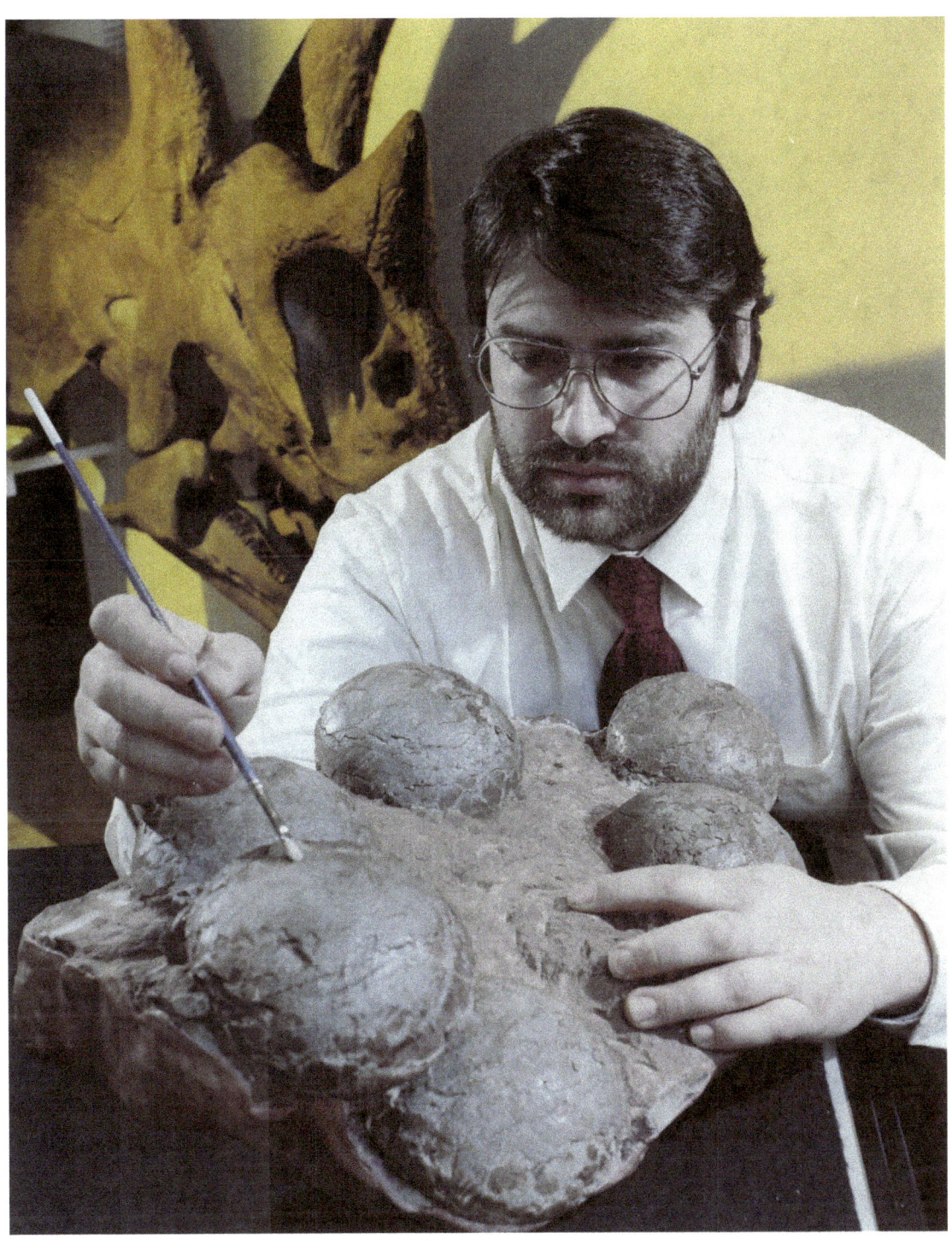

Examining dinosaur eggs at Glasgow University

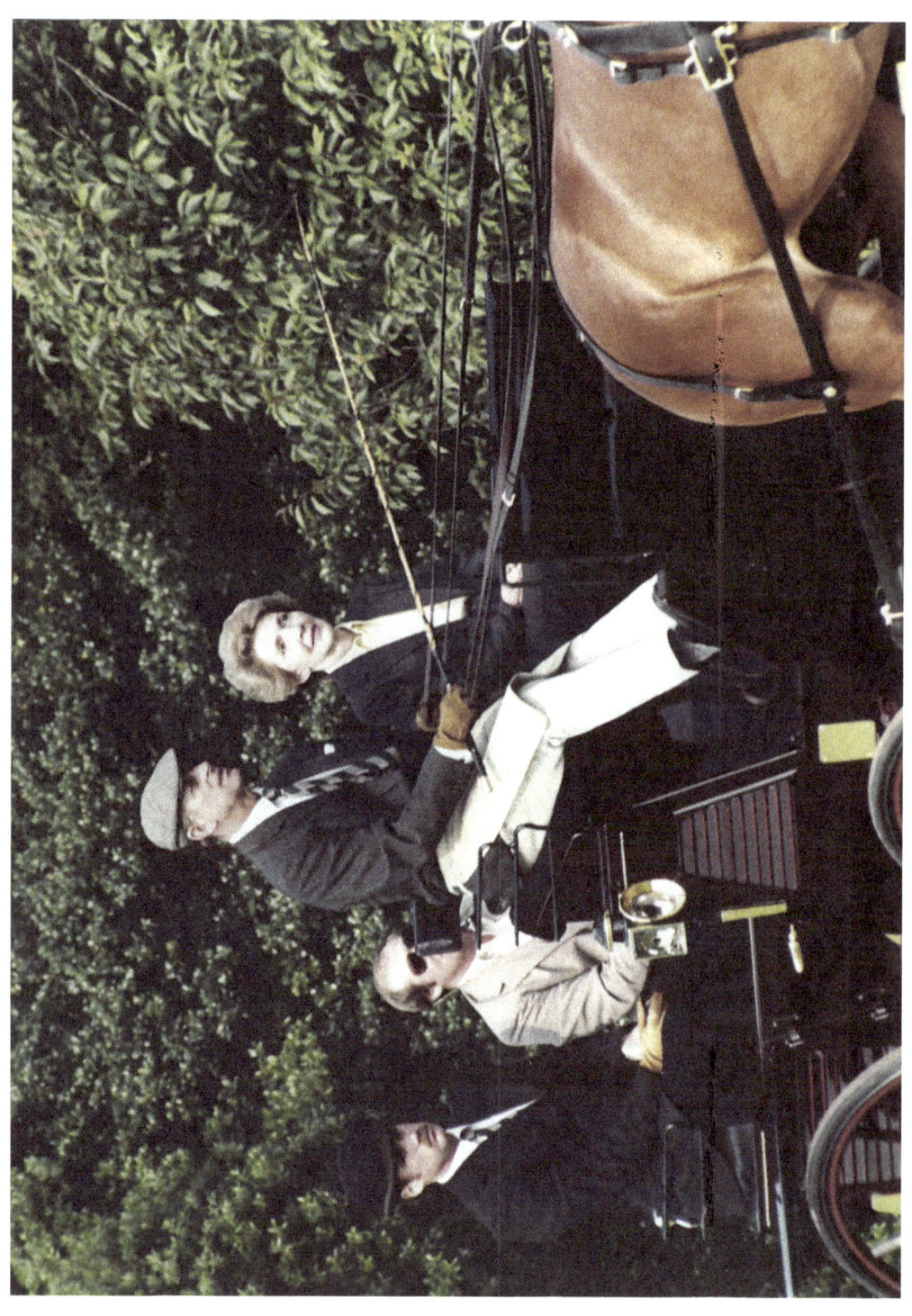

The Duke of Edinburgh and Nancy Reagan driving in a coach and four in Windsor Great Park

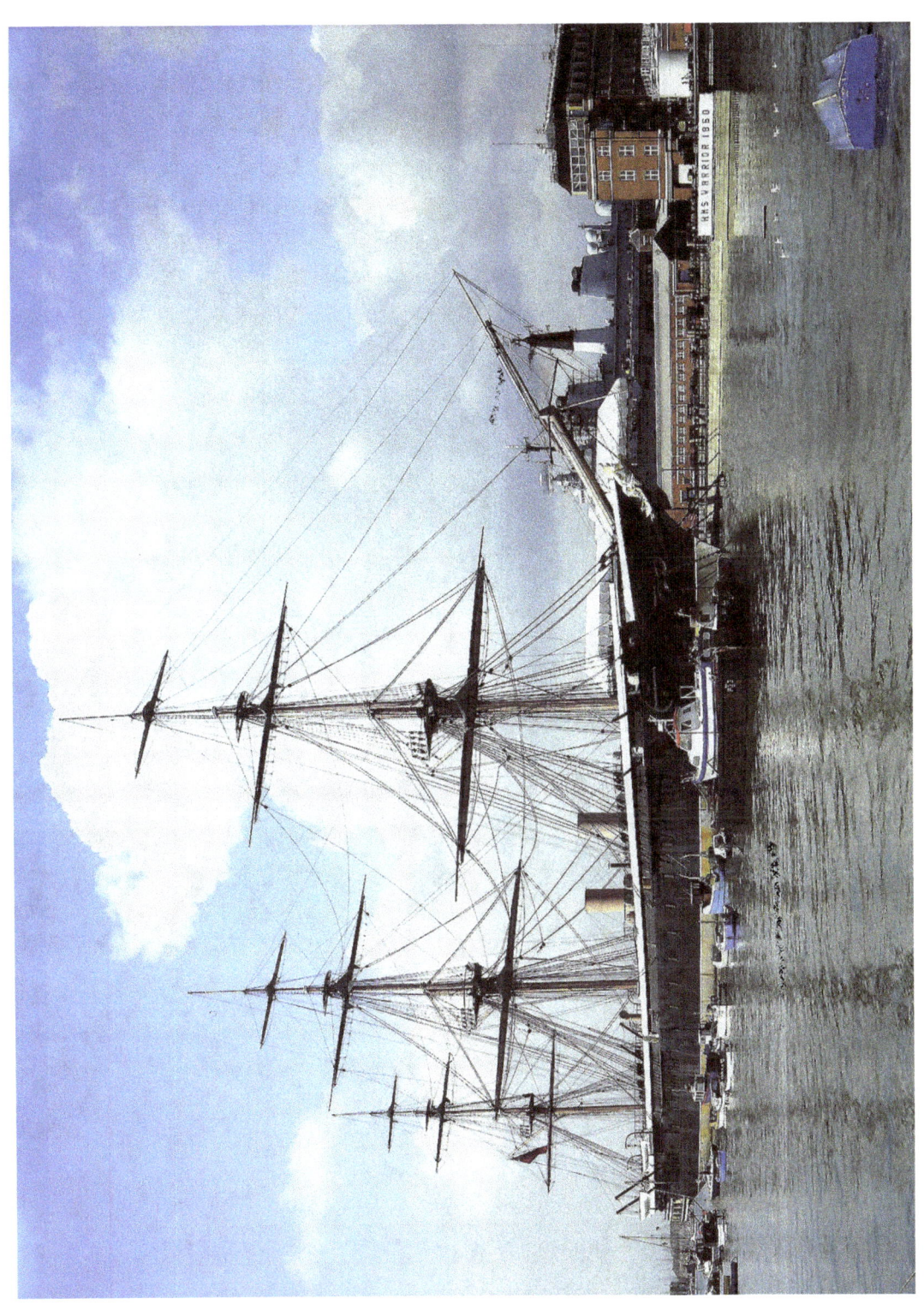

HMS Warrior, Portsmouth Historic Dockyard. The first all metal war ship

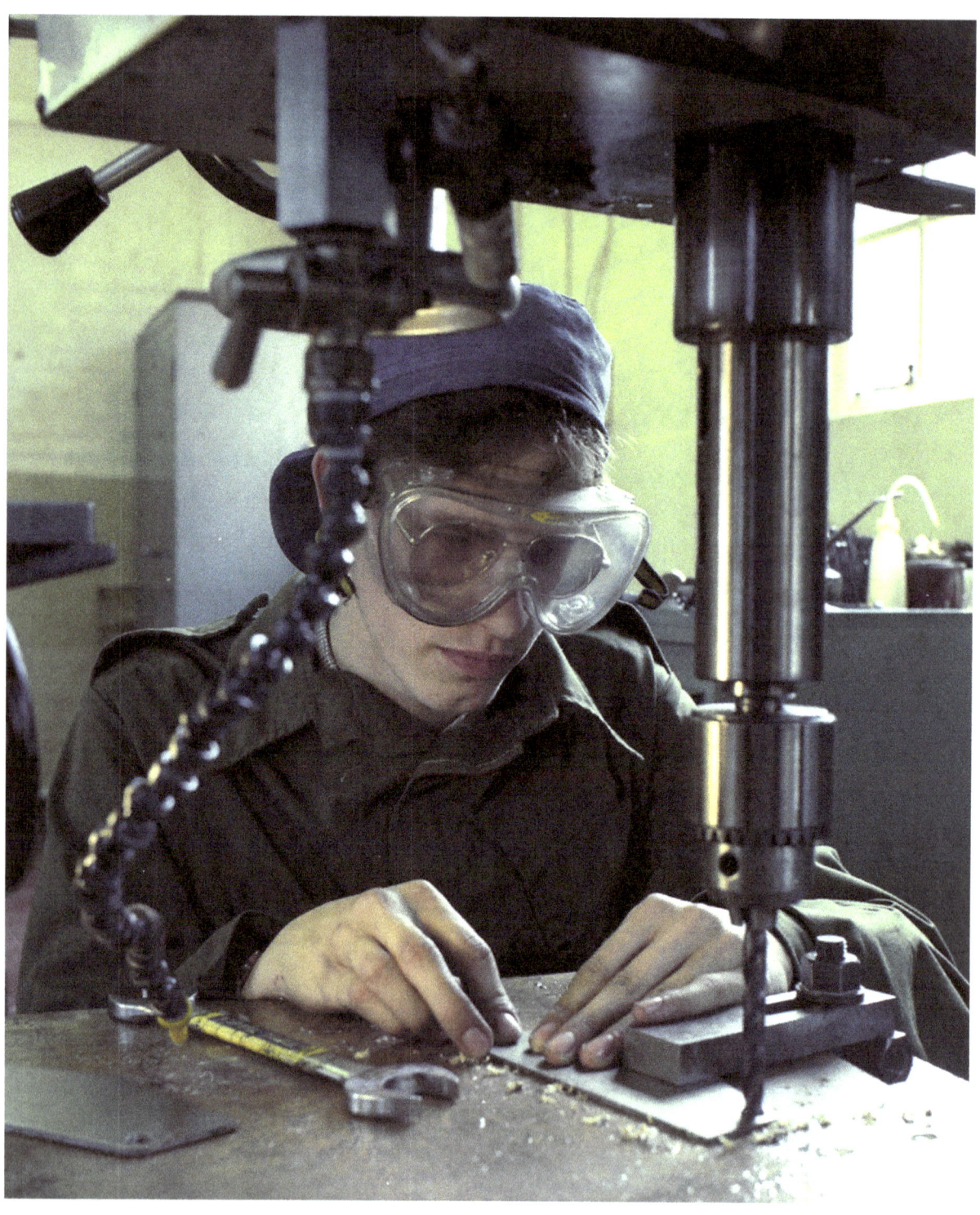

Engineering training at Farnborough

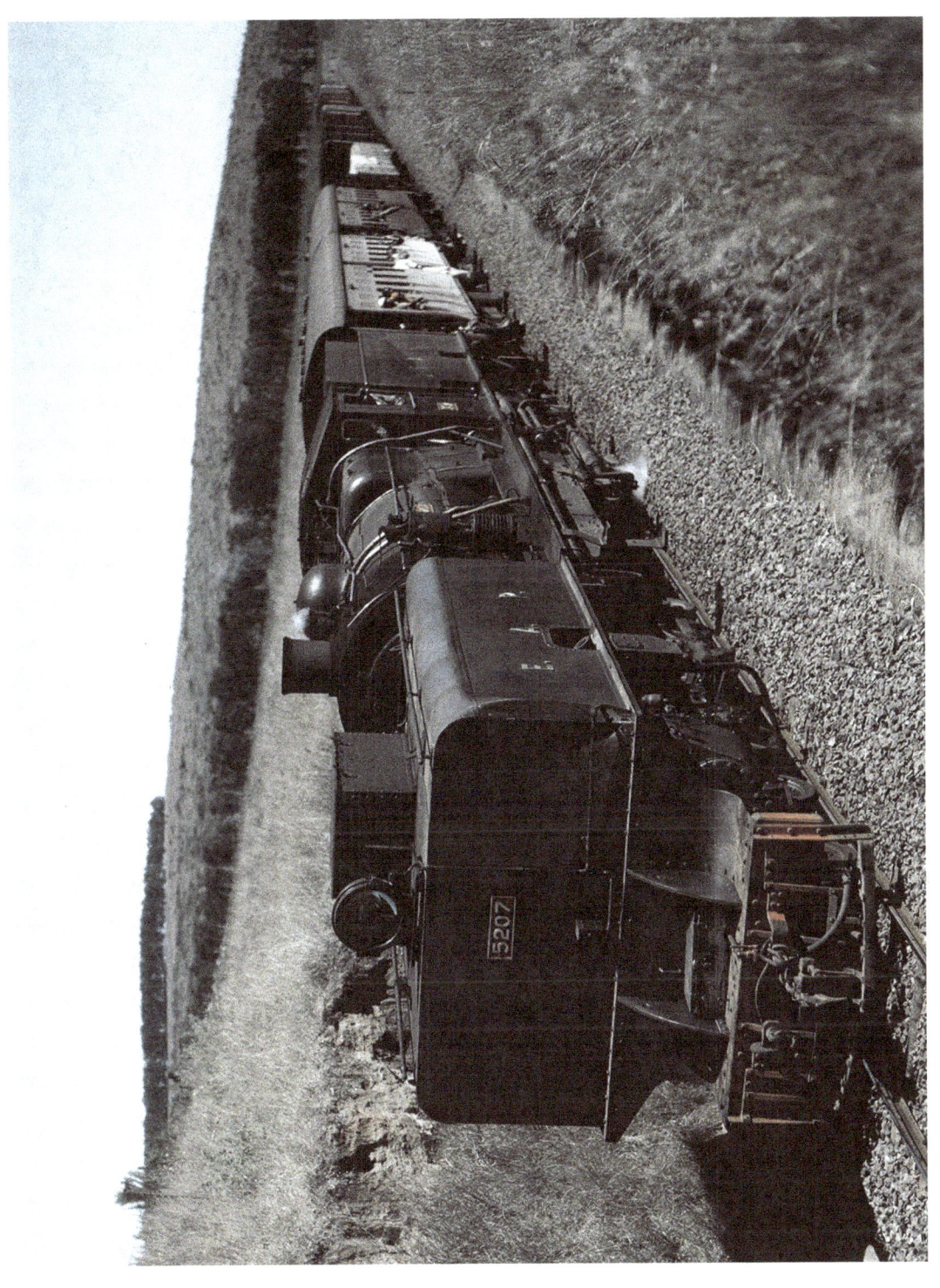

A train climbing up over the Mau escarpment near Nakuru, Kenya

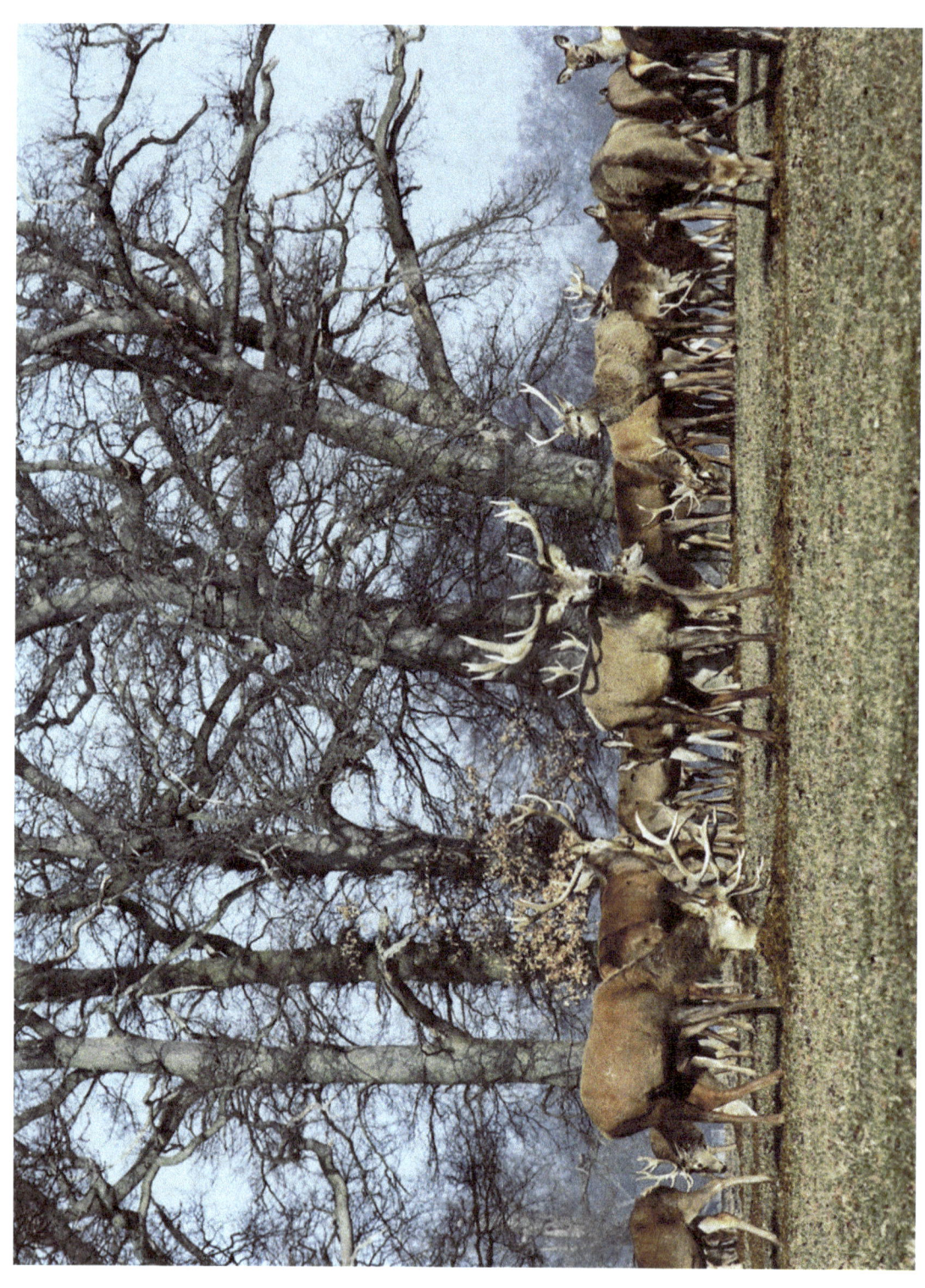

Breeding red deer for export at Warnham, Sussex

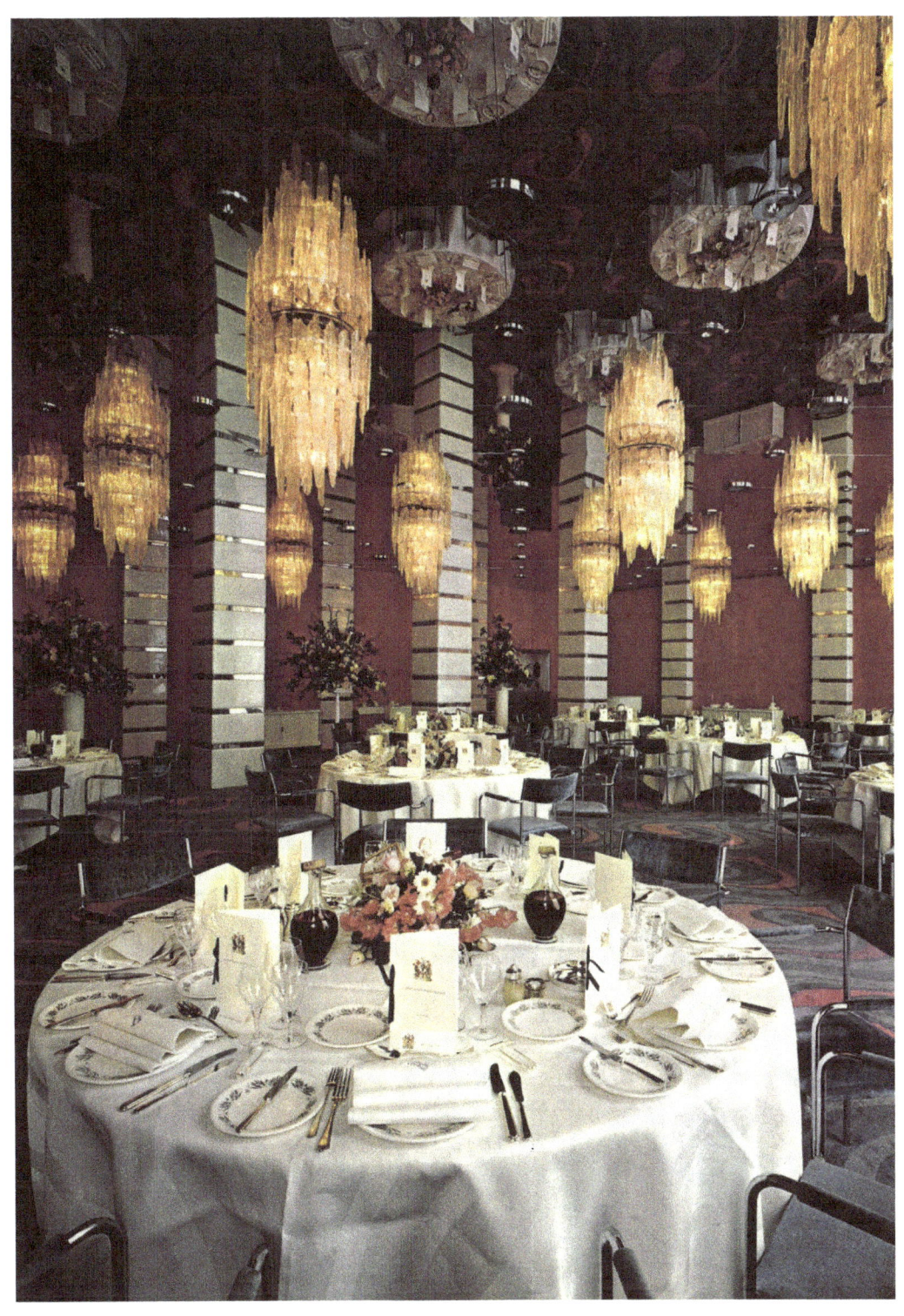

The ICI plastic mirror ceiling in a London hotel

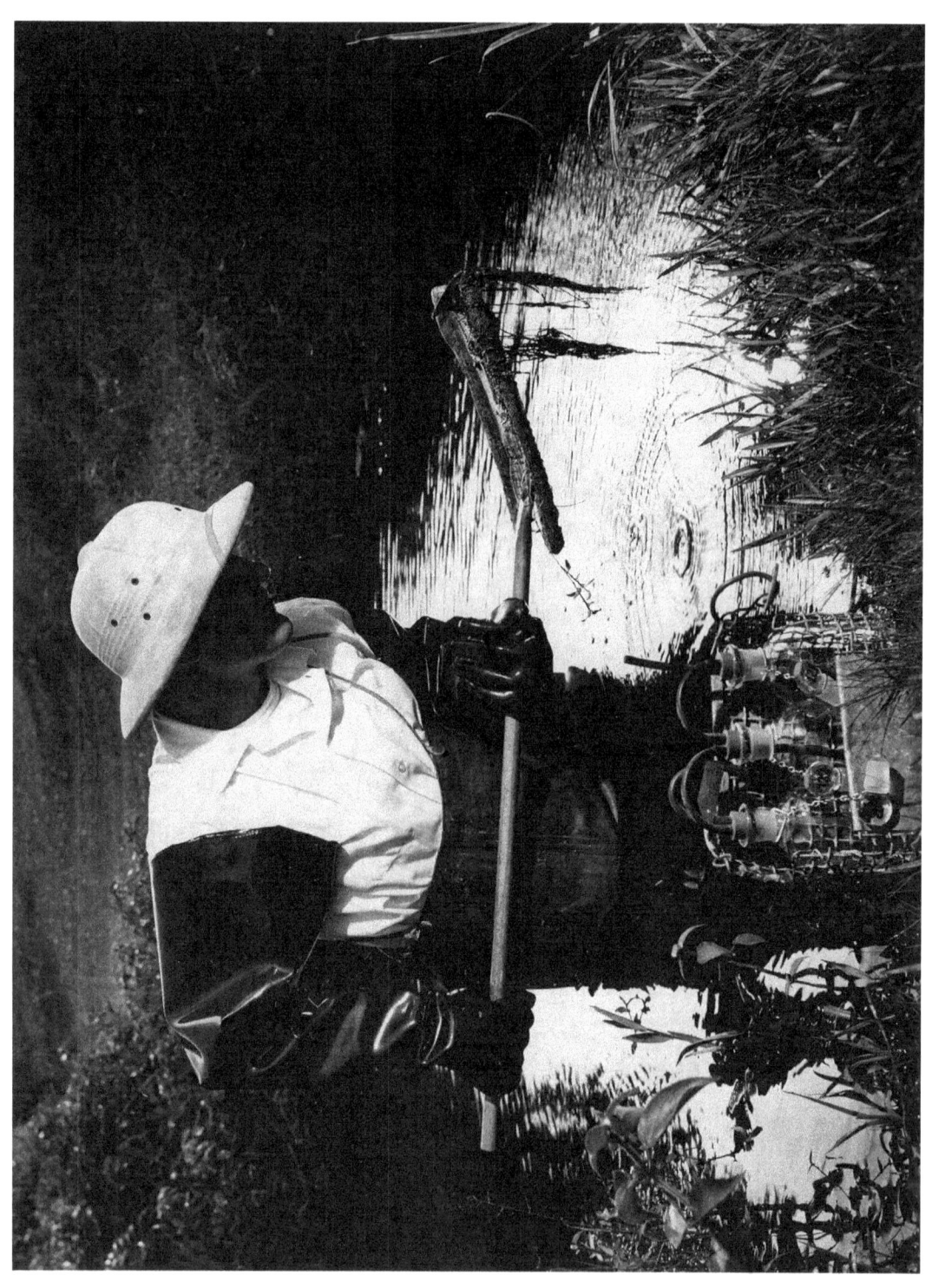

Vet checking for mosquito larvae in a stagnant pool in Monrovia, Liberia

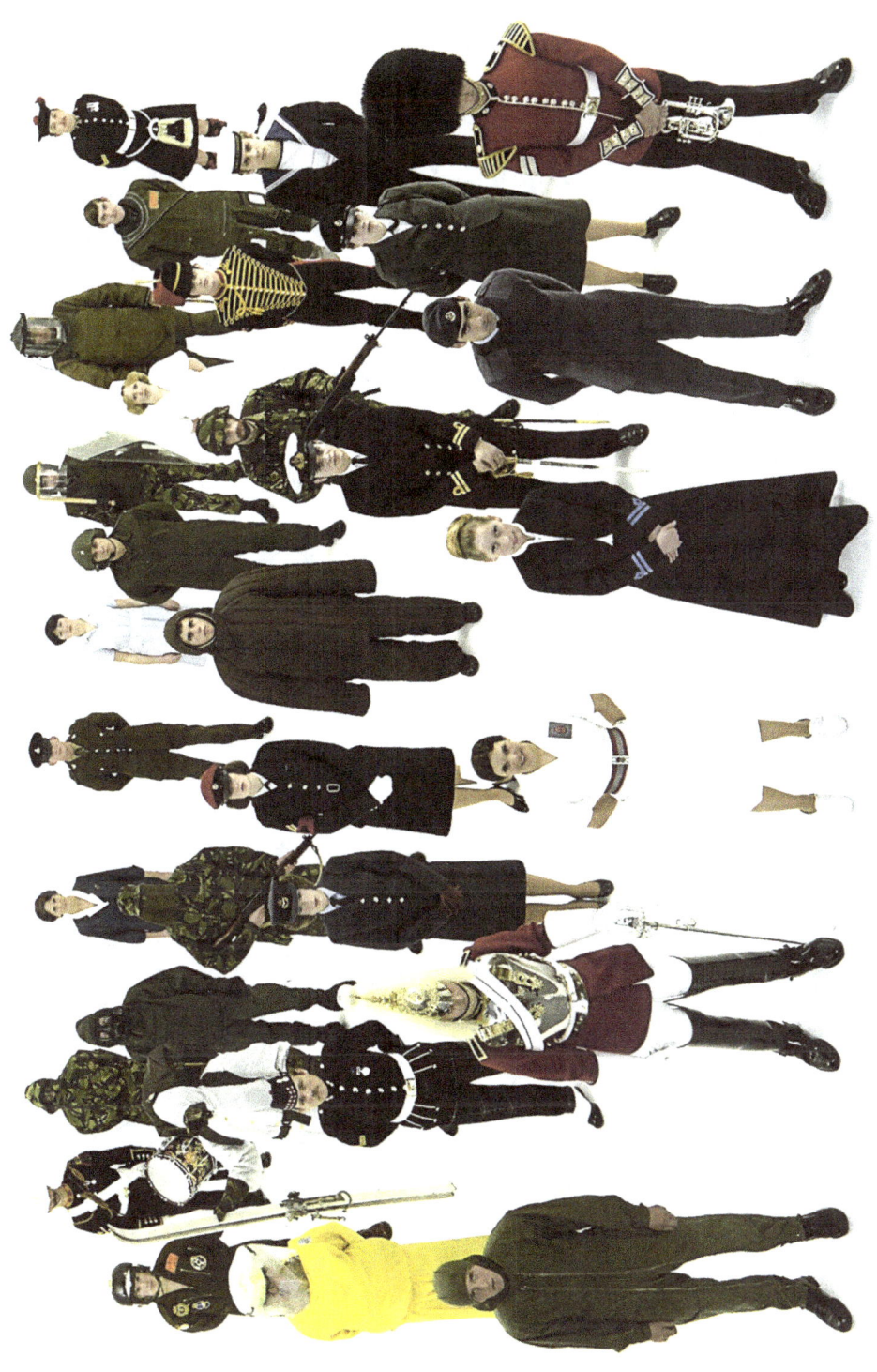

Service uniforms being shown in a studio picture for an MOD brochure

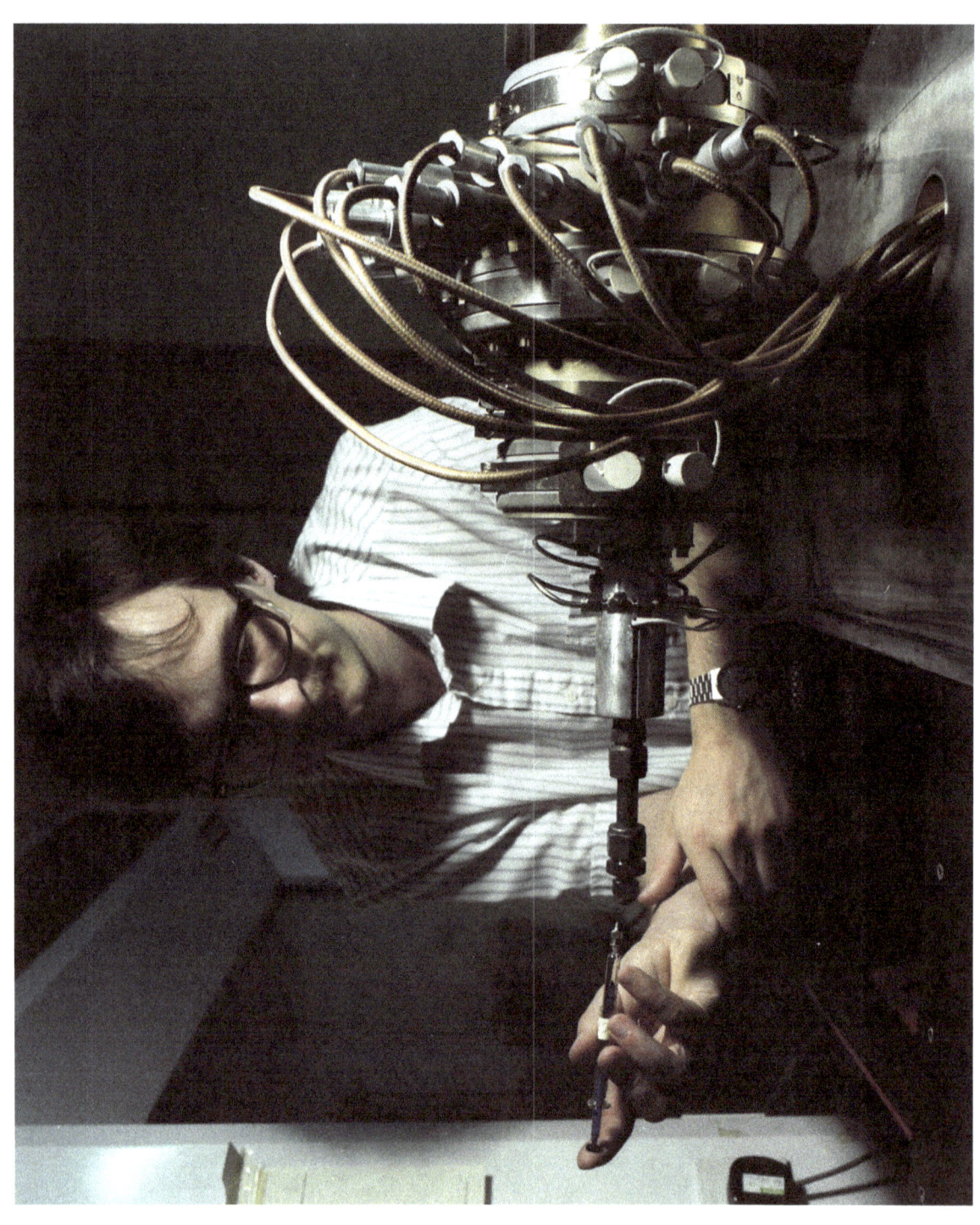

CDE Porton Down – working in the labs

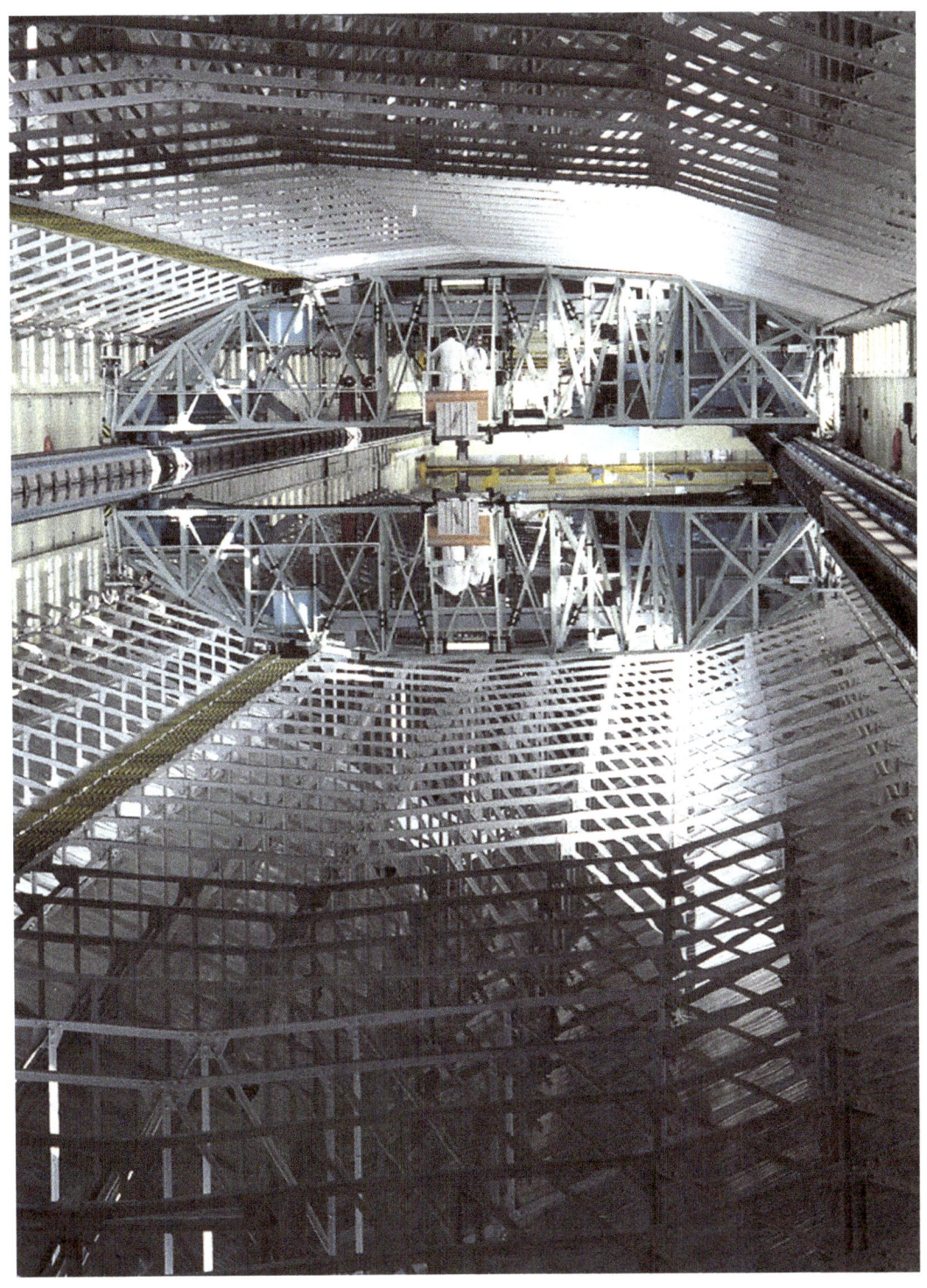

Picture for the Haslar brochure showing a reflection in the still water

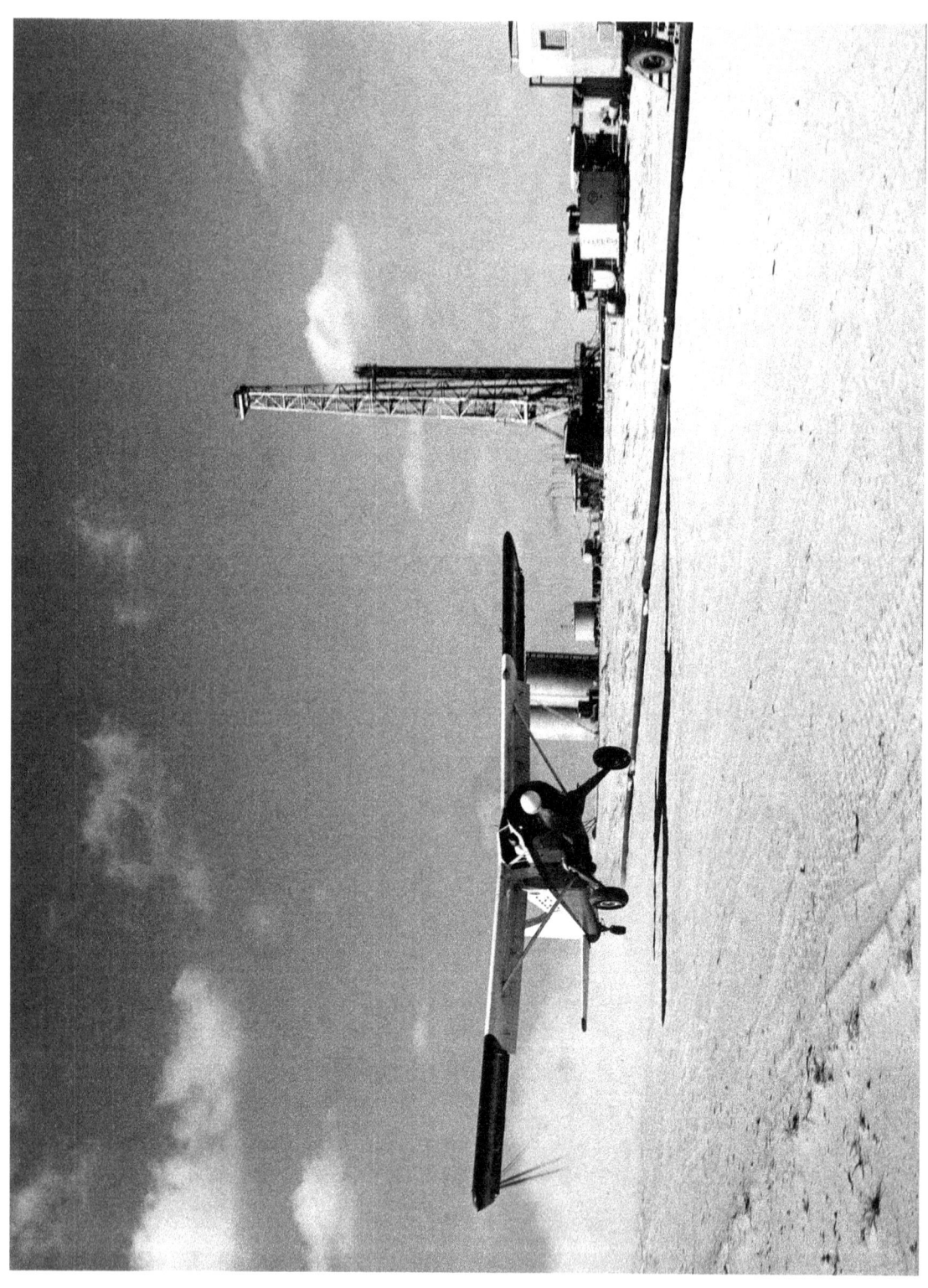

A Beaver aircraft taking off from a small strip in the Libyan Desert having left food for the oil drilling crew

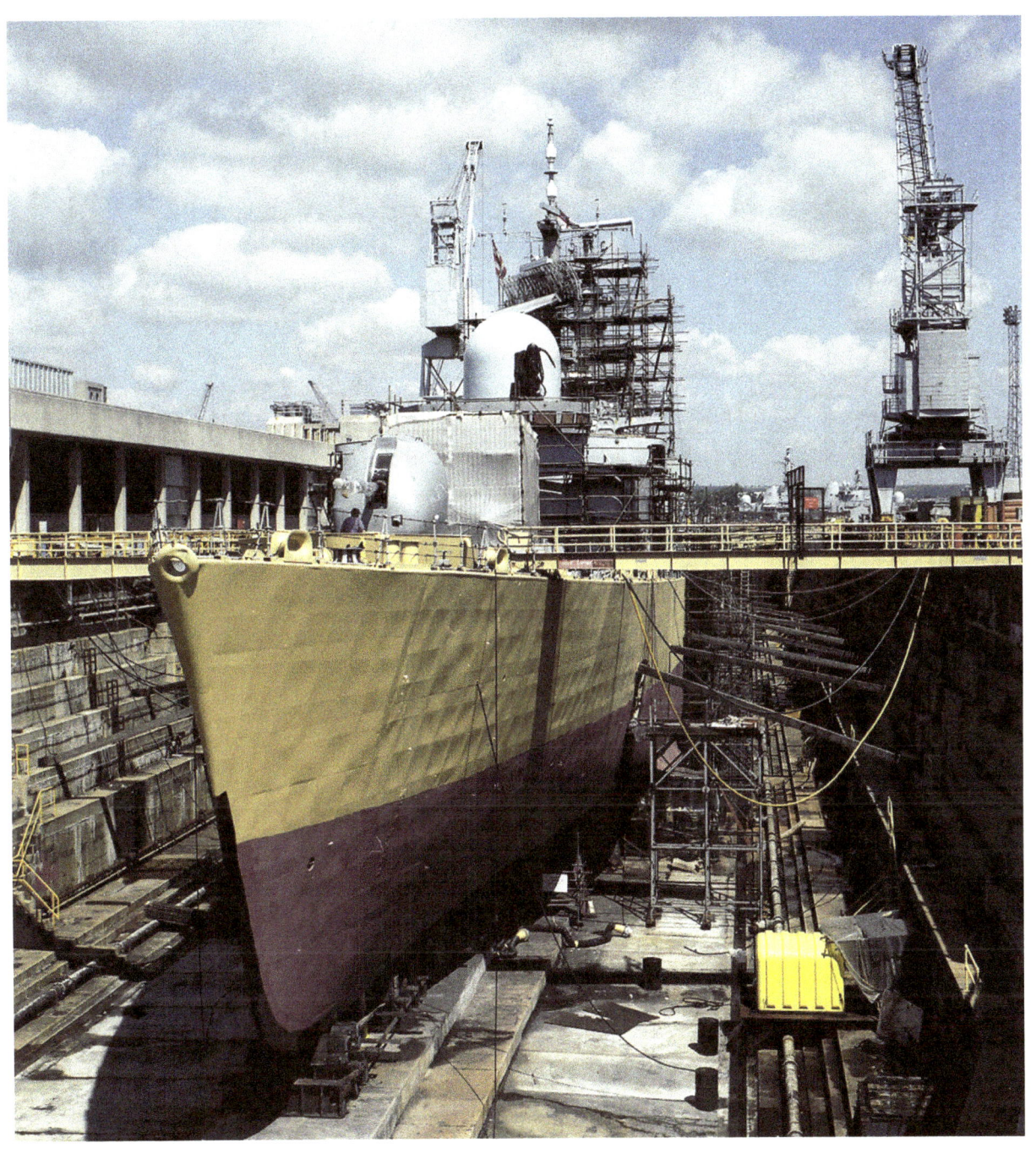

Repainting a destroyer in Portsmouth Dockyard

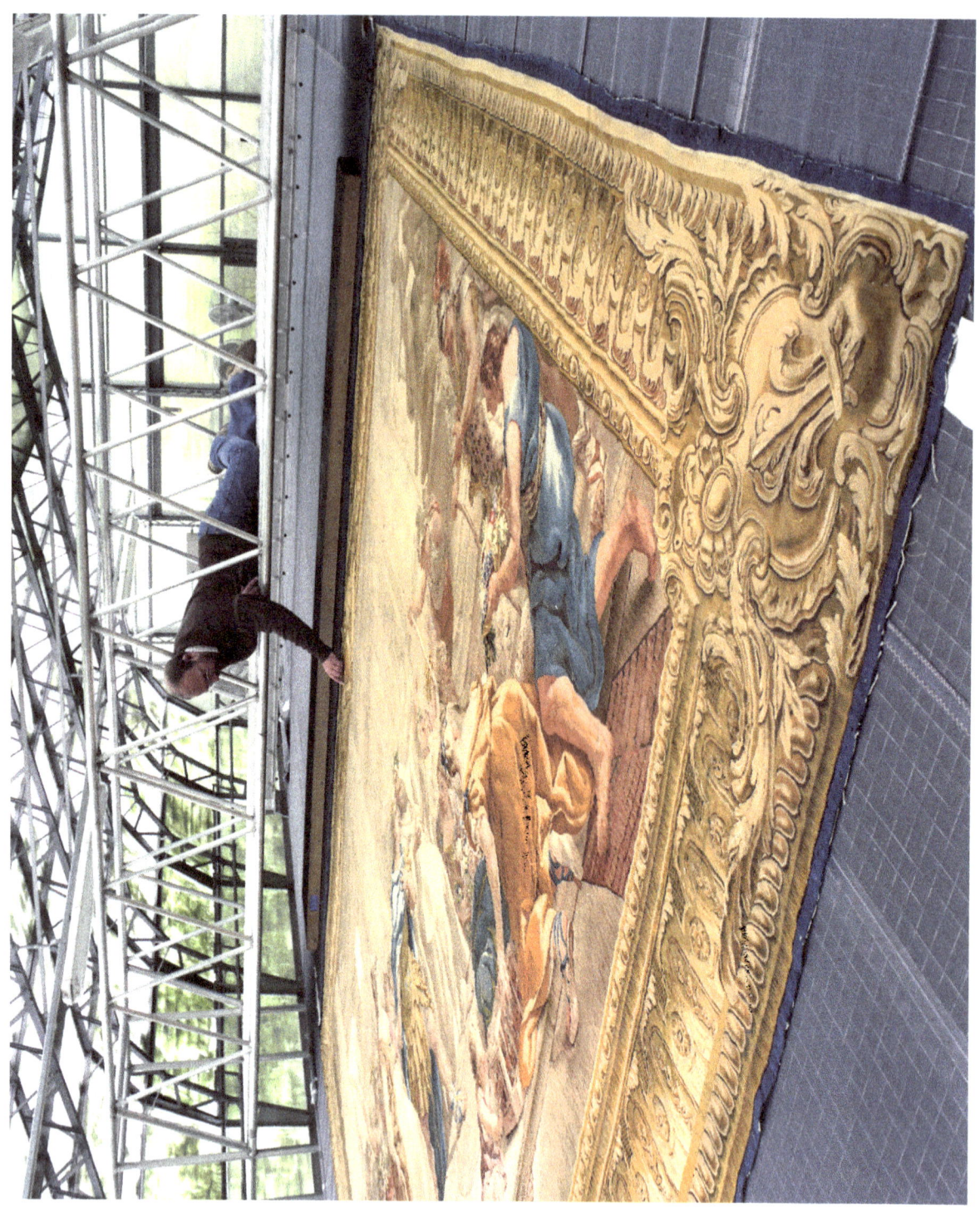

Cleaning and repairing an old tapestry, Hampton Court Palace

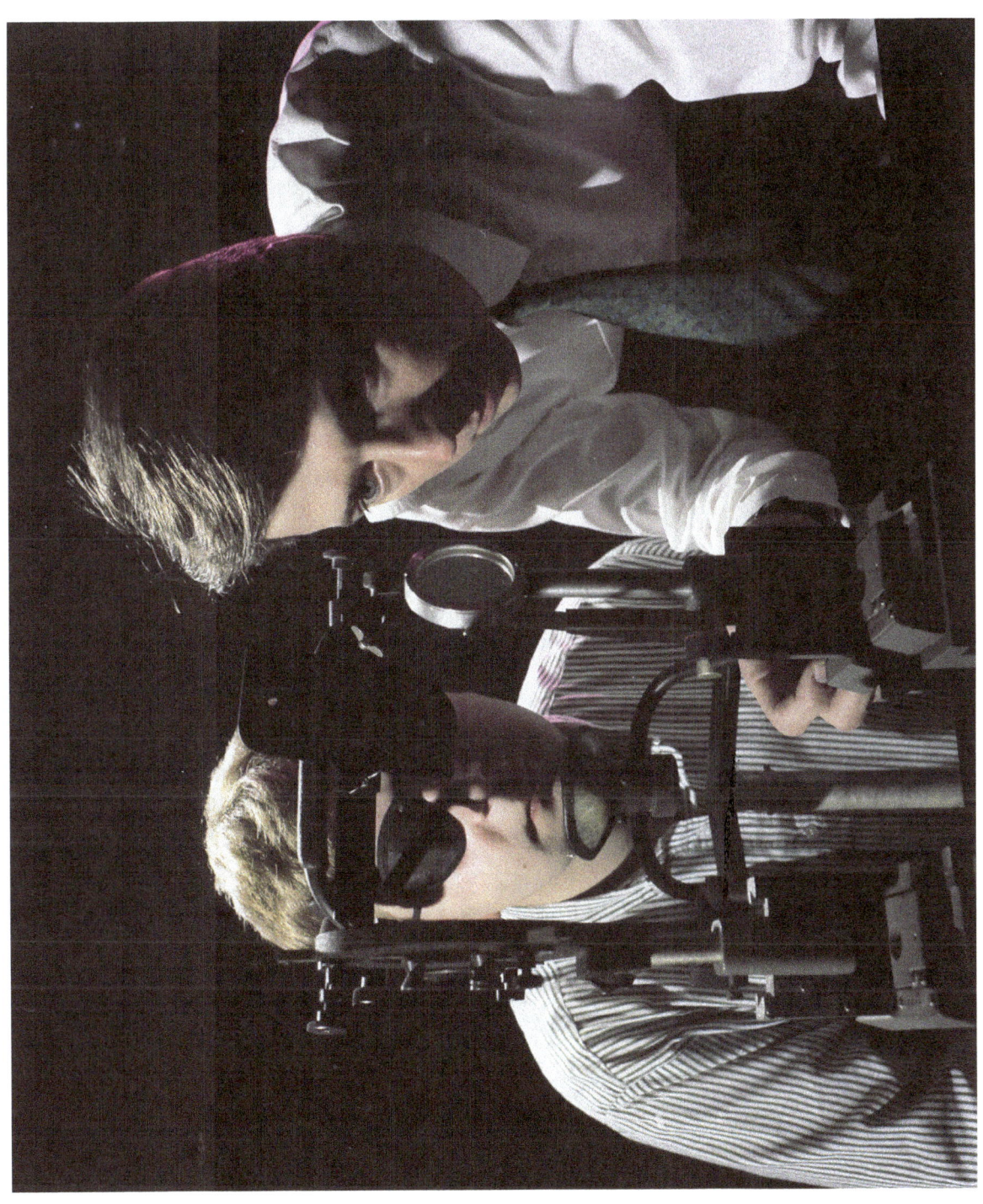

Engineering training at Farnborough

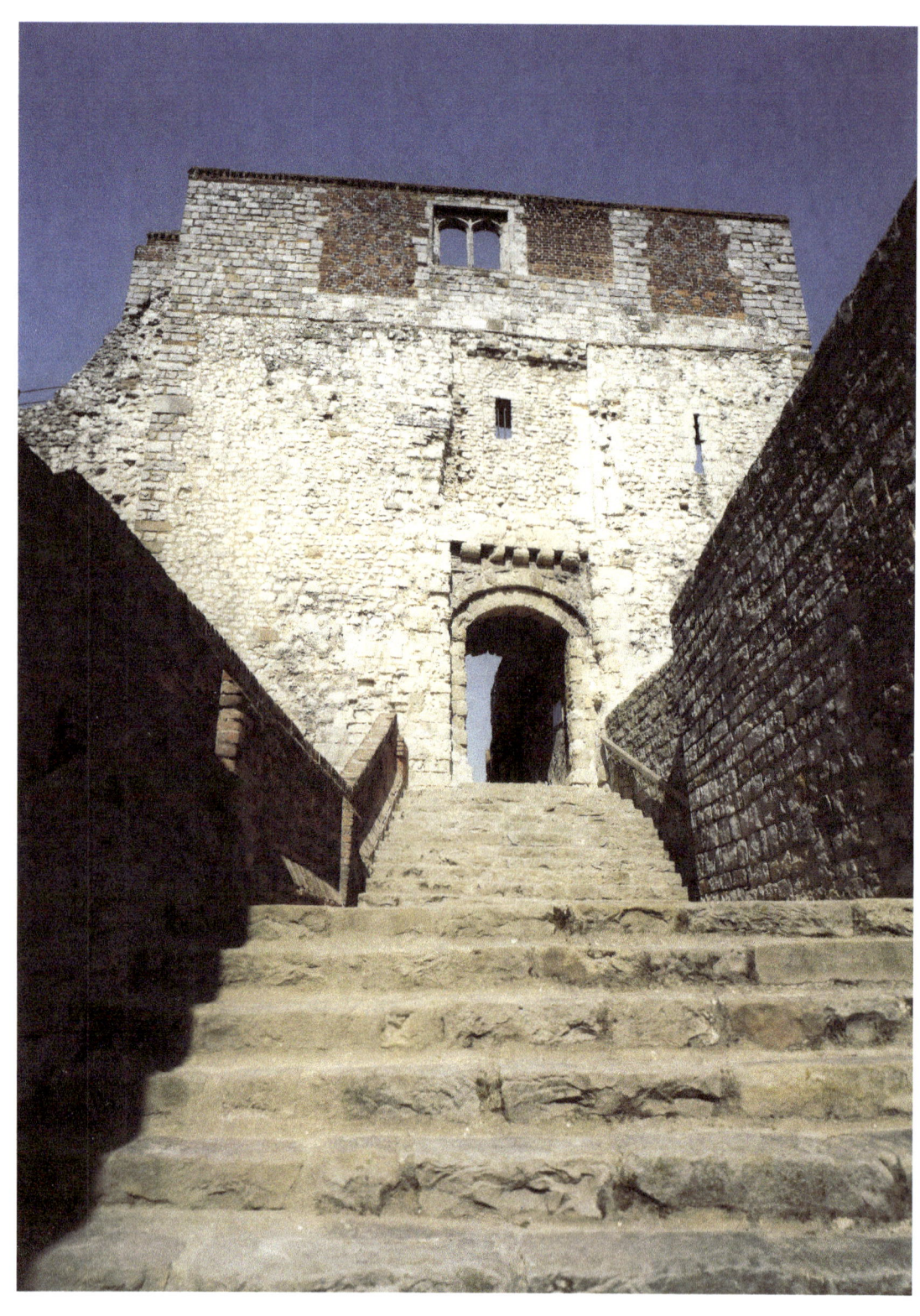

Farnham Castle Keep

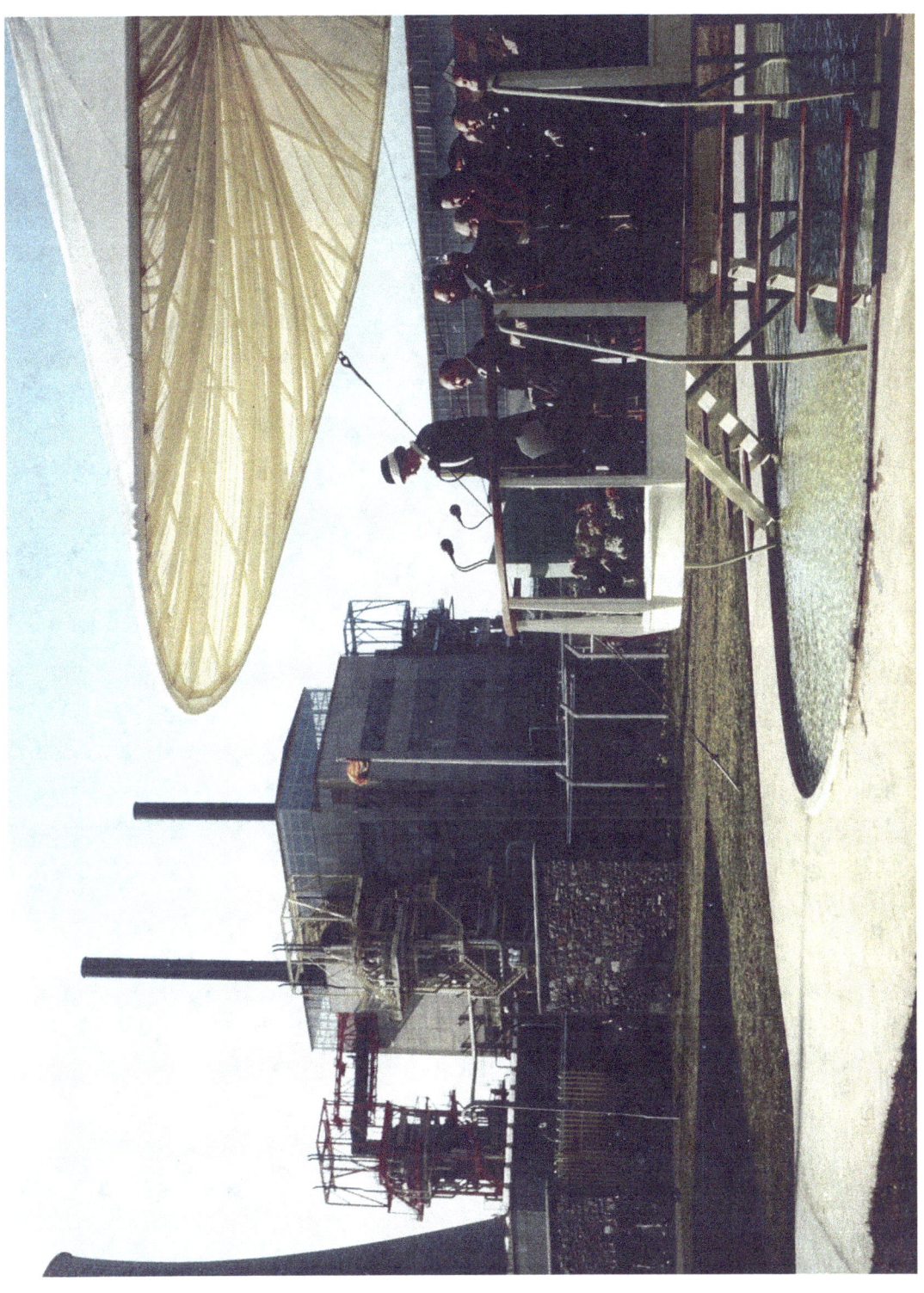

Queen Elizabeth opens Calder Hall, the world's first full scale nuclear power station, 1956

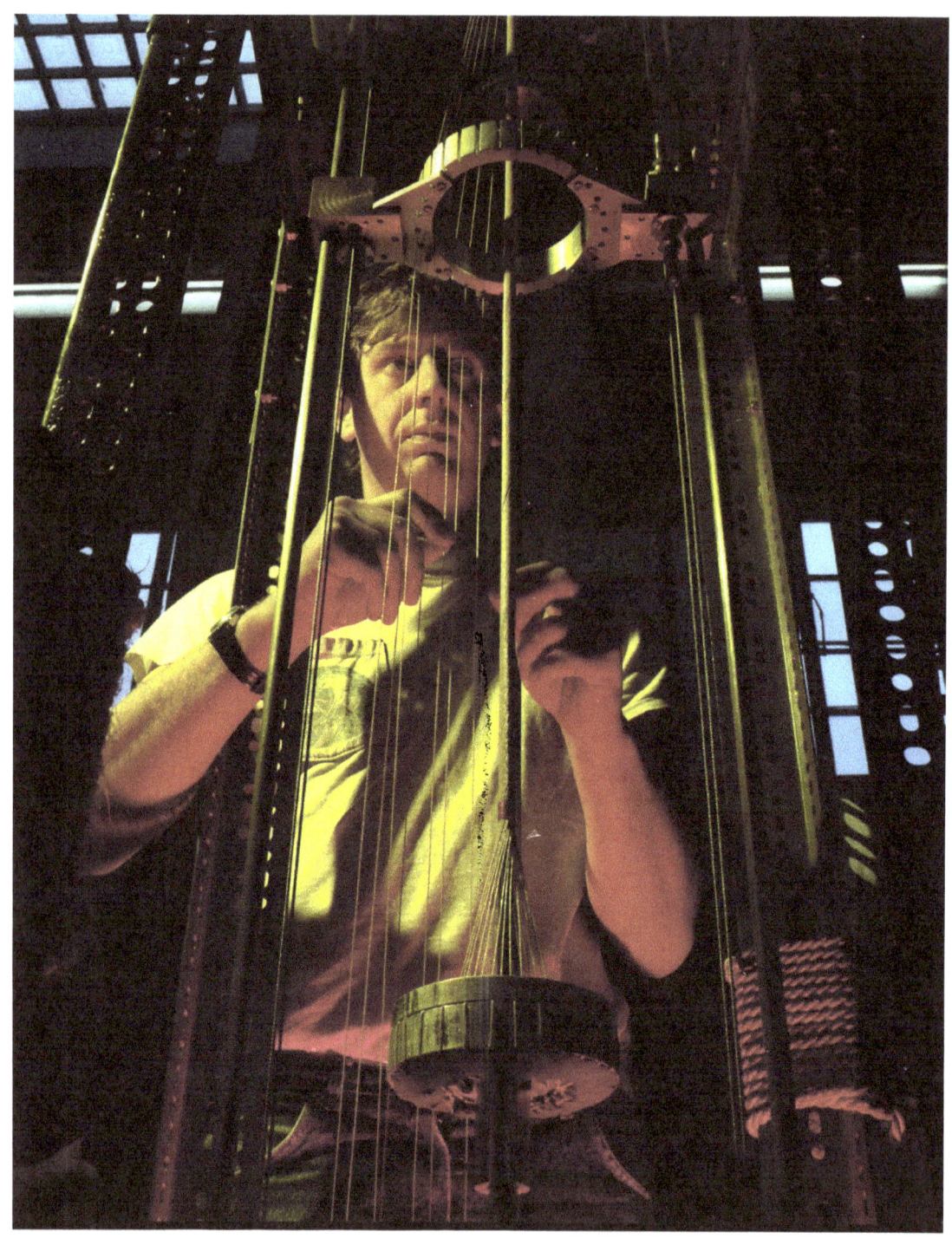

ARE Portland, working in the laboratories

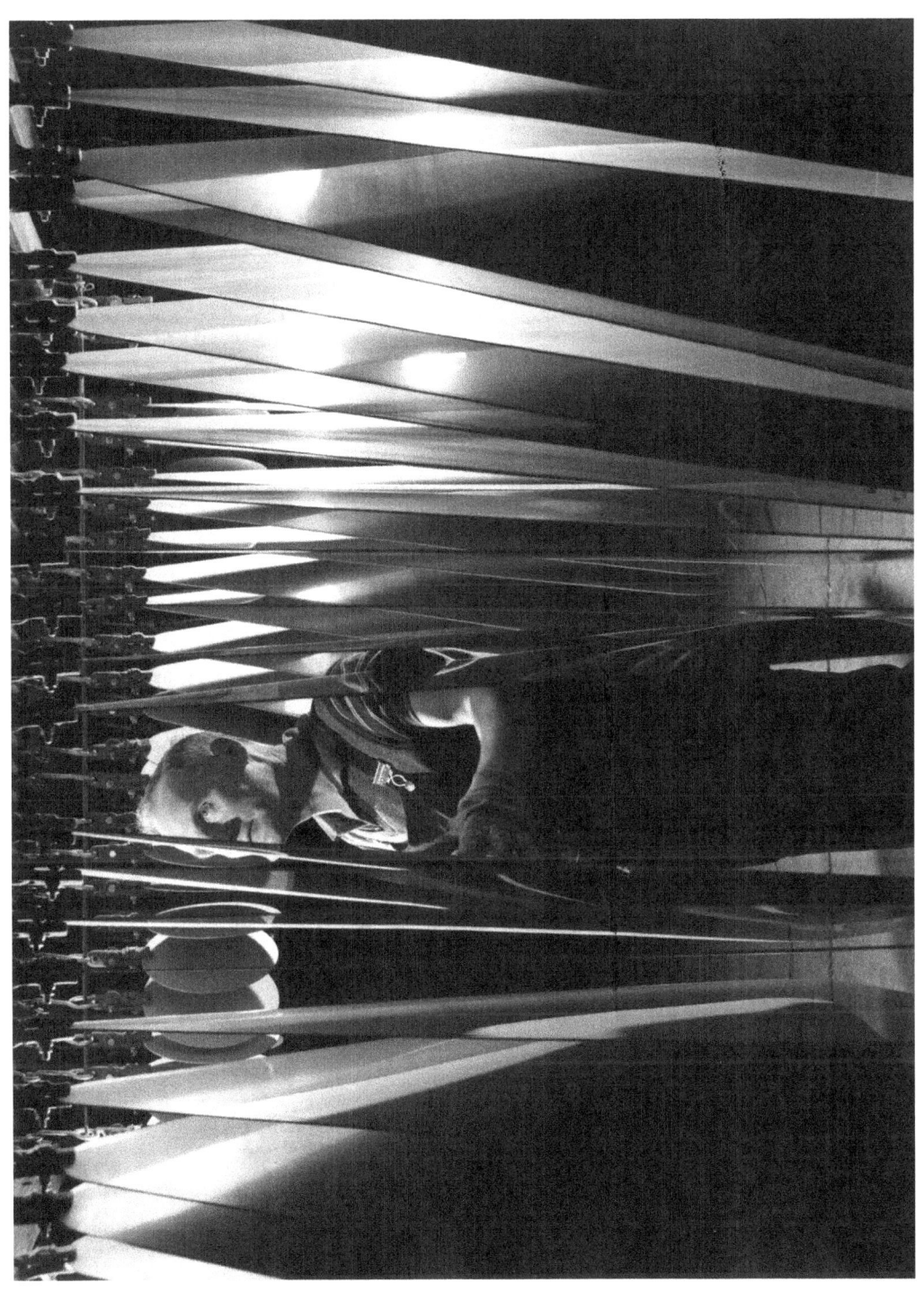

Checking aluminium sheets at British Aluminium, Falkirk

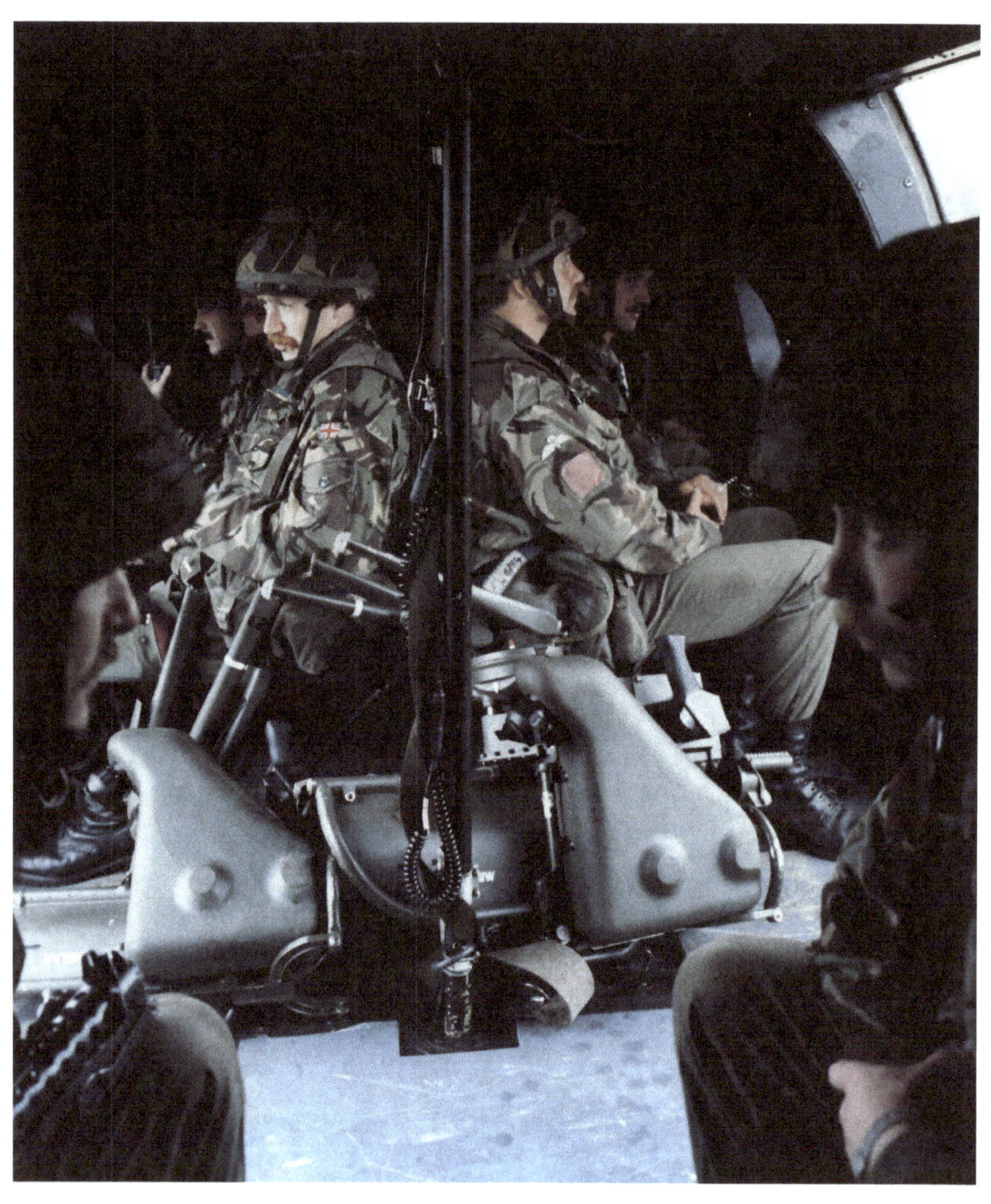

Armed troops in a Puma helicopter

The Tower of London lit for Son et Lumiere, 1967

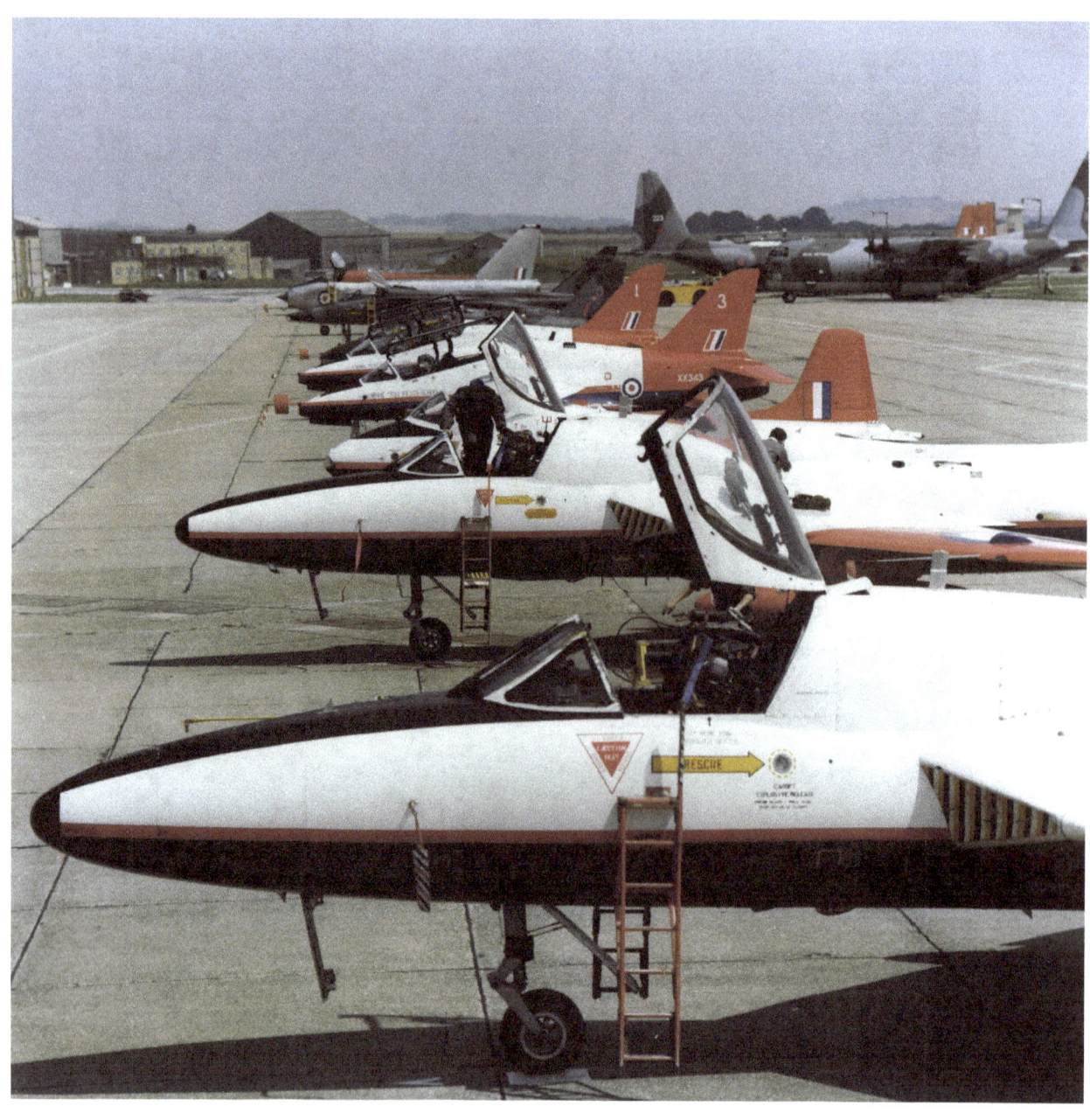

Hawker Hunter aircraft waiting to be flown by students from the Empire Test Pilot's School, Boscombe Down

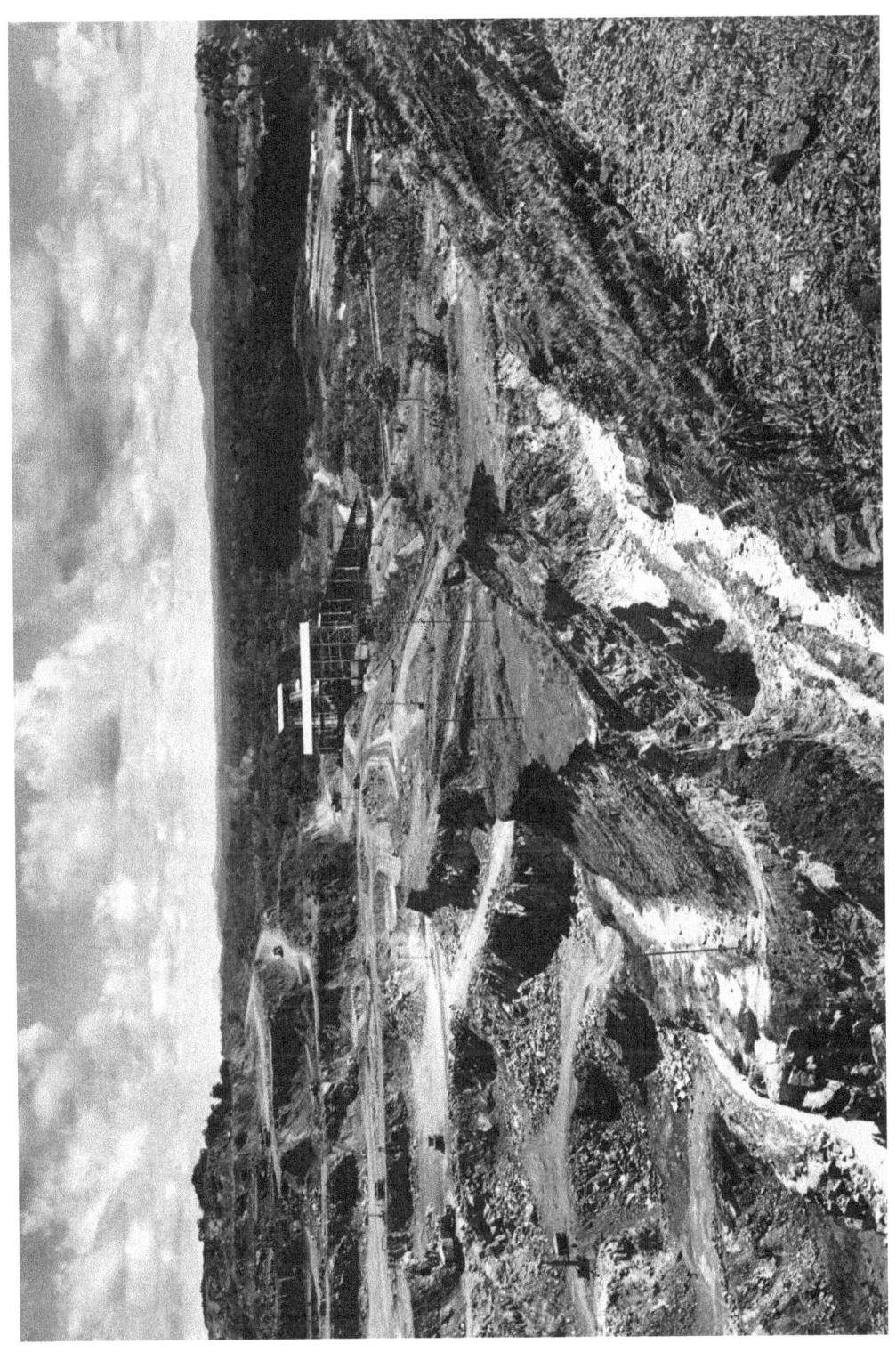

A large copper mine in Liberia

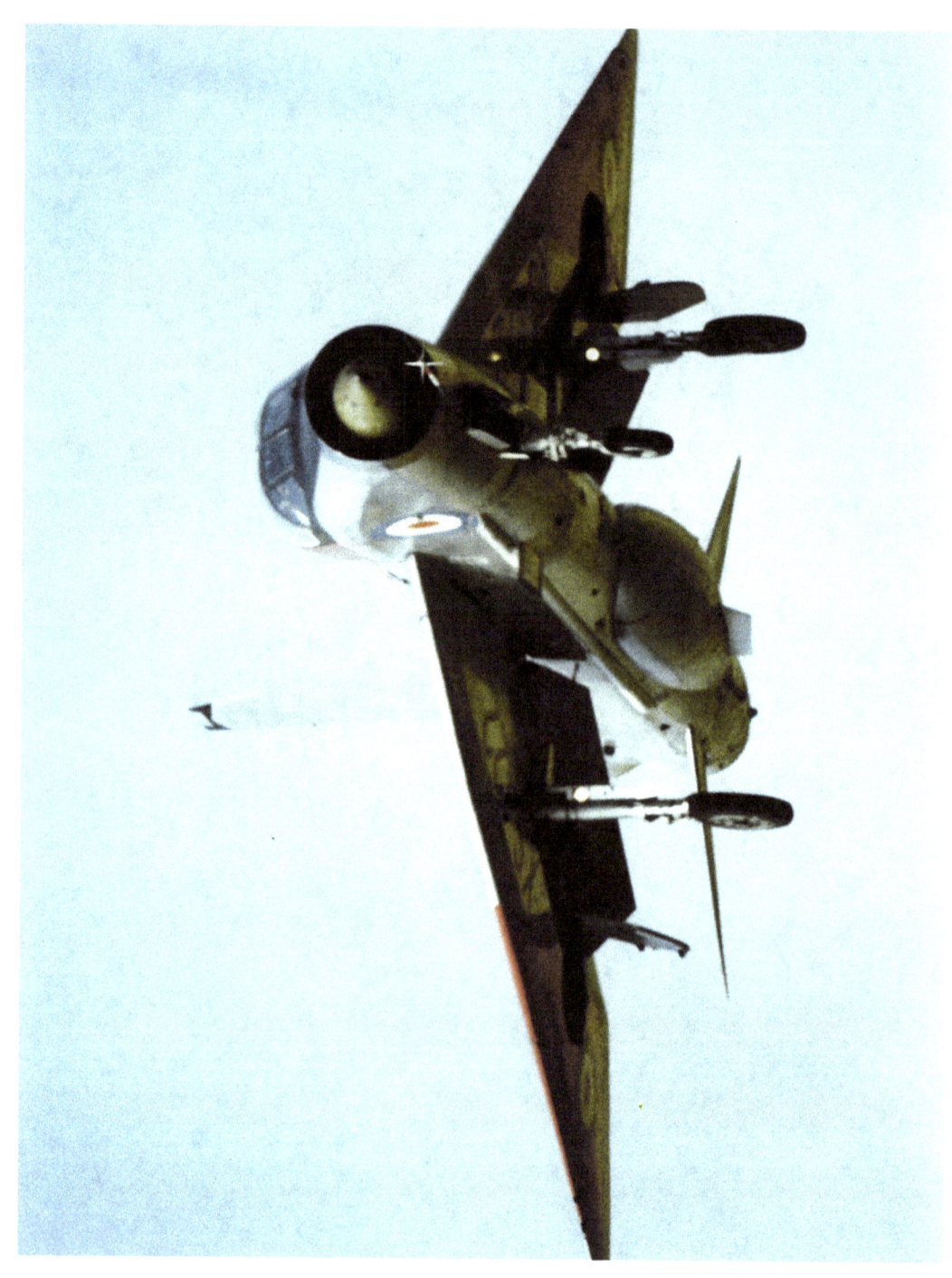

A Lightening fighter coming into land at Boscombe Down

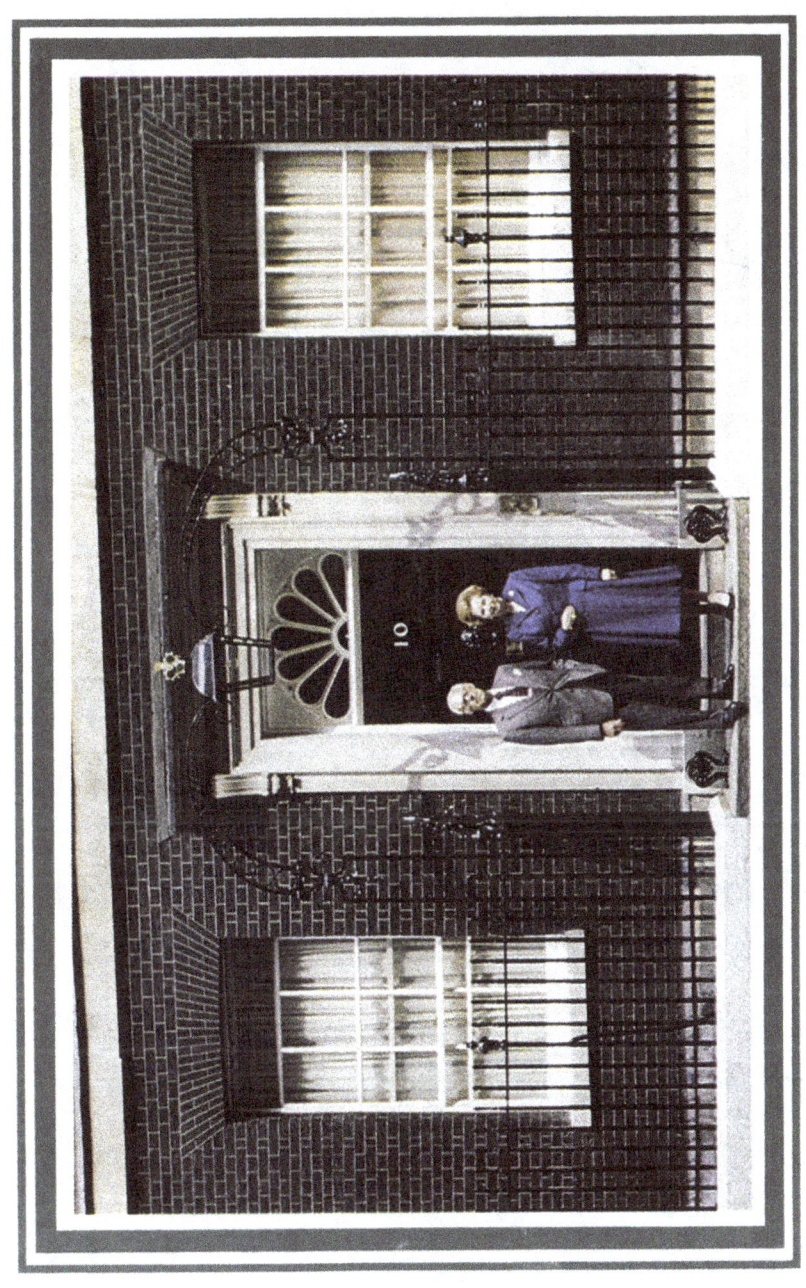

Mr and Mrs Thatcher's Christmas card for 1982

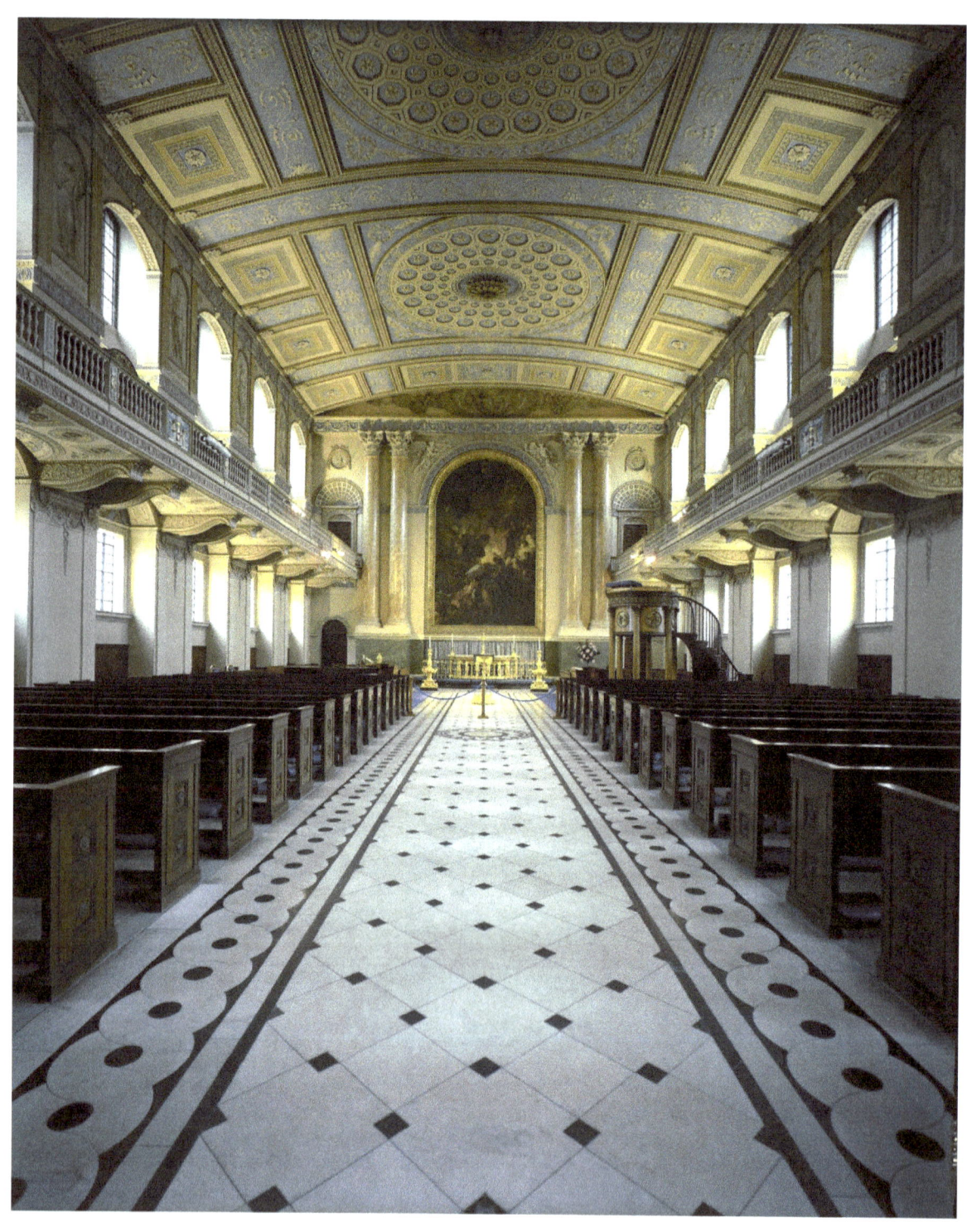

Royal Navy College church, Greenwich

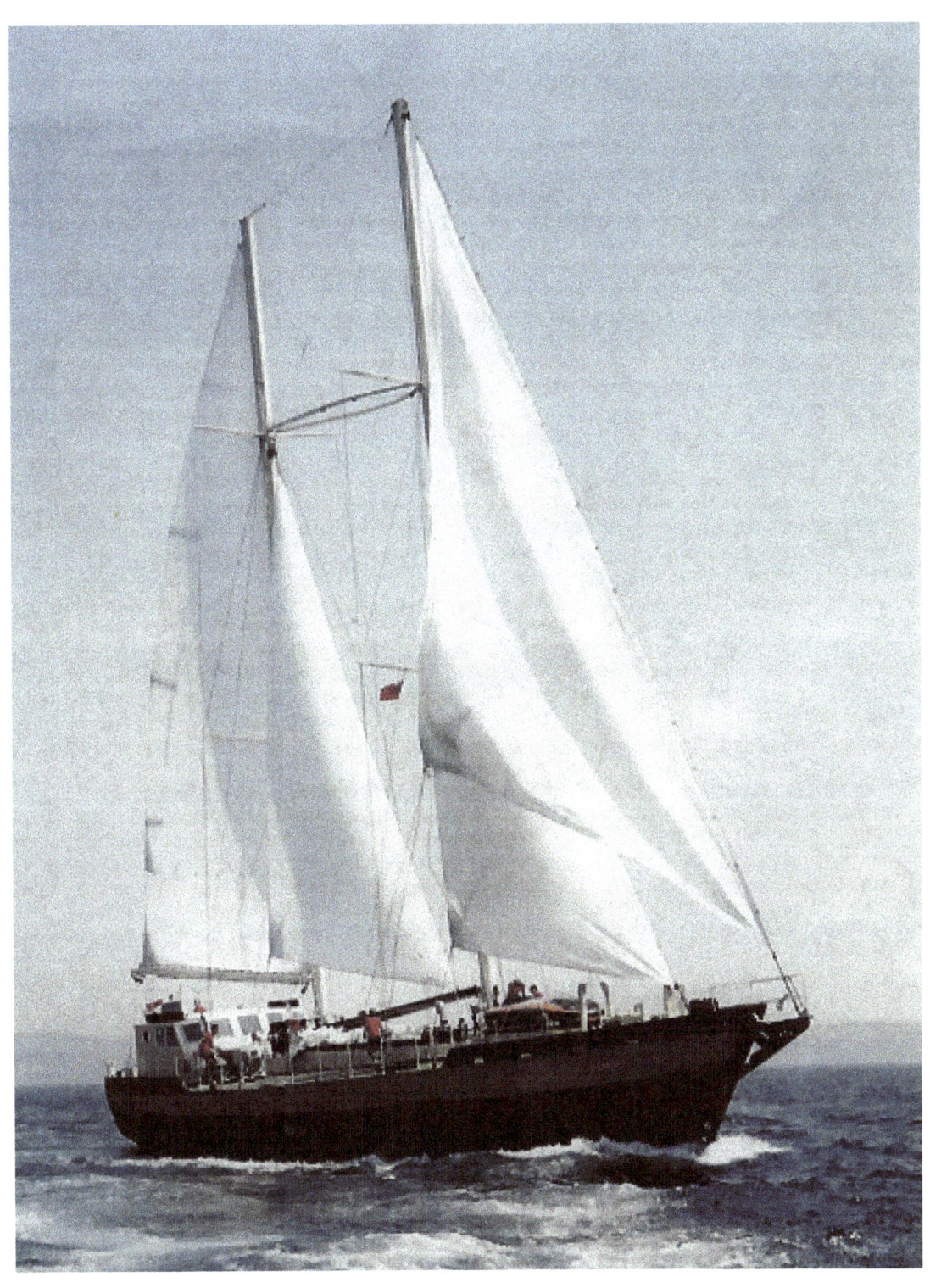

Two-masted sailing vessel on route from Plymouth with exports to West Africa

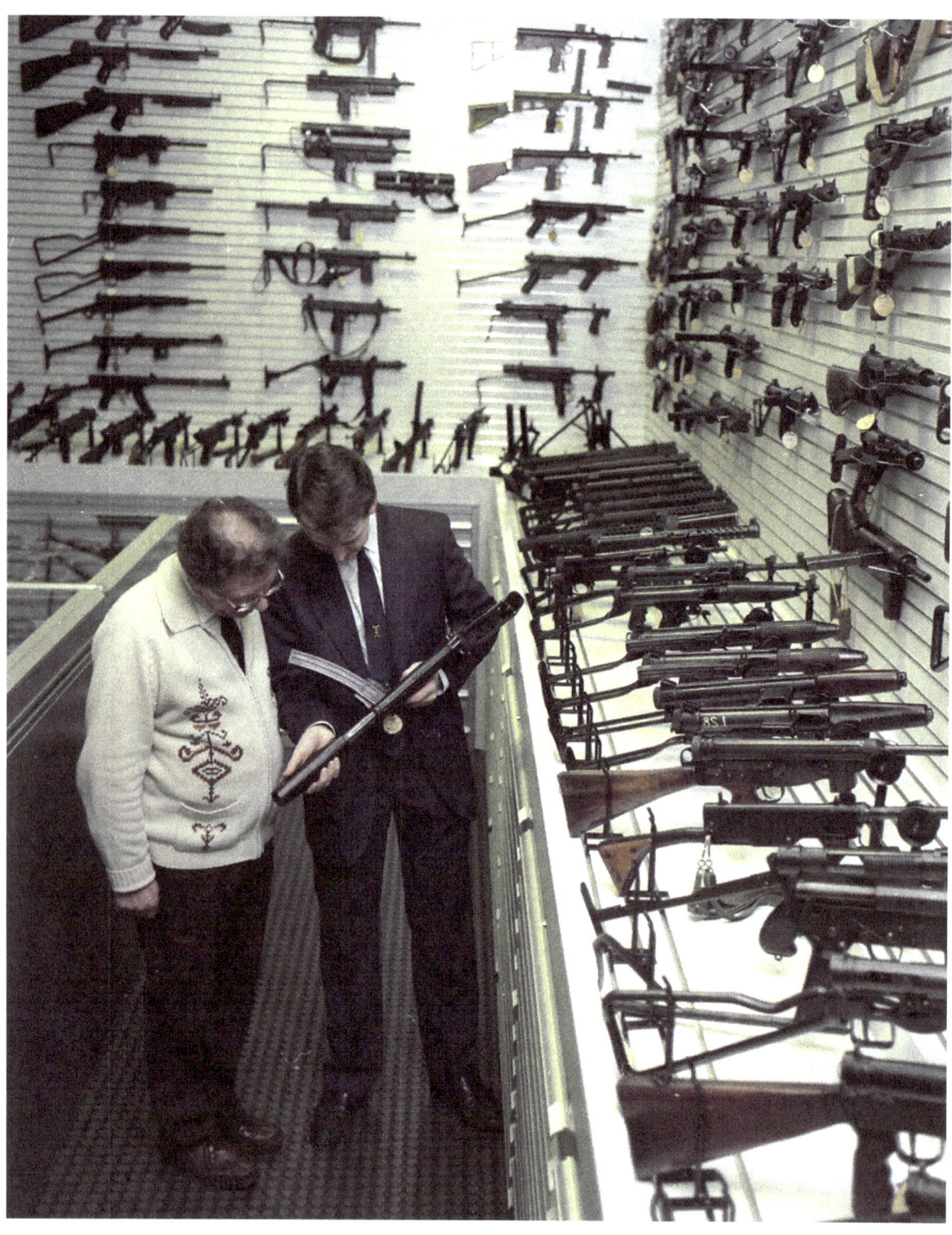

The Pattern Room in Nottingham which houses every hand gun manufactured throughout the world

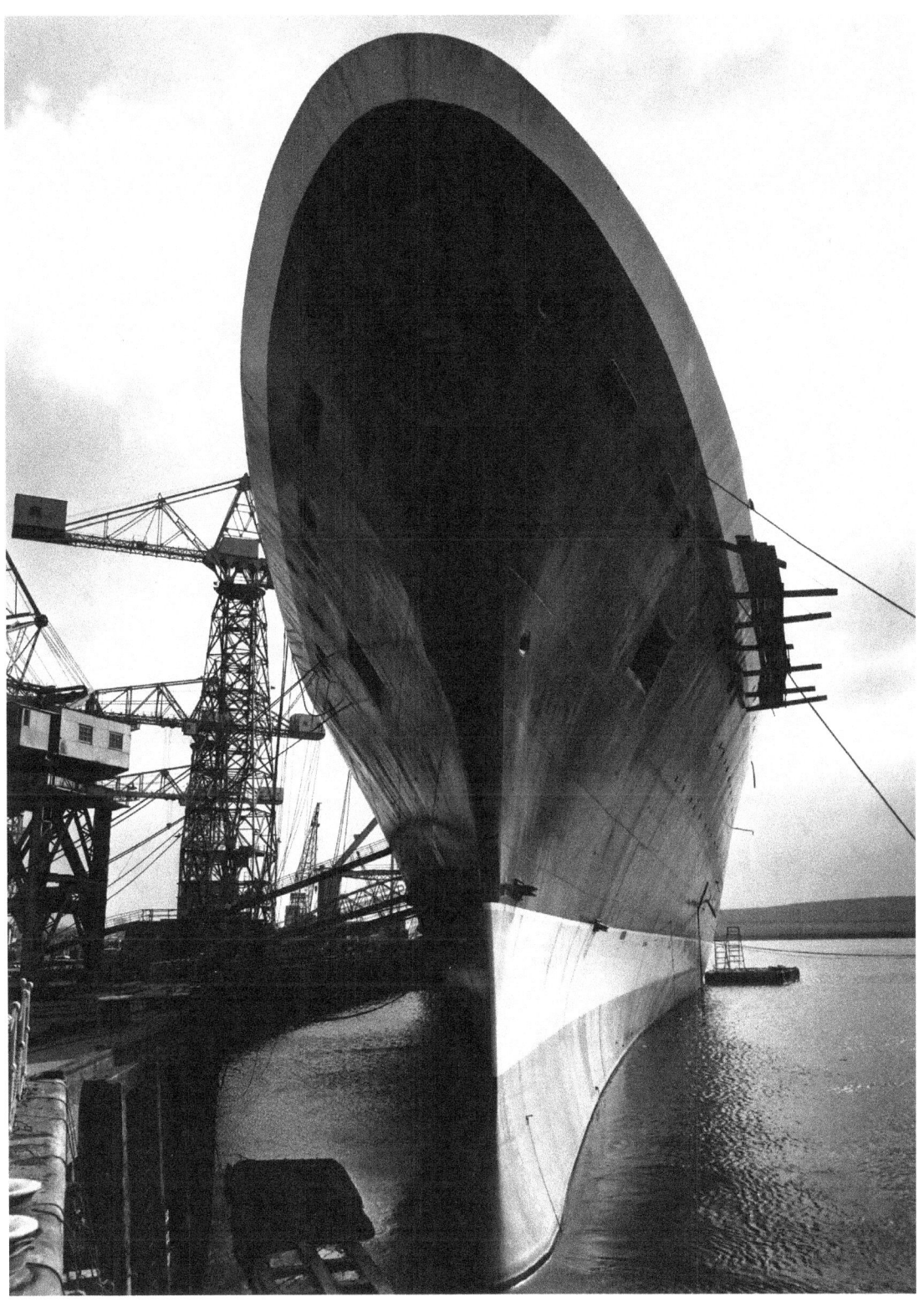

The QE2 under construction at John Browns ship yard, Glasgow

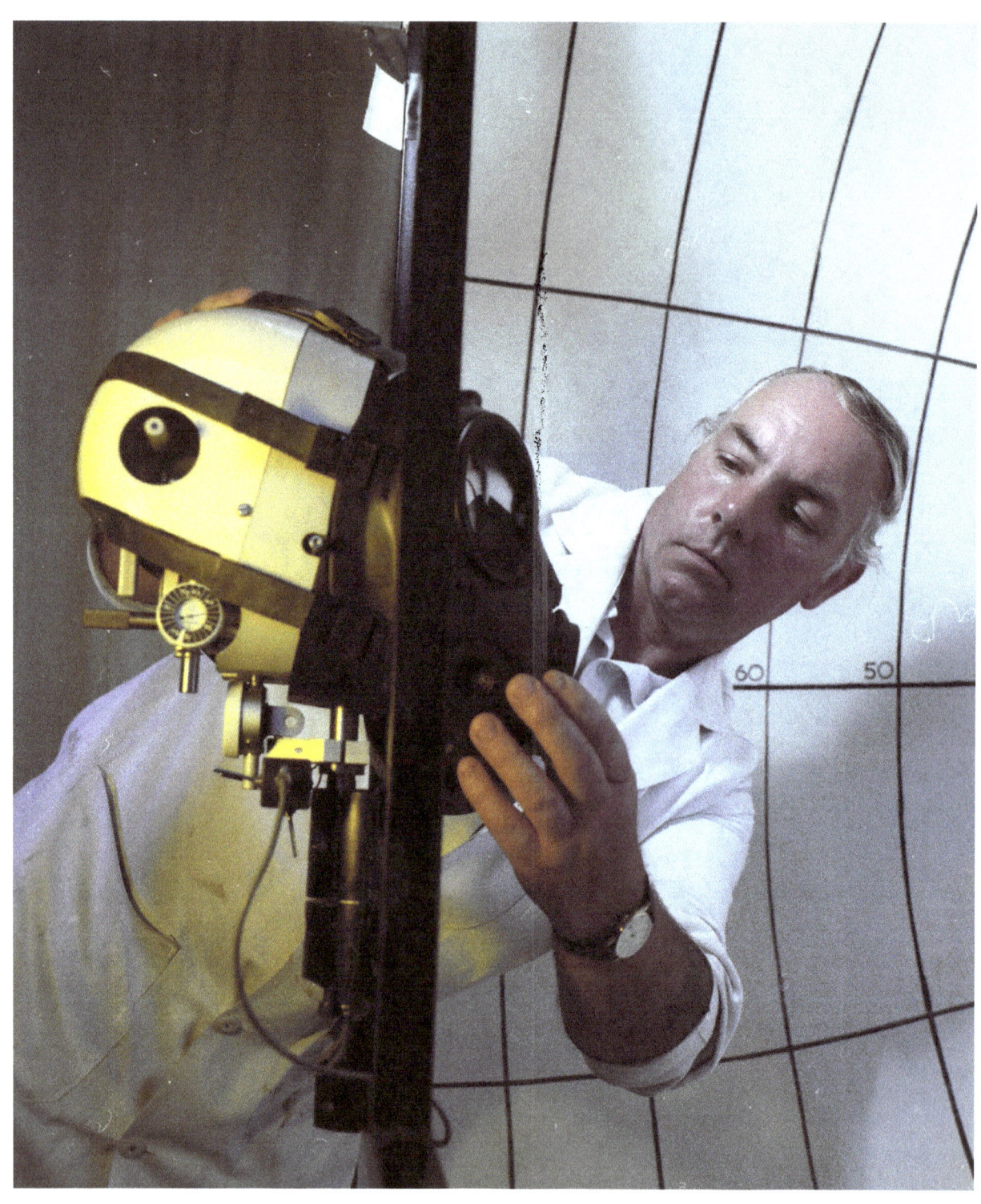

Testing a gas mask at CDE Porton Down for all round vision

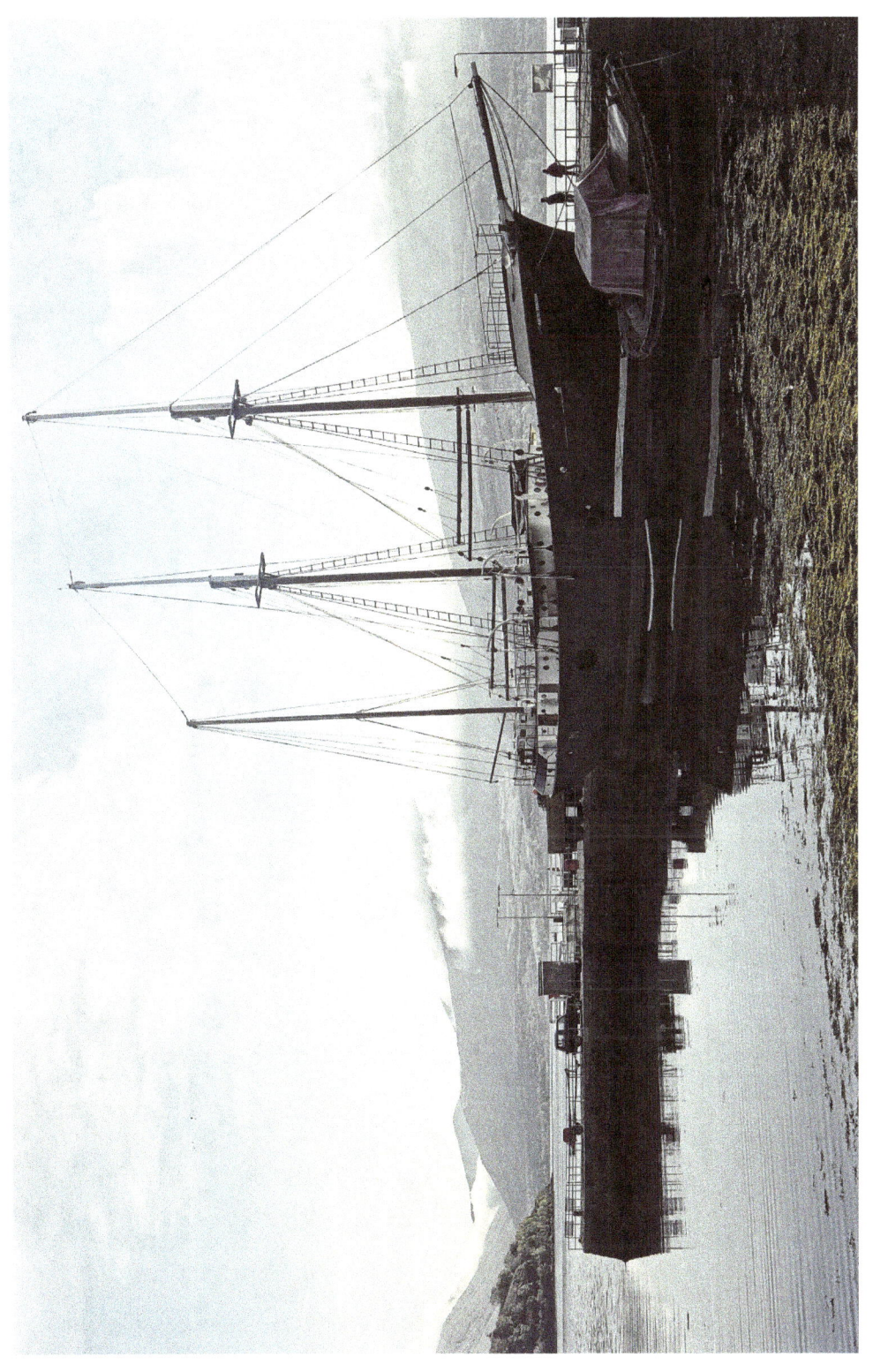

Inverary Pier, Loch Fyne showing the 'Artic Penguin' a boat built in Dublin in 1910

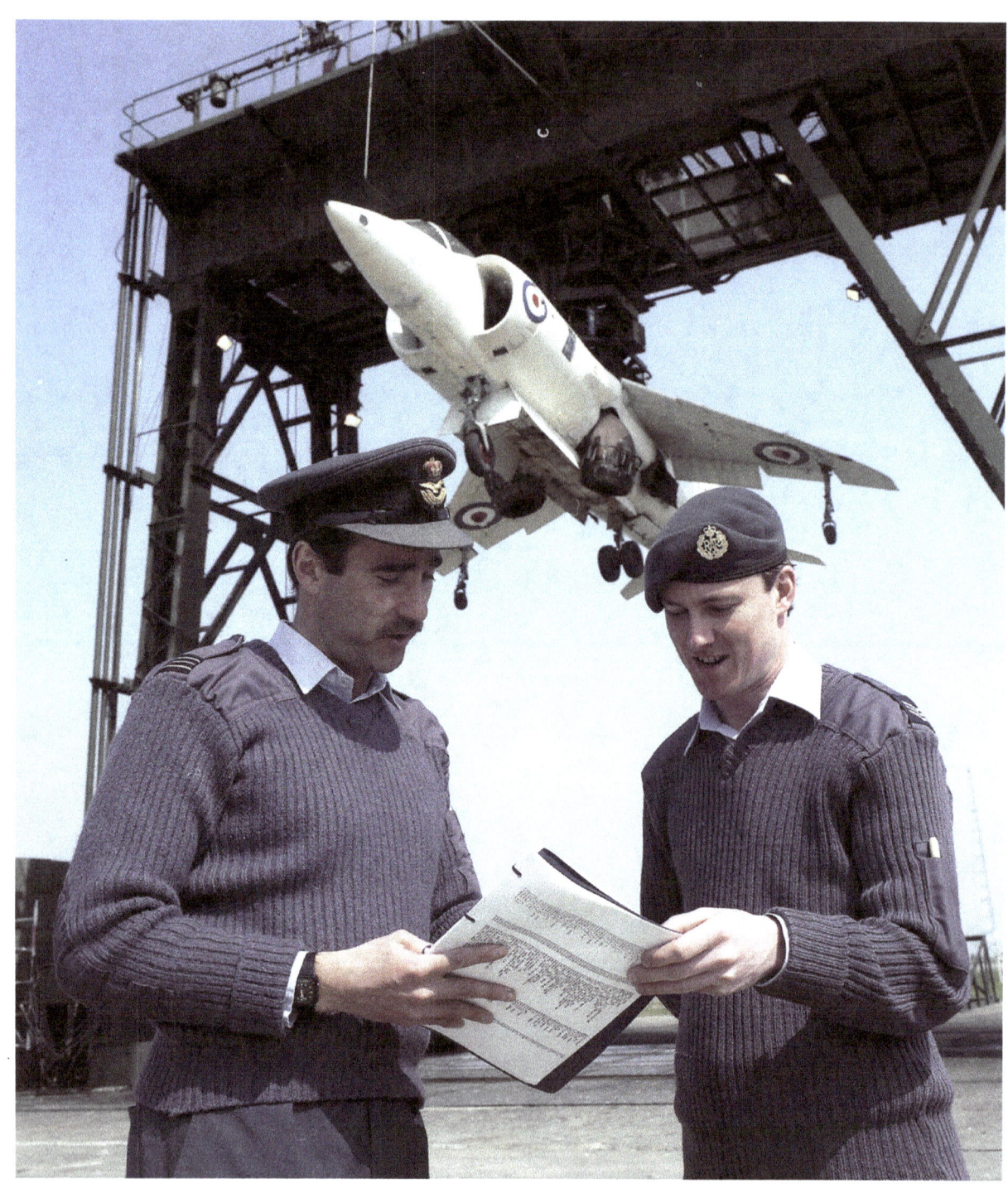

A Harrier fighter slung up for static tests at DPEE Shoeburyness

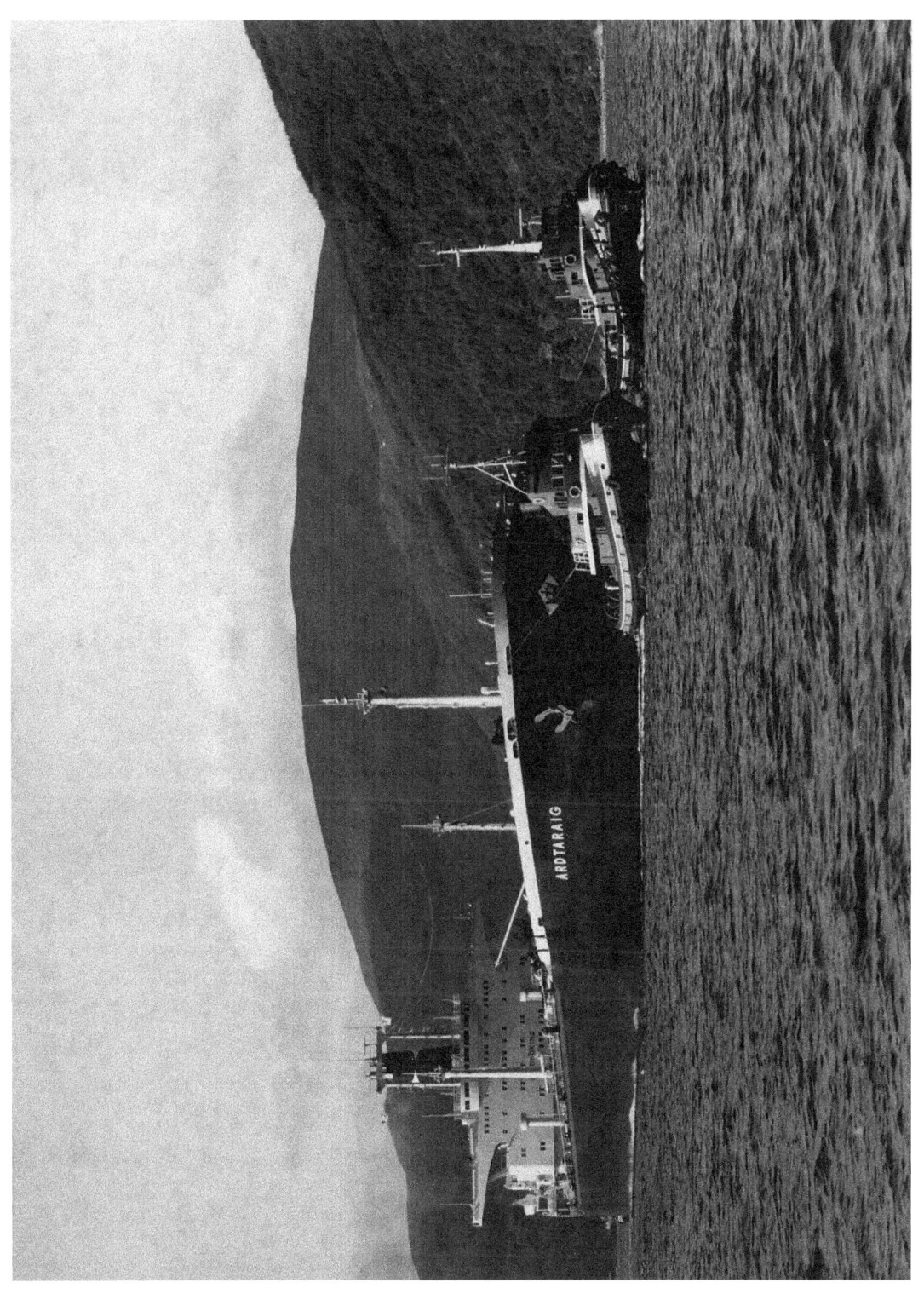

A large tanker under tow going to discharge its load of oil at Grangemouth Refinery, Firth of Forth

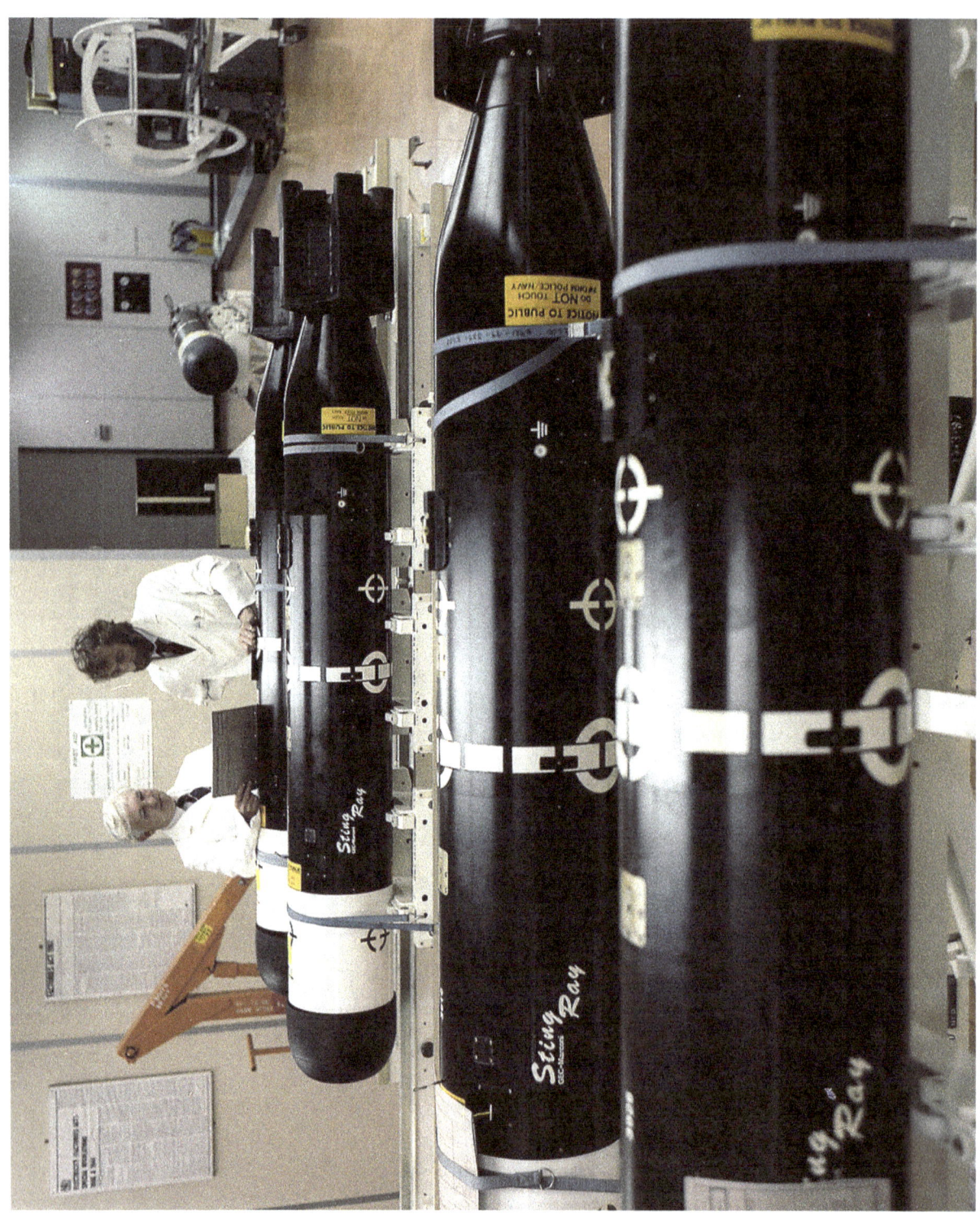

Sting Ray missiles being examined prior to delivery to naval ships from RNTNS Gosport

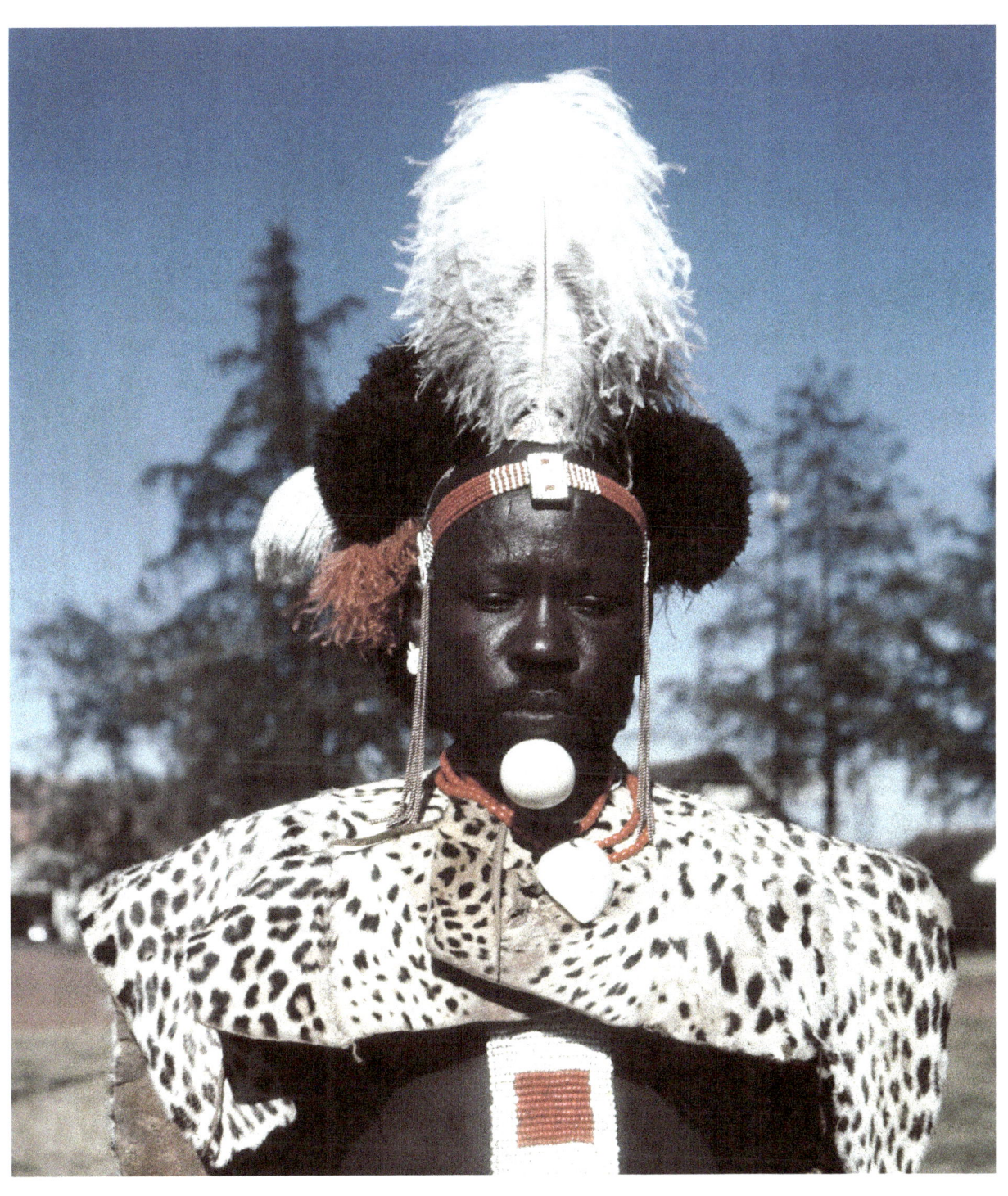

The portrait of a Turkana Chief from the Northern Frontier District, Kenya

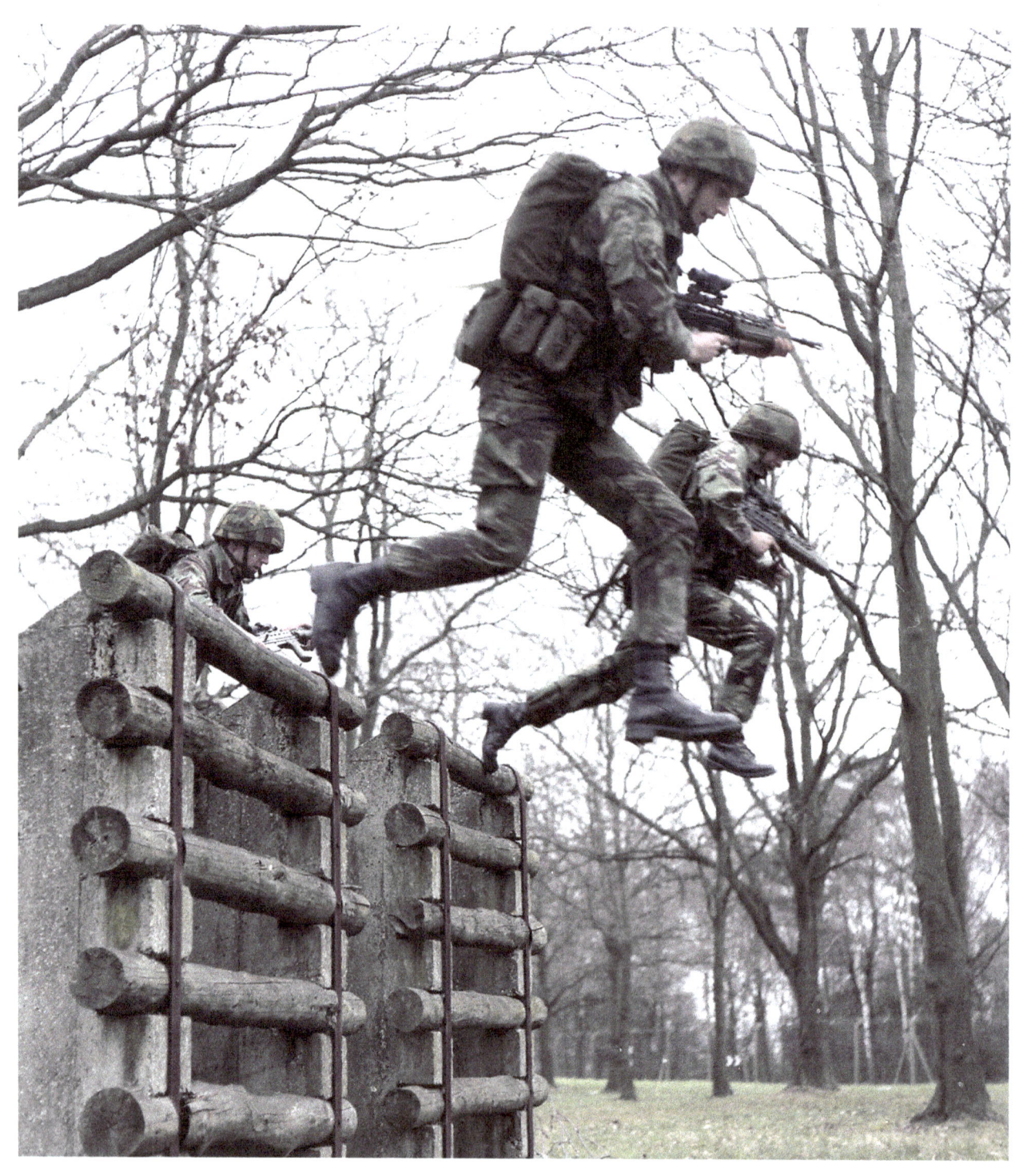

Soldiers on an assault course in Farnborough

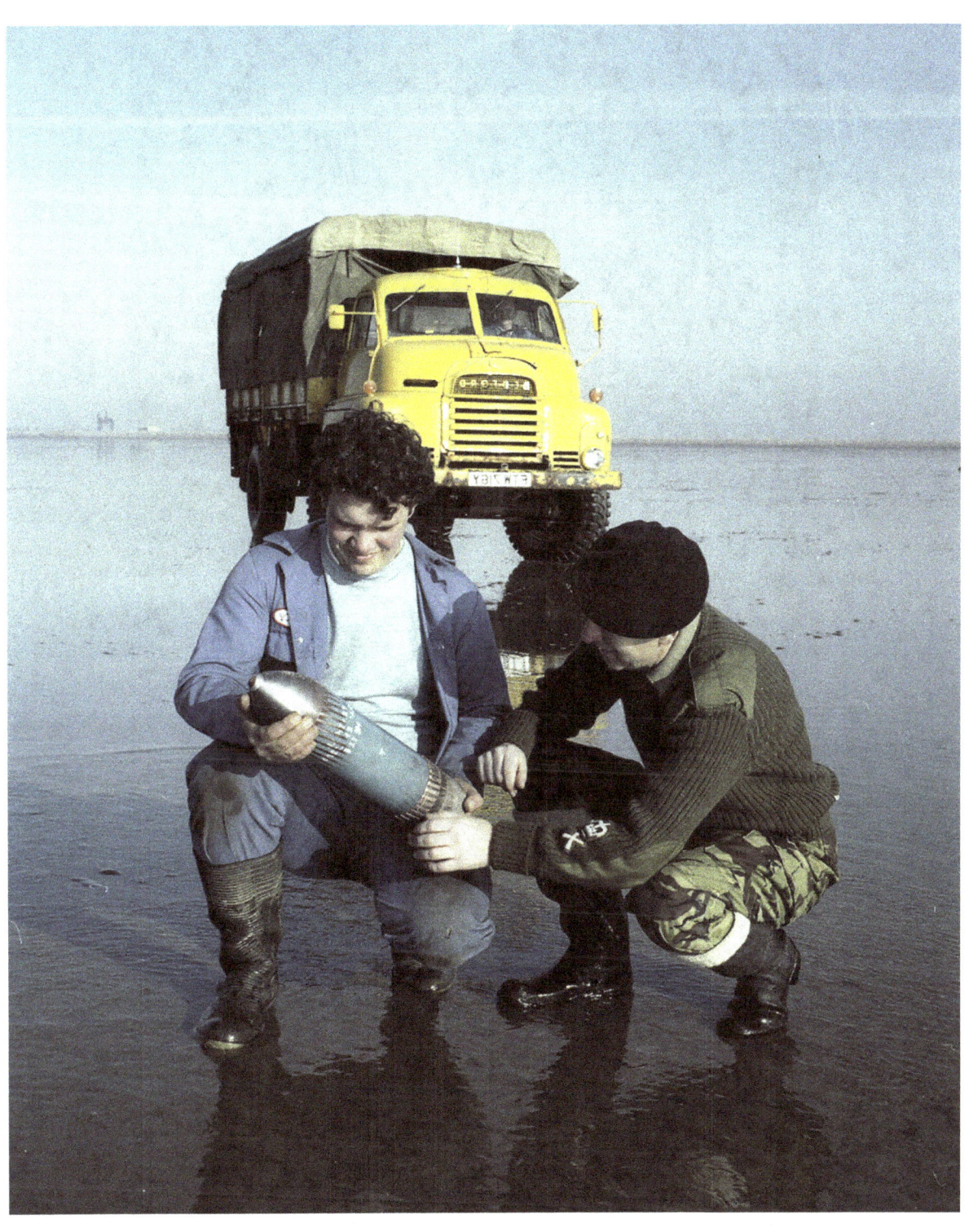

Retrieving a round fired into the sea to check its trajectory at Foulness

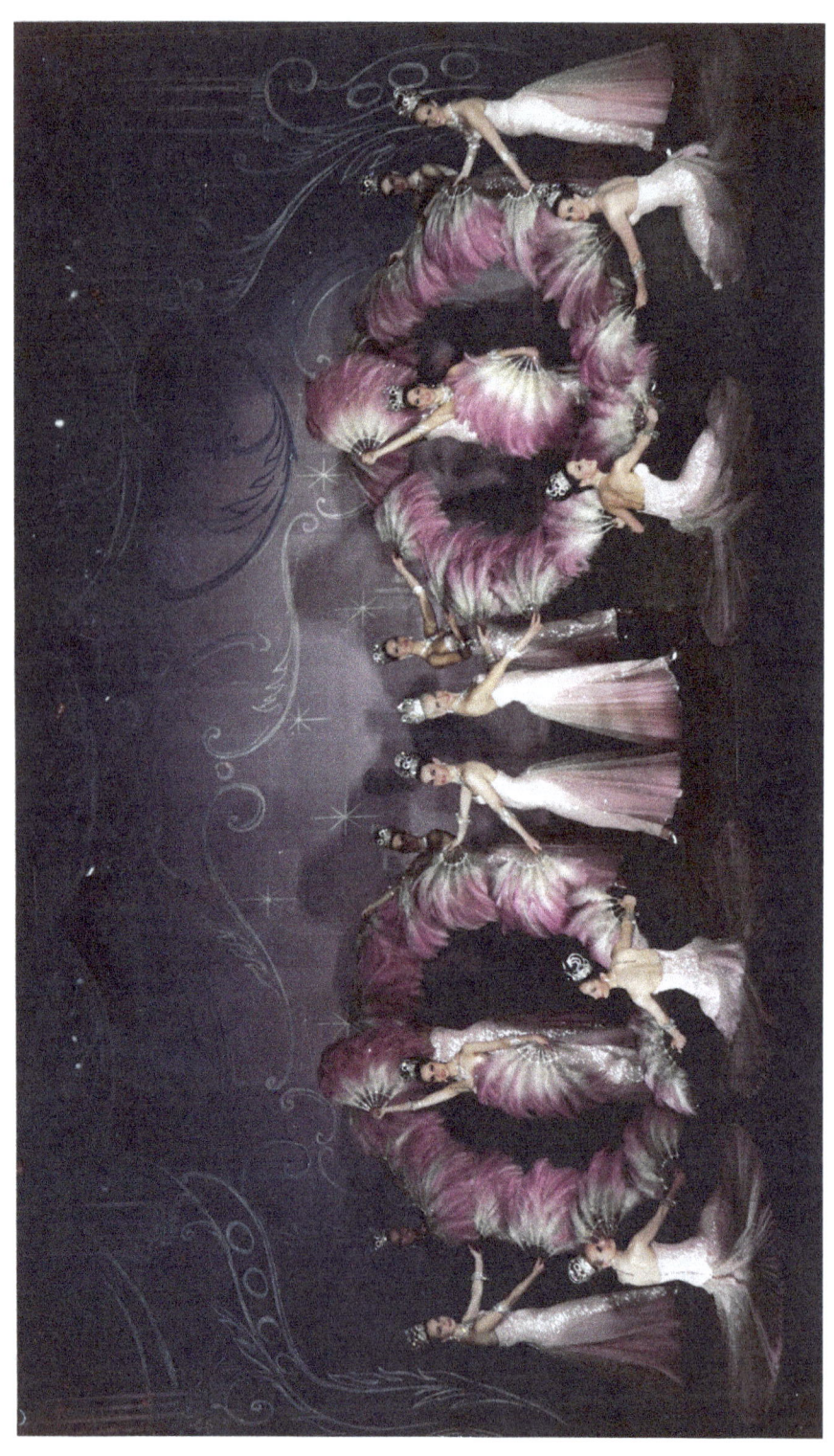

The Blue Bell Girls at the London Palladium, 1967

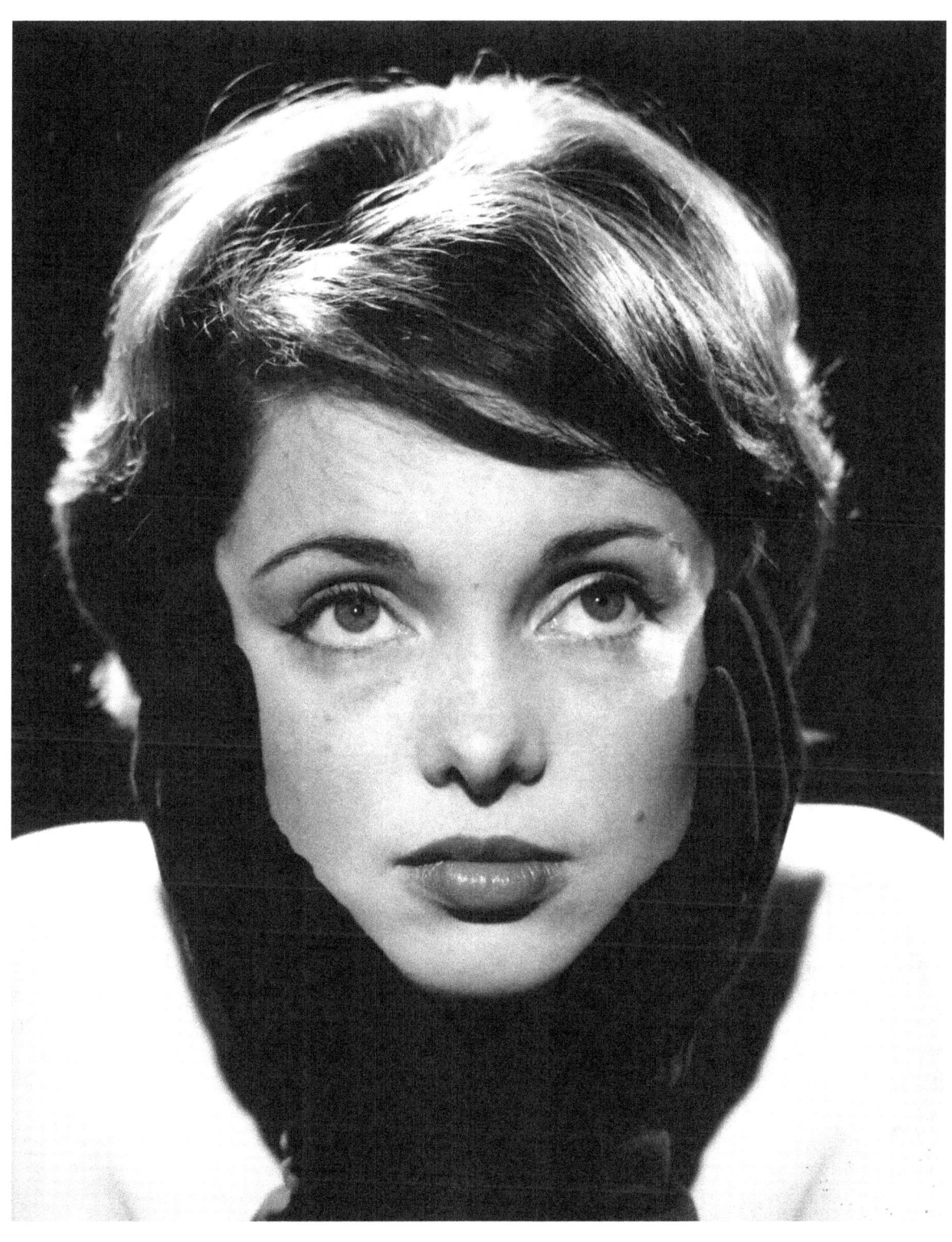

My wife, Chris

Also from John Jochimsen

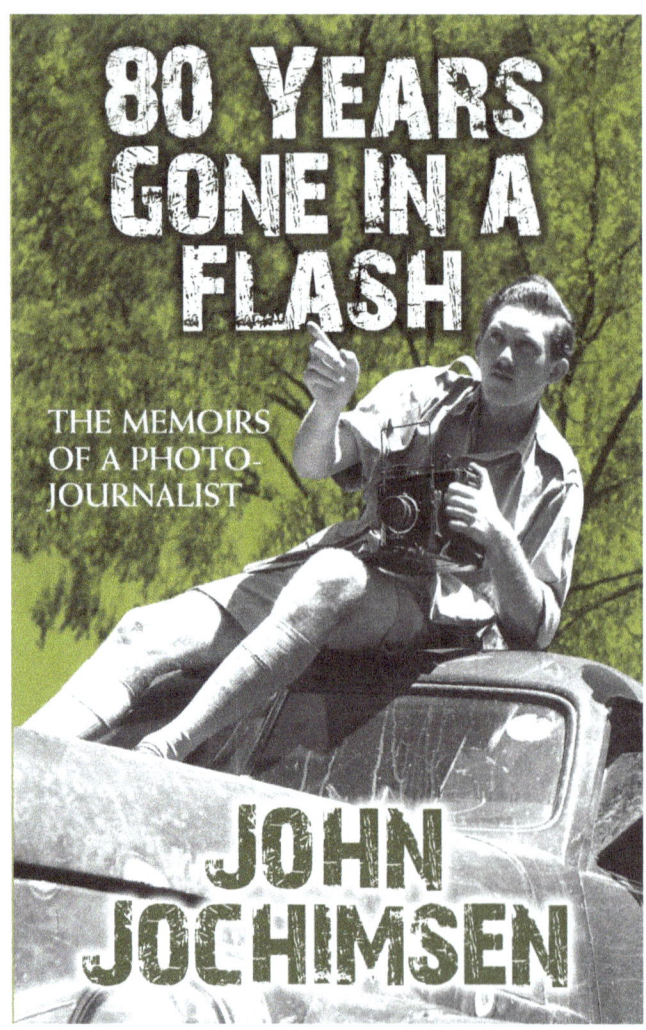

From presidents to royalty, war torn regions to stunning scenery, the camera of John Jochimsen has captured it al Perhaps the last person left alive today who was with Princess Elizabeth the day she became Queen, John is one of the la: remaining old school photojournalists. Eighty Years gone in a Flash traces the remarkable story in his own words, and wit his own incredible pictures. From life at The News of the World to the jungles of Malaya, John provides an honest, wit and touching account of a colourful career spanning more than five decades.

"John's story is the story of one of only a few photojournalists and journeyman photographers who were never drawn u into the hoopla of events around them, but who produced images as iconic as those of their contemporaries who achieve fame on the public stage through fashion or glamour or notoriety of one form or another. His is a remarkable story whic spans the final post war decades of still film photography, covering editorial as well as commercial events both nation and global, encompassing industry and service, pageant and celebration at all levels of society and culture. It is all th more remarkable that this story has not been lost to us, and that John has strived to tell it."
Art's Eye Photographic.

Also from MX Publishing

Stunning travel photography from Keith Hern

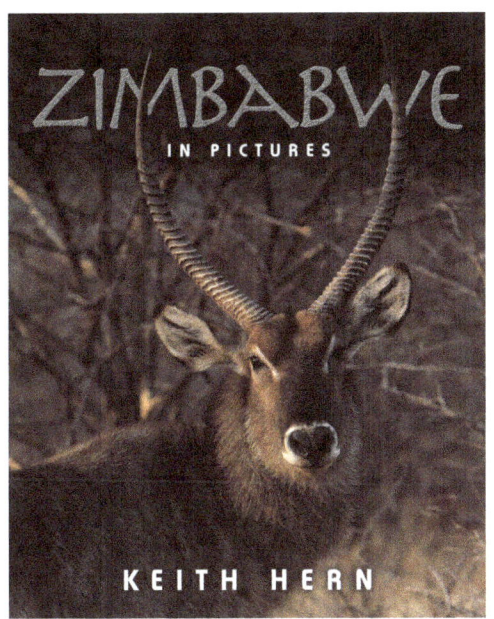
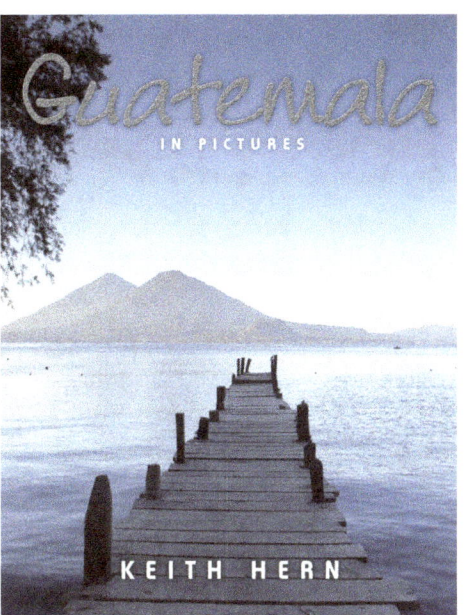
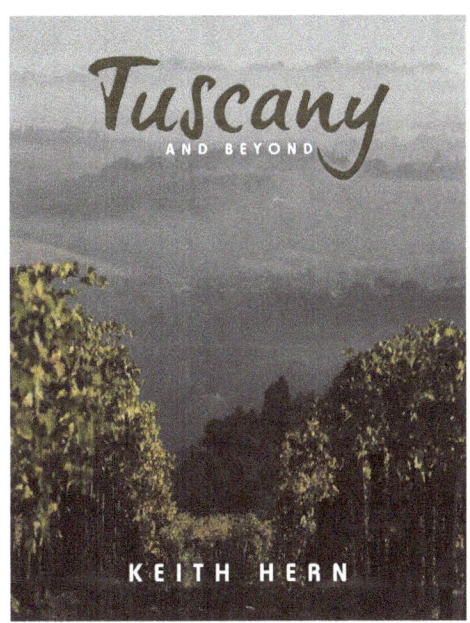

www.ingramcontent.com/pod-product-compliance
Lightning Source LLC
Chambersburg PA
CBHW062327220526
45469CB00008B/2626